JOHN BURIDAN
ON SELF-REFERENCE

JOHN BURIDAN
ON SELF-REFERENCE

Chapter Eight of Buridan's *Sophismata*

Translated, with an Introduction and a
philosophical Commentary, by

G. E. HUGHES

CAMBRIDGE UNIVERSITY PRESS

CAMBRIDGE

LONDON   NEW YORK   NEW ROCHELLE

MELBOURNE   SYDNEY

CAMBRIDGE UNIVERSITY PRESS
Cambridge, New York, Melbourne, Madrid, Cape Town, Singapore, São Paulo, Delhi

Cambridge University Press
The Edinburgh Building, Cambridge CB2 8RU, UK

Published in the United States of America by Cambridge University Press, New York

www.cambridge.org
Information on this title: www.cambridge.org/9780521288644

First published 1982
Re-issued in this digitally printed version 2009

A catalogue record for this publication is available from the British Library

Library of Congress Catalogue Card Number: 81-21637

ISBN 978-0-521-24086-4 hardback
ISBN 978-0-521-28864-4 paperback

UXORI DILECTISSIMAE
BERYL
Amore et gratia

CONTENTS

COMMENTARY

PREFACE

The eighth and final chapter of Buridan's *Sophismata* is devoted to problems about self-referential propositions. Some at least of these have perplexed philosophers for more than two thousand years, and continue to do so today. The best known is probably the so-called *Liar Paradox* – the problem of whether someone who says 'What I am now saying is false' is thereby saying something true or something false. Buridan not only gives us his own distinctive and detailed solution of this particular problem, but also introduces us to a wide range of other self-referential paradoxes, many of which are likely to be unfamiliar to most present-day readers. In addition, he uses his main theme to lead into discussions of such questions as the nature of propositions, the criteria of their truth and falsity, the conditions of the validity of inferences, and the analysis of the concept of knowledge; and in this way the scope of his chapter is much wider than its official topic might suggest.

This book is not intended primarily as a contribution to the history of philosophy or to textual scholarship, but mainly as an attempt to make Buridan's ideas accessible to present-day philosophical readers for the sake of their inherent importance. The issues he deals with are still being discussed, probably more vigorously today than at any period since his own. I believe that his ideas and arguments have a contemporary relevance that is independent of their historical context and that they have a distinctive contribution to make to an ongoing debate.

My work on Buridan has been aided and encouraged by more people than can be mentioned individually here. I have shamelessly picked the brains of many colleagues and visitors here in Wellington, and they have helped me greatly by discussing Buridan's arguments, making suggestions for improving earlier drafts of the book, or casting light on difficult passages in the Latin. Jan Pinborg of the University of Copenhagen generously put his textual and philosophical scholarship at my disposal, and also lent me a vital microfilm at a crucial stage in my work. Peter Geach of the University of Leeds made many valuable comments and criticisms which led me to undertake a substantial revision of the book, both to its own considerable benefit,

I believe, and to mine. He also devised the argument which is suggested on pp. 140–1 as a replacement for a defective one of Buridan's own, and kindly gave me his permission to use it. My wife, to whom the book is dedicated, read and checked the entire typescript, and I am grateful to her for helping me to remedy many inaccuracies and infelicities. The fact that my manuscript went through several drafts made the typing a more massive task than might appear from the book's final form, and I want to thank past and present secretaries in this Department, and especially Lynsie Dollimore and Helen Fleming, for their care and patience in coping with it.

Department of Philosophy
Victoria University of Wellington
New Zealand

May, 1981

INTRODUCTION

I

John Buridan was one of the most eminent philosophers and scientists of the fourteenth century, yet very little is known about his life with any certainty. He was a Frenchman, probably a native of Picardy. In 1328, and again in 1340, he was Rector of the University of Paris, so it seems likely that he was born towards the end of the thirteenth century. His death probably occurred in 1358 or not many years later. The best account of what has been established or conjectured about his life will be found in Faral [1949]. His reputation and influence as a thinker during his lifetime and until the sixteenth century appear to have been enormous, but in later times his works came to suffer almost total neglect. One might, indeed, almost omit the 'almost'; for it seems safe to say that to many generations of students of philosophy his name has brought no more to mind than 'Buridan's ass' – the donkey that starved because it was equidistant between two equally succulent bundles of hay; and yet no one has found this example in any of his writings. In recent years, however, his ideas, especially his ideas in logic and the philosophy of language, have begun once again to attract some of the attention that they deserve.

This revival of interest in him is not an accident, for many of the problems with which he and his contemporaries wrestled have, quite independently of their work, come to the fore again in our own century after a long period of comparative neglect. Among such problems are those that surround the semantic paradoxes of self-reference, and my initial idea for this book grew out of an interest in what Buridan in particular had to say about them.

The simplest of these paradoxes to state is the one commonly called the *Liar*, in which someone is assumed to utter the proposition 'What I am now saying is false'. The main problem here is, put briefly, this. If the proposition in question is true, then since what it asserts is that it itself is false, it seems to follow that it *is* false; but on the other hand, if it is false, then since that is just what it asserts, it seems to follow in turn that it is true. We therefore reach the apparently inescapable but quite intolerable result that it is true if and only if it is false. The problems raised by such paradoxes are grave and vexing, and although a great many solutions of them have been proposed, it seems safe to say that at no time has any of them won general acceptance. They are also profoundly disturbing, not least because they provoke nagging doubts about the very consistency of our notions of truth and falsity. One can ignore the paradoxes if one chooses, but one cannot in good conscience dismiss them as mere curiosities or trivialities.

What makes the proposition in the *Liar* paradox self-referential is the fact that it contains an expression ('what I am now saying') that refers to that very proposition itself. Similar problems, however, are raised when a proposition contains no such expression, but instead contains a reference to some other proposition which in turn refers to the original one (or to a third which refers to the original, etc.), and it is convenient to extend the term 'self-referential' to cover propositions of this kind as well. To distinguish the two kinds we can call them *directly* and *indirectly* self-referential propositions respectively. Buridan discusses examples of both sorts.

Some of the paradoxes of self-reference were formulated in ancient Greek times, and they have perhaps never been wholly ignored since then; but the two periods in which they have been most intensively worked on have probably been the fourteenth century and our own. By Buridan's day a large number of variants on the *Liar* theme had become current, as his own discussion bears witness; and some indication of the range of views canvassed at that time is given by the fact that Paul of Venice, writing at about the end of the century, prefaces his own solution with an outline of fourteen others with which he was familiar (see Bocheński [1961], pp. 238–51).

Mediaeval logicians gave the name 'insolubles' to paradoxes of the kind I have mentioned. Buridan refers to them as the 'so-called insolubles' (*vocata insolubilia*), perhaps because he thought he had a satisfactory solution for them. His fullest and most systematic discussion of them occurs in Chapter 8 of his *Sophismata*, where in Sophisms 7–12 he examines six in detail and mentions several others briefly. (He also deals with the topic, though much less elaborately, in his Commentary on Aristotle's *Metaphysics* (Book VI, Question 9), and there is a brief sketch of a solution in his *Consequentiae* (Book I, ch. 5); but these texts do not express his mature views, and I shall not discuss them in this book.) Put shortly, his contention is that all the paradoxical propositions in question are simply false: he accepts the standard arguments designed to show that if they are true they are false, but he gives reasons for rejecting the *prima facie* equally valid arguments for the converse. One major question, of course, is whether he can maintain all this

consistently. In my opinion he can; but my reasons for thinking so will
have to emerge as we proceed.

In the *Sophismata* Buridan sets his examination of the *Liar*-type
paradoxes in the context of a wide-ranging and yet highly unified
discussion of self-reference in general, which forms the theme of
Chapter 8 as a whole. I have therefore taken that entire chapter, and
not merely one section of it, as the topic of this book. I am well aware
that by confining myself to this one chapter I am presenting the reader
with a text that its author never intended to be read by itself.
Nevertheless it can in fact stand on its own to a remarkable degree.
It is true that it assumes a familiarity with certain background ideas,
but these are ideas which a modern commentator, even if he were
dealing with the complete work, would be under an obligation to
explain to his readers in any case. Moreover, although Buridan no doubt
expects us to have worked through the earlier chapters before coming
to Chapter 8, there are in fact only two passages in them – one in
Chapter 2 and another in Chapter 7 – to which he explicitly refers us
back; and I summarize the arguments of the former later on in this
Introduction, and those of the latter at the appropriate place in the
Commentary.

In its overall structure the chapter falls into four clearly distinguishable
sections. (A) Sophisms 1–6 deal with a miscellaneous group of problems
which are concerned with self-reference but do not involve the
insolubles proper. Their main themes are the conditions of the validity
of inferences and the nature of propositions. Part of Buridan's purpose
here seems to be to establish certain preliminary results to which he
can then refer back briefly in the more complicated arguments that
follow. (B) Sophisms 7–12 consist of discussions of six *Liar*-type
paradoxes. (The *Liar* itself is Sophism 11.) These may conveniently be
called *alethic* paradoxes. (C) Sophisms 13–15 form a group of paradoxes
that involve the notions of knowing and doubting as well as those of
truth and falsity. They may be called *epistemic* paradoxes. Finally (D)
Sophisms 16–20 deal with paradoxes that occur in the context of
action–directed activities or attitudes such as promising or wishing, and
may be called *pragmatic* paradoxes.

Section (B) has an ingenious inner structure of its own. With the
exception of the very brief Sophism 12, which is intended chiefly as
a transition to the next group, each sophism in this section contains
some point that is relevant to all the others, though we are often left
to apply it to them for ourselves. Buridan seems to have felt – and if
so his readers will have no difficulty in agreeing with him – that if he

were to say immediately all he wants to say about Sophism 7, for example, the result would be too complicated to be readily understood, so he reserves some of his points for inclusion in his discussion of subsequent sophisms. The effect is therefore of a gradually unfolding panorama of argumentation; and if one is to understand his complete solution of any one sophism in this section one has to work one's way through them all, or at least the first five. I shall try to set out the details of all this in the Commentary.

The technique of expounding and defending a philosophical position by a discussion of 'sophisms' was a well-established one in Buridan's day, though it has now long gone out of fashion. A sophism, in the technical mediaeval sense of the word, is not a piece of fallacious or 'sophistical' reasoning. Briefly, it is a problem sentence or proposition, where it is possible to advance arguments both for its truth and for its falsity and we are expected to learn something by seeing how the arguments for one side or the other can be refuted. (Buridan sometimes uses the word 'sophism' narrowly to refer to the problem sentence itself, and sometimes more widely to refer to his whole discussion of it. This convenient ambiguity never seems to cause any confusion in practice, and I shall feel free to indulge in it myself.)

The basic or orthodox pattern of the discussion of a sophism is in five steps.

1. The sophism itself is formulated. This is accompanied, where appropriate, by the 'positing of a case' – i.e. the description of some situation in the light of which the sophism is to be considered – and a statement of the question to be discussed. Usually this question is whether, given the posited case, the sophism is true or false.

2. The arguments for one side (e.g. that the sophism is true) are listed, usually without comment on their validity.

3. The arguments for the contrary view are then similarly listed.

4. Buridan states his own opinion on the issue, either in a simple unadorned fashion or else accompanied by some argument or explanation.

5. Finally he presents a refutation of each of the arguments initially stated for the view he rejects.

Steps 1–3 can be called the *exposition* of the sophism, and steps 4 and 5 its *solution*.

This basic pattern can be discerned in nearly all the sophisms we shall encounter, and tracing it out is a great help in following the structure of the arguments; but it seldom occurs quite unmodified, since Buridan is always ready to introduce elaborations or variations as the case makes appropriate. For example, a general discussion of the issues raised by the sophism may be interpolated between steps 4 and 5, and the opposing arguments then answered in the light of this. Or the development of the argument may throw up a further problem which Buridan then proceeds to solve on its own before resuming the overall pattern; sometimes indeed this subsidiary discussion itself takes on the form of a sophism, so that we have a sophism-within-a-sophism structure. Or again, after having completed his solution of the problem as initially stated, he may propose an alteration in the originally posited case and raise the question whether the sophism would then still have the same truth-value as before. Another important variation, which does not occur in Chapter 8 but which he uses frequently in other chapters, consists in grouping together a number of closely-related sophisms, giving first the exposition of each, then a general discussion of the issues, and finally the solution of each sophism in turn; and then moving on to the next batch and dealing with them similarly. In these and other ways, what may seem at first to be a rigid and cramping structure can become, at least when handled by someone of Buridan's genius, a flexible and even imaginative instrument.

II

I shall now try to outline just as much of Buridan's theory of meaning and truth as is necessary for an understanding of the arguments in our text. I want to make it clear that I am doing no more than that, and that his full account of these matters is much more elaborate and subtle than will appear here.

The things that are true or false, at least in any sense of 'true' and 'false' with which Buridan thinks the logician should be concerned (see §6.0.1), are what he calls *propositions*. And a proposition, for him, can be briefly described as a meaningful sentence-token (i.e. a particular utterance or inscription), spoken or written with assertive intent. I shall elaborate this a little.

Firstly, a proposition is a sentence-token. This means that two physically distinct utterances or inscriptions, even if they consist of occurrences of the same words in the same order (as, for example, when you say 'The cat is on the mat' and I say 'The cat is on the mat'), count for Buridan as two propositions, not as one – assuming, that is, that they are propositions at all. He would say that they were *similar* or, to use a useful modern philosophical coinage, *equiform* propositions, but not that they were numerically the same. Very often, of course, two or more equiform propositions have identical truth-conditions, and then it is for many purposes a harmless and convenient looseness of expression, in which Buridan himself sometimes indulges, to speak of them as a single proposition; but sometimes their truth-conditions differ, and then he is scrupulously careful to distinguish them.

One important corollary of regarding propositions as sentence-tokens is that they are things that come into being and go out of existence, and that it is always a contingent matter whether a certain proposition (or indeed any equiform one) exists at a given time or not. Moreover, if a certain proposition does not exist at a certain time, then according to Buridan it cannot be either true or false at that time. It is easy to imagine, for example, that at a certain moment *t* Socrates is in fact sitting, but that no proposition equiform with 'Socrates is sitting' exists at *t*. Then it will be incorrect to say that 'Socrates is sitting', or any equiform proposition, is true at *t*; the most we can say is that if any such proposition had existed at *t*, it *would* have been true then.

Secondly, to be a proposition a sentence-token must be spoken or written with assertive intent. In so far as this requirement is meant to distinguish propositions, as indicative or declarative sentences, from, say, interrogative or imperative ones, which do not express a claim that something is, was or will be the case, it is self-explanatory. But Buridan also wants to insist that for an expression to count as a proposition it is not enough for it to be of a kind that *could* be used to make an assertion; it must actually be used assertively. Suppose, for example, that I say 'Ptolemy said that the sun moves round the earth': Buridan would refuse to regard the expression 'the sun moves round the earth' in that remark of mine as constituting a proposition at all, either a true one or a false one, since I am not using it to assert that the sun moves round the earth, or indeed to assert anything at all. The only proposition to be found in what I say is the one that is formed by my remark as a whole. Quite generally, in fact, he maintains that no part of a proposition is itself a proposition, though it is often convenient to speak of it loosely as such. Strictly speaking, he holds, all we are entitled to say about it is that it *would be* a proposition if it were used assertively on its own. For more on this theme see the Commentary on §4.3.1 on pp. 91–3.

The third requirement, that a proposition be a meaningful sentence, calls for more detailed explanation.

An utterance or inscription is not a proposition in virtue of its sound or shape, or even its grammatical structure, but only because it also has a certain *meaning*. Buridan stresses that it is purely a matter of convention what meaning any word or sequence of words has. The users of a language decide or agree to use words in certain senses, and they could always have decided otherwise. It is indeed always possible, and sometimes even convenient, for a group of people to decide to use certain words in a new way, or for an individual person to announce his intention of doing so. In this way it can happen that *one and the same proposition* can be true given the sense that I attach to it but false given the sense that you attach to it; and the same situation can of course also arise when words have well-established meanings but are ambiguous.[1] Buridan holds, however, sensibly enough, that when there are well-established and unambiguous conventions about the meanings of the words we are using, then in the absence of any explicit agreement or announcement of intention to depart from those conventions it is to be assumed that we are abiding by them, and our propositions are to be assessed for truth and falsity on that assumption.

Language, then, is a system of conventional written or spoken signs. Now we use words, according to Buridan, to express the thoughts or ideas – what he usually calls the *concepts* – that we have in our minds. In his terminology the words are said to *signify* the concepts they are used to express. This kind of signification, which is possessed by all meaningful words or sequences of words, he sometimes calls 'signification within the mind', to distinguish it from another kind of signification, 'signification outside the mind', which is possessed in addition by some meaningful words but not by all. A word has signification outside the mind when the corresponding concept is a concept *of*, or a concept that covers, other things of a certain kind. In such a case the word is said to signify 'outside the mind' the things that are covered by, or that fall under, the concept in question, and these things are said to be the *ultimate significates* of the word. For example, the ultimate significates of the word 'horse' – the things it signifies outside the mind – consist of all the actual flesh-and-blood animals covered by the concept *horse*, i.e. by the concept that is signified in the mind by the word 'horse' when it is used in accordance with our normal conventions. Words that have signification outside the mind are said to be *categorematic* words.

To avoid possible confusion it is worth noting that Buridan does not intend the phrase 'signification outside the mind' to suggest that

---

[1] We might put this by saying that the proposition is true for me but false for you; but this is a sense of 'true for me' which has no connection with the, to my mind, deplorable habit of saying 'That's true for me' to mean merely that one is disposed to agree with what has been said.

the ultimate significates of the words that have such significates are always non-mental things; he uses it merely because they very frequently are. The concept corresponding to a categorematic word might, however, be a concept of things that are themselves mental in character, and in that case those mental things are the ultimate significates of the word, or (in spite of the awkwardness of the expression) what it signifies outside the mind. The word 'concept' itself would be a good example.

Contrasted with categorematic words are what are known as *syncategorematic* ones, whose function is to build up more complex verbal expressions out of simpler ones, and which signify (within the mind) concepts which are not concepts *of* other things but which have the role of building up more complex concepts out of simpler ones in an approximately analogous way. Thus syncategorematic words, like categorematic ones, have signification within the mind, but unlike them have no ultimate significates. Examples of categorematic words are 'horse' and 'white'; examples of syncategorematic ones are 'some', 'not' and 'or'.

(Buridan also recognizes words that are neither purely categorematic nor purely syncategorematic, but mixed in nature. An example is 'someone', where the corresponding concept contains both an element answering to the categorematic term 'person' and also an element answering to the syncategorematic term 'some'. But for our purposes we need not explore this matter any further.)

Among the various kinds of categorematic words there are two that are worth mentioning specially here. Sometimes the corresponding concept is a concept of a certain kind of *object*; 'horse' is an obvious example. In such a case Buridan insists that the ultimate significates of the word include all objects of the relevant kind, past, present and future ones. I think it is easy to see why he says this: not merely all the horses that there now are, but all that there ever have been or ever will be, fall equally under the concept *horse*, and we would not understand the word 'horse' in the way we in fact do if we did not regard it as applicable to Bucephalus and to the animal that will win the Derby in 2010 just as much as to the horses that are alive at the present moment. With some other categorematic words, however – and 'white' would be an example – the corresponding concept is a concept not of a certain kind of object but of a certain kind of *attribute* of objects. In such a case the ultimate significates of the word consist of all instances of that attribute, again past, present and future ones. This means that Buridan regards the word 'white' as signifying (outside the mind) not some

8

abstract universal, and not a collection of white *objects*, but the whiteness that is found in Socrates, the whiteness that is found in this piece of paper, and so on and so forth. (It is not that he thinks that instances of whiteness *exist* independently of their possessors. It is only that our *concept* of an attribute as belonging to an object is a different sort of concept from our concept of an object itself; and the word 'white' signifies within the mind a concept of the former kind, not the latter.)

I have already remarked that the relation between a word and the concept it signifies is a conventional one. It follows that it is also at least partly a matter of convention what the ultimate significates of a categorematic word are. There is nothing conventional, however, about the relation between a concept and the things that fall under it. The point might be put in this way. It is within my power to decide that I shall henceforth use the word 'giraffe' to mean what I and others have hitherto used the word 'typewriter' to mean, and thereby that on my lips it will apply to typewriters and only to typewriters. The worst that will happen is confusion in communication with others, and even that will disappear if I can persuade them to join me in this new usage. But it would be absurd to suppose that I could make my present *concept* of a giraffe cover typewriters and only typewriters: any concept that covered precisely such things would *ipso facto* be a quite different concept from my present concept of a giraffe. Thus although what the ultimate significates of a categorematic word are depends on two relations – one between the word and the concept it signifies and another between that concept and the things that fall under it – yet only a single convention or decision is involved, that which links the word with the concept.

According to Buridan some concepts are simple and others are complex; and he would classify *horse* and *white* as simple concepts, and *dragon* and *white horse* as complex ones. The notion of a simple concept raises difficult problems which it is, fortunately, unnecessary to enter into at any depth for our present purposes. But when Buridan says that *horse*, for example, is a simple concept, I do not take him to be denying that when we think of a horse we think of an animal with a variety of distinguishable parts such as a tail, legs and a mane. Roughly, I take him to be claiming that this concept is not one that we have built up or fabricated by combining various other concepts that we already had, but rather one that we have acquired by abstracting the essential features of objects of a certain determinate kind that we have encountered. By contrast we have constructed the concept *dragon* out of previously given concepts such as *reptile, fire* and *breathing,* and formed the concept *white horse* by putting together the concepts *horse* and *white.*

If we now ask 'What are the ultimate significates of the expression "white horse"?' Buridan's answer is that these consist of all horses together with all instances of whiteness. This may surprise us a little at first: we might perhaps have expected him to say that its ultimate significates consisted only of white horses. Nevertheless I think it is not difficult to see why he says what he does here. He is not concerned with the question of what things we are talking about when we use the expression 'white horse' in a proposition (that question will arise under the heading of *supposition,* which we shall come to a little later on); he is concerned rather with the question of what we *understand* by the expression 'white horse'. Now we do not understand that expression unless we understand each of its component words; and we do not understand the word 'horse' unless we recognize that it applies to all horses, no matter what their colour may be, or the word 'white' unless we recognize that it applies to every instance of whiteness, irrespective of whether it occurs in a horse or in anything else. In general, indeed, the ultimate significates of a complex verbal expression consist of the sum total of the ultimate significates of all the categorematic words that occur in it.

Buridan warns us, however, that the degree of complexity of a verbal expression is no automatic indication of the degree of complexity of the corresponding concept. It quite often happens that we form a complex concept and then decide to use a single word to express it. We can, for example, form the concept of an animal with the head of a lion, the body of a goat and the tail of a serpent, but instead of using the long phrase 'animal with the head of a lion etc.' to express or signify this concept we can decide to use the single word 'chimera'. Then we have a simple verbal expression but a complex corresponding concept. Moreover, the ultimate significates of the word 'chimera' will consist of all the things that fall under the component elements of this complex concept; these will include all animals, heads, tails and so forth – but not, Buridan would insist, chimeras, since there are not, and indeed (he would say) cannot be, any such things. The case of 'dragon', mentioned above, is of course similar.

A proposition, as we have .seen, is a conventionally meaningful sentence, and is therefore a certain kind of meaningful verbal expression.

As such, like all other meaningful expressions, it expresses or signifies a certain concept, in this case a complex concept which we might describe as a thought that something or other is the case. Buridan calls a concept of this kind a *mental proposition*, and he seems to think of it as having a structure somewhat analogous to that of the verbal proposition by which it is signified. There are therefore two kinds of propositions, linguistic (spoken or written) ones and mental ones; and a proposition of either kind can be true or false. With mental propositions, of course, the question of conventional signification does not come into the picture, since they and their elements are themselves concepts, and concepts do not have conventional signification as linguistic expressions do.

It is worth noting that a mental proposition is not a *belief*. I can form the thought – the mental proposition – that $2 + 2 = 5$, but this does not mean that I believe that $2 + 2 = 5$, or that anyone else does, for that matter. In general, if I have a certain mental proposition in my mind, I may either believe it or disbelieve it or have no opinion about it at all; but it will be the same proposition whichever of these three attitudes I have to it. It is also worth noting that although Buridan recognizes linguistic propositions and mental ones, what we do not find in his thought is any notion of a proposition as an abstract or timeless entity, neither linguistic nor mental in character. For him a proposition is always a particular utterance or inscription or else a thought that occurs in the mind of some intelligent being.

There are only a few references to mental propositions in Chapter 8. (When Buridan uses the word 'proposition' without qualification, it is always spoken or written propositions he is referring to; when he wants to speak of mental propositions he always calls them that explicitly; and I shall follow him in this practice.) Nevertheless mental propositions are important for his overall theory, and are indeed more basic than linguistic ones. A spoken or written formula would not be a proposition at all unless it expressed a mental proposition, whereas a mental proposition need not be given any verbal expression at all. Moreover, mental propositions seem to be regarded as the primary bearers of truth and falsity, and verbal propositions count as true or false only in so far as they express true or false mental ones. And he portrays informative discourse between human beings as a process whereby a speaker uses words that express the mental propositions that he has in his own mind with the intention that they will produce similar mental propositions in the mind of his audience.

Like other mediaeval logicians Buridan regarded four propositional forms as basic. These are the A, E, I and O propositional forms of traditional syllogistic logic. A propositions (universal affirmatives) are of the form *Every A is (a) B*, E propositions (universal negatives) of the form *No A is (a) B*, I propositions (particular affirmatives) of the form *Some A is (a) B*, and O propositions (particular negatives) of the form *Some A is not (a) B*. In these forms, *A* and *B* are to be understood as categorematic terms (simple or complex), known as the *subject* and the *predicate* respectively; and each proposition contains in addition a syncategorematic term ('is' or 'is not') known as the *copula*, and also a (syncategorematic) sign of quantity ('every', 'no' or 'some').

Into this scheme it was common to assimilate propositions of certain other closely related forms, in particular those known as *indefinite* and *singular*. Indefinite propositions lack an explicit sign of quantity; they are of the form *(An) A is (a) B* (affirmative) or *(An) A is not (a) B* (negative), where *A* is a common noun or noun phrase, not a proper name. They were normally treated as equivalent to the corresponding particular propositions, though it was recognized that in some cases, such as 'A man is an animal', it was more reasonable to treat them as universals. Singular propositions are of the form *X is (a) B* or *X is not (a) B*, where *X* is a proper name or some other expression that designates a definite individual. They were commonly assimilated to A and E propositions respectively.

Propositions of all the foregoing forms were known as *categorical*. More complex propositions could be constructed out of two or more categorical ones by propositional connectives such as 'and', 'or', 'if' and 'when'; such propositions were called *hypothetical*[2] ones. Further variations could be introduced by the use of modal words such as 'can', 'must' or 'impossible', and also by changing the tense of the copula. (Mediaeval logicians, unlike many modern ones, took the tenses of propositions seriously.)

It was of course recognized that very many indicative sentences in ordinary language do not explicitly conform to any of the above-mentioned forms, but it was commonly held that they could always be reformulated without change of meaning into sentences that do so conform. Buridan does not seem to dissent from this view.

---

[2] This is a wider use of the word 'hypothetical' than is customary among modern logicians, who would restrict its application to conditional propositions. Buridan would in fact be unhappy with the description I have given of hypothetical propositions, but would assent to it as a convenient though loose way of speaking. See the commentary on §4.3.1, pp. 91ff.

So much for what propositions are and what forms they can take. We now have to approach the question, what is it that makes true propositions true and false ones false? One commonly held view in Buridan's day was that a proposition is true if and only if 'as it (the proposition) signifies, so it is' (*sicut significat, ita est*). Buridan, however, insists emphatically that no such account of the truth-conditions of propositions will hold water if 'signification' is understood as he understands it, or in any approximately analogous way. His reasons are spelled out in detail in Chapters 1 and 2 of the *Sophismata*, and are too elaborate to be given here in detail; but very briefly they amount to the following. Since, according to him, signification is a relation between a linguistic expression and the things it signifies, 'as it signifies, so it is' will have to be taken to mean that the things signified by the proposition actually exist. But now (1) suppose that what is intended by 'signification' is signification within the mind. Then 'as it signifies, so it is' will have to mean that the concept that the proposition expresses does actually exist in the mind of the speaker. This, however, gives us the absurd result that every spoken proposition is true, since *every* spoken proposition expresses a corresponding concept (in this case a mental proposition) that exists in the mind of the speaker. Suppose, however, (2) that signification outside the mind is intended. Then 'as it signifies, so it is' will have to mean that the ultimate significates of the categorematic words in the proposition do in fact exist. But then two absurd results follow. (a) Since 'not' is a syncategorematic word with no signification outside the mind, a proposition and its negation will signify precisely the same things and hence have the same truth-value. And (b) a patently false proposition such as 'A man is a donkey' will turn out to be true, since what it signifies are precisely men and donkeys, and all of these exist. Buridan also considers (3) a theory, to which he himself does not subscribe but which was held by some of his contemporaries, to the effect that a proposition as a whole signifies some abstract entity, distinct both from its ultimate significates and from the mental proposition it expresses. Thus, for example, 'Plato is fair-haired' might be held to signify something like *Plato's being fair-haired* or *the fair-hairedness of Plato*. But then trouble arises when we ask whether this abstract entity exists or not: for if we say it does not, then the proposition will be left without any signification; and if we say it does, then the proposition will thereby automatically be made true — 'Plato is fair-haired', for example, will be true irrespective of whether the actual man Plato has fair hair or not.

A theory of truth-conditions in terms of signification, Buridan thinks, is defective on two main counts: it fails to mark out adequately what thing or things are being spoken about or referred to by a proposition, and it fails to make clear what has to hold of these things if the proposition is to be true. To remedy these defects, he maintains, we have to formulate our theory in terms not of signification but of what mediaeval logicians called *supposition*.

The topic of supposition-theory in mediaeval logic is a complicated one, but Buridan's basic ideas in this area, which are all we have to consider here, are straightforward enough. We have seen that the word 'horse' *signifies* indifferently all past, present and future horses; but if I say

(1) A horse is running

then *in that proposition* (provided that we take the tense of the verb seriously) I am not speaking of all past, present and future horses but only of present ones, in the sense that the behaviour of any presently existing horse is relevant to the truth of (1) but the behaviour of past or future horses is quite beside the point. This is expressed by saying that *in the context of* (1) the term 'horse' *stands for (supponit pro)*, or that its *supposition*[3] consists of, present horses only. It still, of course, *signifies* all past, present and future horses, for even in (1) – or in any other proposition, or in a non-propositional context for that matter – we understand it to express a concept that covers all of these; yet as it occurs in (1) it *stands for* only some of the things it signifies, and precisely which of these it stands for is determined by other elements in the proposition. Analogously, in

(2) A horse was running

'horse' stands for present and past horses but not for future ones; and in

(3) A white horse is running

it stands for presently existing white horses only. The past tense of the verb in (2), that is, extends or 'ampliates' the supposition of 'horse' to cover past horses as well as present ones, and the presence of the

---

[3] Thoughout this book I use 'stand for' to translate *supponere pro*, and avoid using it in any other sense; but I translate the abstract noun *suppositio* by 'supposition', since no other English word seems to be readily available. (I follow Scott [1966] in this; some other authors translate *supponere pro* as 'supposit for', 'suppone for', or 'suppose for'.) Buridan also uses *supponere* in a non-technical way, when it can usually be rendered simply as 'assume' or 'suppose'.

word 'white' in (3) restricts it to horses that are white. (Sometimes Buridan prefers to say that in a proposition such as (3) it is the whole phrase 'white horse', rather than 'horse' itself, that has this restricted supposition; but the point is not of much importance to us here.) Again, in

(4) Plato is running

the word 'Plato' both signifies and stands for the man Plato, but in

(5) Plato's horse is running

although 'Plato' still signifies Plato it does not stand for him, since it is not he who is said to be running. Its role in (5) is rather to restrict what 'horse' stands for to a single horse, the one owned by Plato. In (5), in fact, 'Plato' does not *stand for* anything at all. Moreover, if Plato does not own a horse, then 'horse' in (5) does not stand for anything either. It can thus easily happen that a word signifies one or many things, and yet in a given proposition does not stand for anything (*pro nullo supponit*), or has no supposition. There are even significant words and phrases that never have any supposition in any proposition: 'chimera', as we saw, signifies a great many things, but it never stands for anything since there are no such things as chimeras. In general, a categorematic term in a given proposition stands for each member of a certain sub-class (possibly empty) of its ultimate significates, a sub-class that consists of just those objects that have to be taken into account in determining the truth or falsity of the proposition. Precisely what objects fall into this sub-class is determined by various features of the proposition as a whole.

The above account has to be modified in one respect for terms that signify attributes rather than objects. Such terms, as we have seen, *signify* all instances of the relevant attributes, but what they are said to *stand for* are not these but the objects that possess them – or some appropriate sub-class of these objects. In (1), for example, 'running' stands for all presently running *objects*; hence both the subject and the predicate of (1) have objects as their suppositions, though only the subject has objects as its significates.

Mediaeval logicians, Buridan among them, devised elaborate rules for determining, from the structure of a proposition, the range of supposition of the terms in it. We need not, however, concern ourselves with the details of these rules here.

Supposition of the kind I have been describing is known as *significative* supposition (from its close connection with signification), or alternatively as *personal* supposition. There is, however, another kind of supposition, *material* supposition. This occurs when a term in a proposition is used to stand not for any of its ultimate significates but for some linguistic expression which consists of either it itself, or another expression verbally identical with it, or an expression derived from it by certain grammatical transformations. For example, if I say

(6) Water has five letters

it cannot reasonably be supposed that I intend thereby to attribute five-letteredness to water itself (the substance), which is what I would be doing if I were using 'water' with significative supposition. To make sense of (6) we have to assume that the word 'water' that occurs in it stands either for itself (i.e. for that very word-token itself) or for some other word-token or word-tokens equiform with it; and this is to take it as having material, not significative, supposition. In some cases each kind of supposition makes good sense of the proposition, and a real ambiguity arises. To adapt slightly one of Buridan's own examples,[4] consider

(7) A name is trisyllabic.

If the subject of (7) is taken in material supposition, (7) is false, since it will then mean that the expression 'a name' is trisyllabic, which it is not; but if the subject is taken in significative supposition, then (7) will mean that at least one name has three syllables in it, which is true.

For a case that involves grammatical transformation, consider

(8) I believe John to be a scoundrel.

According to Buridan the objects of belief are propositions, so the expression 'John to be a scoundrel' in (8) ought to stand for the proposition that (8) says I believe. But it itself is only an infinitive phrase, which does not even have the structure of a proposition, and therefore what it stands for cannot be precisely itself or any other equiform expression. What Buridan says is that such a phrase in such a context stands for a corresponding sentence in the indicative mood (in this case, 'John is a scoundrel'), which *is* a proposition; and this is another variety of material supposition.

The distinction between significative and material supposition is in

---

[4] *Sophismata*, ch. 3, Sophism 5 (*Nomen est trisyllabum*). It has to be admitted that the example runs more smoothly in Latin than in English, but even in English the point is clear enough.

many respects, though not in all, like the one commonly drawn by modern philosophers between *using* an expression and *mentioning* it, and normally marked nowadays by enclosing a mentioned expression in inverted commas. Inverted commas had not been invented in Buridan's day, and I have therefore refrained from using them in my examples. Nevertheless, the logicians of the later Middle Ages, who were, I should guess, more acutely sensitive to the use–mention distinction than anyone else before the twentieth century, had a variety of devices for indicating mention as distinct from use. Of these the one that probably comes nearest to the modern use of inverted commas (though Buridan himself does not use it a great deal, and in our present text not at all) is the prefixing of the sign *ly*, as in *ly equus* for 'the word "horse"'. In some contexts modern readers may also find themselves reminded of the distinction, deriving from Carnap, between the *formal* and the *material* modes of spech; but there is need for care in terminology here, since the material mode is analogous not to material but to significative supposition, and the formal mode to material supposition.

It needs to be added that Buridan also counts it as a case of material supposition when a term is used to stand for the concept that it signifies within the mind; but I shall not discuss this kind of supposition here since it does not enter into the arguments of Chapter 8.

Armed with the notion of the supposition of terms, Buridan lays down in Chapter 2 of the *Sophismata* certain truth-conditions for A, E, I and O propositions which I shall for convenience call *correspondence truth-conditions* (though he does not call them that, and I should not like the associations of the phrase to be pressed too far). These do not, as we shall see, constitute the whole of his account of the truth-conditions even of such propositions, but I shall set them out on their own first of all. They can be summarized as follows.

The correspondence truth-conditions of an I proposition (one of the form *Some A is (a) B*) are satisfied if and only if its subject and predicate 'stand for the same (thing)'. What this means is that there is at least one thing for which each of A and B stands, i.e. that the suppositions of A and B have some common member.

The correspondence truth-conditions of an A proposition (one of the form *Every A is (a) B*) are satisfied if and only if (i) A stands for something, and (ii) everything that A stands for, B also stands for. Buridan sometimes expresses all this briefly by saying that the subject and the predicate 'stand for the same universally'.

E and O propositions are then treated as equivalent to the negations of I and A propositions respectively. That is, the correspondence truth-conditions of an E proposition (one of the form *No A is (a) B*) are satisfied if and only if those of the corresponding proposition of the form *Some A is (a) B* are *not* satisfied; and those of an O proposition (of the form *Some A is not (a) B*) are satisfied if and only if those of the corresponding proposition of the form *Every A is (a) B* are not satisfied.

The extension of these conditions to singular and indefinite propositions is a straightforward matter.

It is worth noting that Buridan interprets all affirmative propositions (A's as well as I's) existentially, in the sense that the 'non-emptiness' of the subject is a necessary condition of their truth, and therefore its 'emptiness' a sufficient condition of their falsity. This appears, indeed, to have been the standard mediaeval way of interpreting such propositions. (See Moody [1953], ch. III.) An A proposition, so understood, cannot therefore be represented by the formula $\forall x(\varphi x \supset \psi x)$ of modern logic, which counts as true if there are no φ's, but is more analogous to $\exists x \varphi x \land \forall x(\varphi x \supset \psi x)$.

Now the satisfaction of the relevant correspondence truth-conditions is, according to Buridan, a necessary condition of a proposition's truth. If the correspondence truth-conditions appropriate to a certain proposition are not satisfied then that proposition is thereby shown to be false (unless of course it does not exist, in which case, as we have seen, it does not qualify as either true or false). But we have not yet, he thinks, got a sufficient condition of truth, for there is another way in which we can show that a proposition is false, and that is by deducing a known falsehood from it, or from it in conjunction with some given true proposition. The principle involved here, to which he appeals many times in Chapter 8, is, in his words, that 'any proposition is false from which, together with something true, there follows something false'. (See, for example, §§ 8.3, 11.5, 14.4, 15.5.1.1.) Typically, when he uses this principle in order to prove that a certain proposition is false, the 'something false' that he deduces from it (or from it together with a given truth) is in fact something self-contradictory, and it would seem that the principle could still do all the work he wants it to do if we were to replace its last word by 'self-contradictory'. So to have a conveniently succinct way of referring to propositions that can be shown to be false in this way, I shall call them *contextually inconsistent* propositions. Now if every contextually inconsistent proposition is false, then a necessary condition of a proposition's being true is that it should be contextually *consistent*, i.e. that it should not (either by itself or in conjunction with any other true proposition) entail anything false. The truth-conditions we have now formulated for categorical propositions are, according to Buridan, not merely severally necessary but collectively sufficient, and we are at last in a position to formulate his theory of the criteria of their truth and falsity. As we have seen, in order to be true or false at all, a proposition must first of all exist. Given then that it does exist, it is true if and only if (1) the relevant correspondence truth-conditions are satisfied and (2) it is contextually consistent; otherwise − i.e. if either the relevant correspondence truth-conditions are not satisfied or it is contextually inconsistent − it is false.

A statement of the truth-conditions of propositions must of course take account of more complex cases than categorical ones. It is worth adding, therefore, that Buridan interprets conjunctive and disjunctive propositions in the truth-functional way that is common in modern logic: that is, *p and q* counts as true if *p* and *q* are both true, and counts as false otherwise; and *p or q* counts as true if at least one of *p* and *q* is true, and counts as false otherwise. (Of course, in view of his doctrine that no part of a proposition is itself a proposition, he would regard all this as loosely expressed.) The truth-conditions of conditional propositions are the subject of lengthy discussions in Sophisms 1−3 and 17−18.

It may perhaps be wondered whether the condition numbered (2) a couple of paragraphs back really adds anything to condition (1). To put the question in another way, is it possible for a proposition to have its correspondence truth-conditions satisfied and yet (on its own or in conjunction with some true proposition) to entail something false? If this cannot happen, then of course condition (2), although it may be interesting and important in its own right, adds nothing of substance to condition (1) in that it does not in any way reduce the number of propositions that count as true. But according to Buridan this is precisely what does happen in the case of the self-referential paradoxes, as we shall see in more detail later on; and that is why he thinks condition (2) is needed in addition to condition (1). On the other hand, he holds that it is *only* in the case of self-referential propositions that this situation can arise at all: this view is made quite explicit in § 15.5.1.3, though he never appears to try to give a proof of it. He therefore thinks that so long as we are dealing only with non-self-referential propositions, the correspondence truth-conditions by themselves will give us perfectly adequate truth-criteria.

It has sometimes been suggested that this means that Buridan is arbitrarily introducing an additional criterion of truth, applicable to self-referential propositions only, that he is therefore employing a different concept of truth and falsity for such propositions, one which requires more stringent conditions for truth and correspondingly more generous conditions for falsity for them than for ordinary, non-self-referential ones, and that his solution of the paradoxes is as a result objectionably *ad hoc*. I do not think that this criticism can be sustained. He intends his criteria for truth to be perfectly general in their application. He is not maintaining that the requirement of contextual consistency is inapplicable to non-self-referential propositions, or that the principle on which it is based fails for them. No proposition whatever, he holds, self-referential or non-self-referential, can be true if it is contextually inconsistent: it is merely that with non-self-referential ones we can be sure that any that have their correspondence truth-conditions satisfied will be contextually consistent as well, and so for such propositions condition (2) is not positively needed in addition to condition (1) in order to sift the true ones from the false ones. Moreover, I can see nothing arbitrary about the requirement of contextual consistency in any case: it seems to be no more than a spelling out of one of the fundamental principles that underlie any sound theory of deductive inference, that true premisses never entail a false conclusion.

Earlier on I referred to some of Buridan's complaints against the idea that a proposition is true if and only if 'as it signifies, so it is'. Another criticism he has to make of this formula is that it misleadingly suggests that there is a single uniform test of truth for all propositions, no matter what their form may be, whereas he himself holds, as we have seen, that the criteria of truth vary in their details from one type of proposition to another. Nevertheless, having delivered his polemics and set out what he thinks is the correct account of what makes true propositions true, he then says that the formula is such a convenient and familiar one that he proposes to go on using it – but in his own sense. And this sense is that to say of a proposition, 'as it signifies, so it is', is to mean simply that the truth-conditions appropriate to that proposition, as he has explained them, are satisfied.[5] Moreover, we must note carefully that it is *not* to be taken to mean that the proposition in question actually exists (or, of course, that it does not); sometimes, indeed, when the need for special care arises, he prefers to say 'as the

---

[5] *Sophismata*, ch. 2, immediately after Conclusion 14.

proposition *would* signify (if it existed), so it is'. This expressly stipulated sense of 'as it signifies, so it is' is the 'good sense explained in Chapter 2' referred to at §1.4.3, and whenever the formula occurs in Chapter 8, as it does with great frequency, this is always the way in which we are to understand it.

For my translation I have tried to find a more natural English phrase which will convey the same general idea as *sicut significat, ita est*, have the same air of spurious generality, and be open to analogous, even if not identical, objections if pressed too closely. What I have used is 'The facts (*or*, Things) are as the proposition says they are', or some minor variant thereof.

In Chapter 8 Buridan sometimes wants a phrase that shall mean merely that a proposition's *correspondence* truth-conditions are satisfied, and not carry the implication that it is or would be contextually consistent. What he uses for this purpose is *sicut significat secundum* (or, *per*) *suam formalem significationem, ita est* (literally, 'as it signifies by its formal signification, so it is'). I have translated this as 'The facts are as by its formal meaning it says they are'.

I remarked earlier that, given Buridan's conception of what a proposition is, it is possible for one and the same proposition to be both true and false, in the sense that two people may attach different meanings to it and it may be true under one interpretation but false under the other. It is also possible, without any variation in interpretation, for one and the same proposition to be true at one time but false at another, since the things to which it refers may change in relevant ways; the proposition 'Socrates is sitting', for example, becomes false when Socrates stands up. But Buridan holds that, given a fixed interpretation of a proposition, it is quite impossible for it to be both true and false at the same time. Moreover he is also a strict bi-valentist in the sense that every proposition is at any given time either true or false (assuming of course that it exists at that time). There is no trace in his thought of any truth-value other than truth and falsity, or of any notion that a proposition might exist but have no truth-value at all.

There is one other matter which I shall say something about before concluding this Section, since it is concerned with truth-conditions and plays a major role in Chapter 8. In Sophism 7 Buridan raises the question of the relation between a proposition itself and a proposition to the effect that that first proposition is true. The conclusion that he comes to is this (for the details see §7.7.3 and the commentary on it and on §7.7.2): Suppose we take any proposition, and suppose we give it the name 'A'; then the conjunction of the original proposition and a proposition asserting that A exists entails a proposition asserting that A is true. This principle seems to deserve a name of its own; I shall call it *the principle of truth-entailment*, and I shall refer to 'A is true' as *the implied proposition*. One use to which Buridan puts the principle is to help to derive a self-contradiction from the paradoxes. That, I think, is a straightforward matter, and I shall illustrate it in the next Section. But he also repeatedly says that it is a necessary condition of the truth of any proposition that not merely should the facts be as it itself by its formal meaning says they are, but also that the facts should be as its implied proposition says they are. Now in one way this seems entirely reasonable, for (granted the principle of truth-entailment) it seems to be simply an application of the principle that what is true cannot entail anything false. But in another way it is puzzling. For since the implied proposition is not self-referential, saying that the facts are as it says they are merely amounts to saying that its correspondence truth-conditions are satisfied; and since it is an affirmative singular proposition this will simply mean that its subject and its predicate 'stand for the same'. But its subject – i.e. 'A' – stands for the original proposition and for nothing else, and therefore to say that its subject and predicate stand for the same is to say no more and no less than that the original proposition is a true one. So Buridan appears to be saying that one of the necessary conditions of the truth of a proposition is that it should be true, and this seems to be a totally vacuous thing to say.

There is a way of looking at the matter, however, which makes his claim not vacuous at all. As we have seen, he thinks it is possible for a proposition to have its correspondence truth-conditions satisfied and yet (together with a given truth) to entail a self-contradiction. When this happens, the deducibility of the self-contradiction does not in any way show that the correspondence truth-conditions of the original proposition are not after all satisfied (i.e. it does not show that things are not as by its formal meaning it says they are); but it does show that the proposition is *false*, and therefore that in the implied proposition ('A is true') the subject and the predicate do not stand for the same, i.e. that *its* correspondence truth-conditions are not satisfied, or that things are not as *it* says they are. So Buridan's insistence that for a proposition to be true the subject and predicate of its implied proposition must stand for the same becomes in effect a way of reminding us that there may be another way in which a proposition can fail to be true than by the non-satisfaction of its own correspondence truth-conditions. The point is non-vacuous only if there *is* such another way; but of course he believes there is.

The requirement that the subject and predicate of the implied proposition should stand for the same is therefore not to be thought of as a third necessary condition of truth in addition to the two we noted earlier on. Given the principle of truth-entailment, and the principle that whatever in conjunction with a given truth entails a falsehood is false, it could take the place of the requirement of contextual consistency; and in Chapter 8, more often than not, Buridan in fact prefers to let it do so. The reason for this preference may lie in the fact that he can then give a complete account of what makes a proposition true in terms of the satisfaction of correspondence truth-conditions alone. For although he cannot say that a proposition is true if and only if its own correspondence truth-conditions are satisfied, he can say that it is true if and only if the correspondence truth-conditions of *it itself and whatever is entailed by it and the context* are satisfied; and this may well have struck him as a neater way to formulate his theory.

III

I shall now try to outline the essential points in Buridan's solution of the *Liar* and allied paradoxes. As I have already mentioned, he deals with several paradoxes of this kind in Sophisms 7–12, and in the Commentary I discuss his treatment of them in some detail. So to avoid unnecessary repetition what I shall do here is to try to work out the way in which he would solve two versions of the *Liar* which he does not mention but which have become well known in recent years.

The first of these examples is adapted from Black [1948], though the way in which I envisage Buridan deriving the paradox is not the same as Black's way, and the solution I attribute to him is very different indeed from Black's.[6] The posited case, as Buridan would put it, is that there is a rectangle, which I shall call 'X', within which is written a proposition to the effect that the proposition written in X is false, and nothing else. The case can therefore be illustrated by the following diagram:

X → | The proposition written in X is false |

[6] The earliest occurrence of this example, as far as I know, is in Thomas Oliver, *De Sophismatum Praestigiis Cavendis Admonitio* (1604). (See Ashworth [1974], p. 114.)

I shall use the letter 'A' as a name of the proposition in X, and of nothing else. Moreover, by the ordinary conventions of English, any token of the definite descriptive phrase 'the proposition written in X' – including the first five words of A itself – will also stand for that same proposition, and for nothing else.

Now *prima facie* we can prove about A that if it is true it is false and if it is false it is true, and therefore that if it is either true or false it is both true and false. This indeed is what constitutes the paradox. It would be Buridan's contention, however, that A is simply false and not true at all. He would be entirely happy with a deduction of its falsity from the hypothesis of its truth, but he would deny the validity of any inference in the reverse direction.

I shall outline the way in which he would argue that A is false, and then show why he would reject the standard inference from this to the conclusion that it is true.

Several arguments for the falsity of A can easily be extracted from Chapter 8, and I shall mention two of them. The first runs like this. Since by the hypothesis of the case A exists, it must be either true or false. If it is false, we have our result immediately. If on the other hand it is true, it follows that the facts are as it says they are; but what it says is simply that it itself is false; so it follows that it *is* false. Hence on either supposition A is false.

The second argument uses what I have called the principle of truth-entailment. This principle holds for any proposition whatsoever, and hence in particular for A. A and 'A exists', therefore, together entail that A is true. But A and 'A exists' also together entail that A is false (since that is just what A itself asserts). So A and 'A exists' together entail that A is both true and false. Now this conclusion is self-contradictory, and therefore, since 'A exists' is given as true by the initial statement of the case, A is contextually inconsistent and hence false.

So far, of course, there is nothing paradoxical. Paradox arises only if we can also prove that if A is false it follows that it is true. So the success of Buridan's solution must in large measure depend on whether he can consistently deny the validity of any such inference.

The standard argument is simply this. Let us assume that A is false; but now what A asserts is just this (that A is false) and nothing else; so everything that A asserts to be the case is the case, and hence it is true. It should be clear from what I have said in the previous Section what Buridan's reply to this would be. It would be that the falsity of A does indeed show that its subject and its predicate stand for the same, and therefore (since it is a singular affirmative) that its correspondence truth-conditions are satisfied, but that this is not enough to prove that it is true. To do that we should also have to show that it is contextually consistent, but our second proof of its falsity consisted precisely in a demonstration that it is not. Moreover, both of our proofs showed that the subject and predicate of the implied proposition ('A is true') do not stand for the same. So although from the supposition that A is false it follows that A satisfies some of the necessary conditions for its truth, it does not satisfy them all.

I think we can gain a better insight into Buridan's position here by confronting it with what seems at first to be a very powerful objection. Clearly he wants to accept

(1) A is false

and to reject

(2) A is true.

But, we may ask, can he consistently do so, especially in the light of his acceptance of the principle of truth-entailment? For it seems possible to deduce (2) from (1) *even on his own principles*, in the following way. Since A just is the proposition written in X, (1) yields

(3) The proposition written in X is false

– which is simply A itself. Next, by the principle of truth-entailment, we can infer from (3) (since the existence of A is given by the posited case):

(4) 'The proposition written in X is false' is true.

And finally, by our convention for the use of 'A' we can re-write (4) as

(5) A is true

– which is simply (2) itself. So (1) does entail (2) after all, contrary to what Buridan wants to maintain.[7]

Buridan does not tackle such an argument directly, but he comes so close to doing so that I think one can work out with reasonable

---

[7] If I may venture a personal remark here, I thought at one time that this argument was irrefutable and that it showed Buridan's theory to be inconsistent. My enthusiasm for him dates largely from the moment when it struck me that he could reply to it along the lines suggested here.

confidence what his reply to it would be. (In doing so I take my main clues from §§ 8.4.3, 13.5–13.6, and 15.8.2.) The crucial step he would reject is, I think, the identification of (3) with the original proposition A. The point here is not the trivial one that these are physically distinct inscriptions; that would not matter if they had the same truth-conditions. The point is rather that A is self-referential but (3) is not; for the subject of A (its first five words) stands for A itself, but the subject of (3) (*its* first five words) stands not for (3) but for A. As we have seen, Buridan holds that the fact that a proposition is self-referential can lead it to have a truth-value different from the one it would have if it were not self-referential, or from the one that an equiform but non-self-referential proposition has; for with self-referential propositions, unlike others, there is the possibility of their being contextually inconsistent even though their correspondence truth-conditions are satisfied.

Let us run through the steps of the objection one by one. The derivation of (3) from (1) seems straightforward, and I do not imagine that Buridan would wish to challenge it. But I think he would say that whether (4) follows from (3), and whether in turn (4) can be re-written as (5) (or as (2)), depends on how we interpret (4). For (4) is ambiguous. Its subject – i.e. everything from the first inverted comma to the second one inclusive – could be taken as a name of (3), in which case (4) does indeed follow from (3) (given the existence of (3), which poses no problems), but it cannot be re-written as (5), or as (2), but only as something like

(6) B is true

where 'B' is a name of (3), not of A. Alternatively, the subject of (4) could be taken as a name of A, the original proposition in X, in which case (4) *can* be re-written as (5) or as (2), but does not follow from (3). So the inference from (1) to (2) breaks down at one point or at another.

On Buridanian principles, indeed, (3) is a straightforward, non-paradoxical *true* proposition. It and A are of course equiform. Like A, (3) has its correspondence truth-conditions satisfied, for its subject stands for A and only for A, and A, according to Buridan, is false, as (3) says it is. But whereas we were able to deduce a self-contradiction from A, we do not seem to be able to deduce one from (3) in any analogous way, or in any other way either, as far as I can see. The parallel procedure would be to deduce both the truth and the falsity of (3) from (3) itself together with the assertion of its existence. But although, as we have seen, we can from this deduce

(6) B is true

(where 'B' is a name of (3)), there seems to be just no way of deducing

(7) B is false.

All we can obtain is that *A* is false, for A is the only proposition in X, but that does not contradict (6).

My second example, which is perhaps the best known of all modern expositions of the *Liar* paradox, occurs in Tarski [1944]. Here I shall follow Tarski's own derivation of the paradox closely, though I shall spell out some of his abbreviations and for obvious reasons I shall alter the page and line numbers in his example. It will, I think, be instructive to try to work out what Buridan's comments on the argument might be. According to Tarski our concept of truth ought to lead us to accept every 'equivalence of the form (T)', i.e. every sentence obtainable from the schema

X is true if and only if *p*

by replacing '*p*' by a declarative sentence and 'X' by a name of that sentence. His example of a paradoxical sentence is

(8) The sentence printed in this book on p. 27, l. 18 is not true.

He then offers as an equivalence of the form (T):

(9) 'The sentence printed in this book on p. 27, l. 18 is not true' is true if and only if the sentence printed in this book on p. 27, l. 18 is not true.

But now, he says, we find empirically that the sentence printed in this book on p. 27, l. 18 just is 'The sentence printed in this book on p. 27, l. 18 is not true'. So by what is sometimes called Leibniz' Law we can obtain from (9):

(10) 'The sentence printed in this book on p. 27, l. 18 is not true' is true if and only if 'The sentence printed in this book on p. 27, l. 18 is not true' is not true.

Thus we seem to be committed to the self-contradictory result that (8) is true if and only if (8) is not true.

A Buridanian critique of this argument would, I think, proceed by claiming that (9) is ambiguous – that on one interpretation it is a genuine equivalence of the form (T) but does not generate any paradox, while on the alternative interpretation it does indeed generate a paradox but is not a genuine equivalence of the form (T) and we do not have to accept it. The crucial question is, what is the expression at the beginning of (9) ('"The sentence...not true"') a name of? This question could have two answers: the expression could be construed *either* as a name of (i) the original sentence (8) *or* as a name of (ii) the right-hand side (RHS) of (9) itself (i.e. everything that succeeds the 'if and only if' in (9)); and (i) and (ii) are not to be identified, because the latter, not being printed on p. 27, l. 18, is not self-referential, but the former is.

Now if (9) is to be an equivalence of the form (T) then its initial expression must be taken in the second of these ways, i.e. as a name of its RHS and not of something else instead. But with this interpretation no trouble arises for Buridan at all. For he would certainly want to maintain that (8) is not true, and hence that the RHS of (9), which non-self-referentially says just that, is true. That being so, the left-hand side (LHS) of (9) will also be true, since it correctly, and again non-self-referentially, says that the RHS of (9) is true. So on this interpretation both sides of (9) will be true. Moreover, if we derive (10) from (9) in the way that was indicated, still using this interpretation of (9), then (10) will turn out to be true, not self-contradictory as was suggested. For the first occurrence of '"The sentence...not true"' in (10) will name the RHS of (9), and the whole LHS of (10) will say correctly of this that it is true; but the second occurrence of it will name not the RHS of (9) but the whole of (8), and the RHS of (10) will say correctly of (8) that it is not true; so both sides of (10), and therefore (10) itself, will be true.

If however, (9) is to generate the desired paradox, then its initial expression must be taken to name not the RHS of (9) itself, but (8). Under this interpretation the falsity of (8) will indeed ensure that the LHS of (9) is false and its RHS is true; so (9) as a whole will be false – in fact self-contradictory, as (10), with a corresponding interpretation, brings out clearly. But with this interpretation (9) is not an equivalence of the form (T), and nothing seems to force us to accept it.

The problem of their truth-value is not the only problem that Buridan raises in connection with the *Liar*-type paradoxes, nor are these paradoxes the only ones he deals with. Nevertheless, a grasp of the principles underlying his solution to this particular problem provides valuable clues to understanding his treatment of other problems and paradoxes. That is one reason why I have singled out this issue for special discussion here. Another reason is that this is the problem which is likely to be most familiar, and of greatest interest, to a modern reader. Most of the modern treatments of paradoxical self-referential sentences maintain either that they are not (or do not express) genuine propositions at all, or that in spite of appearances they are not really self-referential, or that they are neither true nor false but possess some third truth-value distinct from truth and falsity, or that they have no truth-value at all. In contrast with all such views, Buridan maintains that they are genuine propositions, that they are genuinely self-referential, and that they have a determinate classical truth-value. This is what gives his view its importance, if he can maintain it consistently; for *prima facie* the paradoxical sentences are propositional in nature and are self-referential, and whether or not we believe in third truth-values or propositions that have no truth-value at all, it is at least gratifying to find a solution that involves none of these things.

It is not part of my intention in this book to suggest that Buridan has produced *the correct* solution of the *Liar* or any other paradox. Indeed, I am doubtful whether there is or even could be any such thing. The issues raised by the paradoxes of self-reference seem to me to be profound, complicated and ramified, and I suspect that they can be adequately dealt with only by a variety of interrelated approaches which make contact with many other problems, philosophical, logical, linguistic and mathematical. But in that network of argumentation which, if I am right, is needed, Buridan's ideas can, I believe, form an important and distinctive part.

IV

My main reason for deciding to write this book was a conviction that Buridan has something important to say about many of the issues with which twentieth-century philosophical logicians have been concerned. The more I read him the more contemporary he seems to me to be, and what I should like most of all to think is that I had done something to help him to take his place in a present-day debate. I should make it clear that I am not, and have no wish to pose as, a historian of mediaeval philosophy. Although I have of necessity tried to explain certain mediaeval terms and ideas, and have referred occasionally to controversies in which Buridan may have been engaged, I have made no attempt in this book to relate his thought to that of other mediaeval thinkers or to trace his influence on later writers. My concern with him is philosophical rather than historical, and the kind of reader I have had mainly in mind is one who wants to grasp the nature of the problems he raises and to understand just what his arguments are, for the sake of their philosophical interest and importance. On the other hand I have not tried to turn my discussion of him into an independent philosophical treatise on the issues he deals with. I have criticized his arguments when they seem to me to be faulty, and I have sometimes called attention to alternative views, but I have not used his ideas as pegs on which to hang my own.

My purpose, in short, is to let Buridan speak for himself, but I have tried to help him to do so in a way that will be as intelligible as possible to modern readers. Such readers, even when they may suspect that a mediaeval author has much of value to offer them, commonly have to struggle with a terminology, a set of background ideas, and even a style of expounding an argument, that have become unfamiliar and baffling; and I have tried to do what I can to help them to surmount these barriers. This aim has guided me not only in the Commentary but also in the translation. The version I have given *is* intended as a translation, not a mere paraphrase, in that I have tried to make every phrase in the Latin be reflected somehow in the English; but it is deliberately free in style, and I have used as much modern idiom and terminology as I could without distorting the sense. I have also introduced various sub-headings and a system of numbering paragraphs in the hope of making the structure of Buridan's arguments easier to follow, and also to provide a means of easy reference in the Commentary. On the other hand I do not now think it is possible to do what I had at first hoped to do – namely to make a completely modern-sounding book out of Buridan's text – without abandoning the idea of translation altogether and falling back on paraphrase instead; so I am conscious that stylistically my version is something of a compromise.

Perhaps ironically, the *Sophismata* is the only one of Buridan's works of which an English translation is already available. This translation was made by T. K. Scott, and appeared in 1966 under the title *Sophisms on Meaning and Truth*. A reader who cares to compare Scott's translation of Chapter 8 with mine will find a large number of divergences between them, occasionally amounting to a complete reversal of sense. Some of these are accounted for by the differences between the Latin texts with which we were respectively working (about which I shall say something in a moment); others are due to the fact that he was obviously aiming at a far more literal translation than I have been; others again represent genuine disagreements in interpretation. I hope, however, that none of my disagreements with him about either the text or its meaning will be taken as detracting from the debt I owe to his work for making me aware of the excitement and precision of Buridan's thought.

The sources for a Latin text of the *Sophismata* can be briefly indicated as follows. Seven manuscripts of the complete work are known to survive, all dating from the late fourteenth or the fifteenth centuries. Then, during the closing years of the fifteenth century, no fewer than five printed editions appeared, all in Paris. After that the work does not seem to have been printed at all until a modern edited text, produced, like the translation I have mentioned, by T. K. Scott, was published in 1977; this text, however, for the most part follows closely the wording of one of the incunabula (that printed by Denidel and Barra), though it modifies it in the light of some of the manuscript readings.

For the present book I have compiled a fresh Latin text of Chapter 8. In doing so I have compared word by word six of the seven complete manuscripts, the Denidel and Barra edition, and Scott's text. What I have tried to do with this material, however, is simply to assemble a version that seemed to me to make the best *philosophical* sense at each point. I can lay no claim to expertise in textual criticism, and I have therefore not attempted such tasks as establishing priority of manuscripts or trying to reconstruct what Buridan actually wrote; though no doubt those who have as much respect as I have for his intellectual powers will be sympathetic to the idea that what makes best philosophical sense is most likely to have come from his own hand.

This book, of course, deals only with a single chapter, though the longest one, of the *Sophismata*; but whether even the *Sophismata* as a whole should be regarded as a self-contained work on its own is a trickier question than might appear at first sight. Buridan tells us that he planned it as the ninth and final Tract of his long general treatise on logic, the *Summulae de Dialectica*, and that is the position in which it appears in most of the known manuscripts. Nevertheless, its structure is quite different from that of the other eight Tracts, and he himself seems sometimes to have thought of it as a distinct work. In §4.3.1, for example, he refers to the *Summulae* as if it were a different book. There are also a number of places in the *Summulae* in which he mentions the *Sophismata* by name, again as if he were speaking of another book. There is even a passage in the *Summulae* (Tract v, Chapter 6, Part 8) where he explicitly corrects what he says is a mistake in the *Sophismata* – an astonishing thing to do if he were talking about a later section of the very book he was then writing. There is, however, some reason to think that he prepared two versions of the *Summulae*, an earlier one that included the *Sophismata* and a later one that did not (see Pinborg [1976], p. 72), and this may explain some of the apparent anomalies.

I remarked earlier that there are certain features of Buridan's style of argumentation which present-day readers are likely to find unfamiliar and by which they may even be misled. I want now to make some comments on two of these. Neither is peculiar to Buridan; both were among the stock-in-trade of logicians of his period.

The first is his frequent use of stock true and false propositions. A good example occurs in his statement of Sophism 10. A modern writer would be likely to pose the problem by saying something like: 'Suppose there are only four propositions, two of which are uncontroversially true, one of which is uncontroversially false, and the fourth of which is "There are the same number of true and false propositions"'. Buridan, however, simply lists the first three propositions as 'God exists', 'A man is an animal', and 'A horse is a goat', without any comment on their truth or falsity. It is important to realise that the only point that is relevant to the problem is that the first two should be taken as true and the third as false. In particular, by using the first of the three Buridan is not trying to raise any theological questions. 'God exists' is, in fact, one of the favourite stock true propositions used by mediaeval authors, but a reader who is not a theist can always substitute for it any proposition that he does take to be uncontroversially true, and the argument will be unaffected. The examples I have mentioned would in fact be regarded by Buridan as necessarily true or necessarily false; but he also uses a number of stock contingent propositions. Among his favourites are 'Socrates is sitting' (see, for example, Sophism 14) and 'A horse is running'. Again, nothing turns on the content of these examples.

The second feature concerns the ordering of the steps in an argument. A modern reader, when told that a certain proposition, z, is going to be proved, is apt to expect a more or less linear chain of reasoning in which various premises are stated and argued for where necessary, and z is deduced from them at the end. In the style of argument I am concerned with here, z is first announced as what is to be proved, and then we are immediately given an inference, usually with a very simple structure, having z as its conclusion. That is, the argument runs something like: 'z, because (*quia*) p, q, therefore z'. The modern reader, seeing 'therefore z', is apt to suppose that this is the end of the proof, and to find himself bewildered because at least one of p and q is not at all obviously true, has not been argued for before, and may even seem to beg the question at issue. But in fact we are only at the beginning, for the next step is to tackle p and q themselves. Perhaps one of them, say p, is obvious, and we need only to be reminded of this fact; but q may need its own proof. And the proof of q in turn may take the form of deducing it from a number of premisses, some of which may need their own proofs, and so on. Thus we may have a structure like this.

To prove z:

$p, q, \therefore z$

p is an established logical principle.

Proof of q:

$r, s, t, u, \therefore q$

r is given by the posited case.

u is obvious.

Proof of s:

$v, w, \therefore s$

v follows from r.

w is an established logical principle.

Proof of t:

$x, y, \therefore t$

x and y have been proved previously.

Everything needed for the derivation of z is there, and quite explicitly stated; it is only the order of assembly that is unfamiliar. Examples in our text of arguments in this style will be found in §§8.3 (which has almost exactly the form of the above example), 9.3, 14.4.1 and 15.5.1ff, and these are analysed in detail in the Commentary. But essentially the same kind of structure, though in a much simpler form, can be seen in such passages as §2.1.2.

CHAPTER EIGHT

This chapter will be concerned with propositions that are self-referential because of the meanings of their terms. It will include a discussion of the so-called *insolubles*, but some easier sophisms will be presented to begin with. The first is this:

1.0 *Every proposition is affirmative, therefore no proposition is negative.*

1.1 *Arguments in favour of the sophism:*

1.1.1. The first is based on a principle about contraries. 'Everyone is ill, therefore no one is well' is a valid inference because it is impossible for one and the same person to be both well and ill at the same time. In the same way, the sophism is valid because it is impossible for one and the same proposition to be both affirmative and negative at the same time.

1.1.2. The usual way of proving that an enthymeme is valid is to find a necessary proposition which, if added as an extra premiss, will turn the inference into a formally valid syllogism. For example, we say that 'A donkey flies, therefore a donkey has wings' is a valid inference, because 'Everything that flies has wings' is a necessary proposition and if we use it as the major premiss we have a valid syllogism in *Darii*. Now the present sophism is an enthymeme, 'No affirmative proposition is negative' is a necessary proposition, and if we make it the major premiss the result is a valid syllogism in *Celarent*.

1.1.3. It is a universally sound principle about inferences that if the negation of the conclusion entails the negation of the premiss then the inference is valid. Now the sophism clearly satisfies this condition, for 'Some proposition is negative' obviously entails 'Not every proposition is affirmative'.

1.2 *Arguments against the sophism:*

1.2.1. What is possible never entails anything impossible. Now the premiss in the sophism – 'Every proposition is affirmative' – is possible; for God could annihilate all negative propositions and leave the affirmative ones alone, and then every proposition would be affirmative. On the other hand the conclusion – 'No proposition is negative' – is impossible, since there is no situation in which it could

34

be true: for when it does not exist it is neither true nor false, and when it does exist then some proposition (namely it itself) *is* negative; so it must be false to say that no proposition is negative.

1.2.2. If the premiss of an inference could be true without the conclusion's being true, then the inference is not valid. Now in the present case the premiss could be true but the conclusion could not be true at all, so obviously the premiss could be true without the conclusion's being true. This is clear for another reason as well: if God were to annihilate all the negatives then 'Every proposition is affirmative' would be true, but the conclusion of the sophism would not be true, since it would not even exist. So plainly the premiss could be true without the conclusion's being true, and therefore the inference is not valid.

1.2.2.1. One reply to this has been that what makes an inference valid is not the fact that the premiss could not be true without the conclusion, or without the conclusion's being true; rather it is the fact that the premiss could not be true without the conclusion's being true *when these are formulated at the same time* – and the case we are considering does satisfy *this* condition.

1.2.2.2. But this view is open to the objection that if that were the reason why an inference is said to be valid, then the inference 'No proposition is affirmative, therefore there is a stick standing in the corner' would be valid. For it is impossible that its premiss and conclusion should be formulated at the same time and the premiss be true at all; and if the premiss cannot itself be true it follows that it cannot be true without the conclusion.

1.2.3. To resume the arguments against the sophism: If the premiss of an inference is true, but adding the conclusion to it would make it false, then the inference is not valid; for in such a case the conclusion would seem to be more in conflict with the premiss than in agreement with it. But that is how it is with the present sophism. For if we first assume that 'Every proposition is affirmative' is true and then add 'No proposition is negative' to it, that will make it false. So the inference is not valid.

1.3. I maintain that the inference is a valid one, for the reasons given above. But then there is a problem about the conditions under which an inference should be considered to be valid or invalid. I shall now briefly set down some conclusions on this topic.

1.4.1. An inference in which the premiss can be true without the conclusion's being true (or, without the conclusion) may nevertheless be a valid one; for 'A man is running, therefore an animal is running' is a valid inference, yet the first proposition could be true even if the second one did not exist but had been annihilated.

1.4.2. There can even be a valid inference in which the premiss could be true but the conclusion could not possibly be true at all. The present sophism is a clear case in point: 'Every proposition is affirmative' could be true, but 'No proposition is negative' could not; and yet the latter follows from the former. In many other cases something similar would hold too; e.g. 'Every syllable is several letters, therefore no syllable is only a single letter'.

1.4.3. There are propositions that are possible but cannot possibly be true. The proof is this: A premiss which is possible never entails a conclusion which is impossible (see Book I of the *Prior Analytics*). But 'Every proposition is affirmative' is a possible proposition, and it entails 'No proposition is negative'. So the latter is also possible; and yet it cannot be true. This makes it quite clear that what leads us to call a proposition a *possible* one is not the fact that it can be true, nor is what leads us to call a proposition an *impossible* one the fact that it cannot be true. Rather, a proposition is said to be possible because the facts could be as it says they are (taking those words in the good sense explained in Chapter 2), and impossible because they could not.

1.4.4. In a valid inference it is impossible for the premiss to be true but the conclusion false. (This, incidentally, is how we ought to understand the statement in Book II of the *Prior Analytics* that what is false cannot follow from what is true.) So it is quite correct to say that in a valid inference it is impossible for the premiss to be true without the conclusion's also being true, when they are both formulated at the same time. In spite of this, however, it has to be admitted that we can have cases in which something true entails something false. For even if we suppose that 'Every proposition is affirmative' is true, it can still entail something false, namely 'No proposition is negative'. But the point is that when we actually come to state this conclusion, the premiss will no longer be true but will then have become false.

1.4.5. It is not, however, *sufficient* for the validity of an inference that it should be impossible for the premiss to be true without the conclusion's also being true, when these are formulated at the same time. The earlier argument about the stick in the corner showed that. Another example will also make the point clear: 'No proposition is negative, therefore no proposition is affirmative' is obviously not a valid inference, since the negation of the conclusion does not entail the negation of the premiss; yet the premiss cannot be true without the conclusion's being true, simply because the premiss itself cannot be true at all. Something more is therefore required for the validity of an inference, and that is that the facts cannot be as the premiss says they are unless they are also as the conclusion says they are. (Of course we decided earlier on that these words are not really accurate; but we use them here – though in the sense explained elsewhere – because it is impossible to capture in a single formula what it is that makes all true propositions true or all false ones false. We have said all this in another place.)

1.5. In the light of these remarks we can now refute the arguments that were brought against the sophism. To the first one we can reply that 'No proposition is negative' is a *possible* proposition, though not one that is *possibly true*. The answer to the second should be clear from what we have said above. And what needs to be said about the third is this: the propositions in question are indeed in conflict with each other as far as *being true* is concerned; nevertheless they are not in conflict as far as *the facts being as they say are* is concerned (always using these words in the proper sense). Indeed in that respect they agree together perfectly well, since if the facts are as the first one says they are then they are also bound to be as the second says they are.

2.0 *No proposition is negative, therefore some proposition is negative.*

2.1 *Arguments in favour of the sophism:*

2.1.1. Let us assume that every proposition entails that it itself is true. (This seems to be Aristotle's view in the chapter on the term 'prior' in the *Categories*, where he says that if a man exists then it follows that 'A man exists' is true, and conversely; and the same would hold in all other cases.) Then the argument proceeds as follows: From 'No proposition is negative' it follows that 'No proposition is negative' is true; if that proposition is true, it follows that it exists; and if it exists it follows that some proposition *is* negative. So, following the sequence through, we have the result that if no proposition is negative it follows that some proposition is negative.

2.1.2. It is impossible for things to be as the premiss of the sophism asserts them to be unless they are as its conclusion asserts them to be; therefore the inference is valid. This whole inference itself seems to be clearly valid – it simply states the reason we gave in discussing the preceding sophism for saying that an inference is valid, and you could not express this reason in any other way. But now we can prove *its* premiss as follows: if things are as the premiss of the sophism asserts them to be, it follows that it does assert something; if it asserts something, it follows that it exists; and if it exists then things are as the conclusion asserts them to be.

2.2 *Arguments for the opposite view*:

2.2.1. What we said in the preceding sophism refutes this one; for things *could* be as the premiss says they are and yet not be as the conclusion says they are, since this would be the case if every negative proposition were to be destroyed. Hence the inference is not valid.

2.2.2. A possible proposition never entails its own contradictory; but the premiss of the sophism is a possible proposition, and the conclusion is its contradictory; therefore etc.

2.3. I maintain, briefly, that the sophism is false, since the arguments just given prove that the inference was not a valid one.

2.4 *Replies to the arguments for the sophism*:

2.4.1. My reply to the first of these arguments is that the principle stated there, that every proposition entails its own truth, is not strictly speaking correct. From 'A man exists' it does not follow that 'A man exists' is true; for a man could exist even though there were no propositions, and so it is possible for the facts to be as 'A man exists' says they are (or would say they are if it were actually stated), and yet not to be as '"A man exists" is true' would say they are, since the former would still hold if there were a man but no propositions.

2.4.1.1. You may then wonder how Aristotle's rule should be understood. In my opinion it should be understood on the assumption that the proposition in question actually exists; i.e. it should be taken to mean that from the conjunction of any given proposition and another one that asserts that it exists, it always follows that the first one is true. For example, from 'A man exists' and '"A man exists" exists' there follows '"A man exists" is true', for the facts cannot be as that conjunction says they are unless they are as the conclusion says they are (always speaking in the good sense).

2.4.2. The second argument, however, is a troublesome one. The first thing I have to say is that an inference is never valid or invalid unless it actually exists, and this means that for an inference to be valid both its premiss and its conclusion must exist. It is on that hypothesis that we have the rule that an inference is valid if it is impossible for the facts to be as the premiss says they are unless they are as the conclusion says they are. But now the second point is that this rule can be interpreted in either of two ways. (a) It might be an impossibility-proposition in a *composite* sense (in a broad understanding of that term).

I.e. it would mean that an inference is valid if the following is impossible: given that the inference has been actually formulated, the facts are as the premiss says they are, and they are not as the conclusion says they are. Now that rule is not a sound one, since it would yield the result that the sophism is valid; and what was wrong with the argument we are considering is that it was based on that incorrect rule. (b) Understood in the other way, however, the rule would be an impossibility-proposition in a *divided* sense. I.e. it would mean that an inference is valid if the facts cannot possibly be just as the premiss says they are unless they are as the conclusion says they are. And it is clear that this rule would not give the result that the sophism is valid; for the facts *can* be just as 'No proposition is negative' would say they are, without being as the second proposition says they are. This would in fact be the case if all negative propositions were annihilated and the affirmative ones survived; and that is possible.

The third sophism is concerned with what follows from a posited proposition. It is this: Suppose it is posited that every man is a donkey; then this follows:

3.0 *Every man is running, therefore a donkey is running.*

3.1 *Arguments in favour of the sophism*:

3.1.1. It can be proved by the following syllogism in *Darapti*: 'Every man is running; by hypothesis, every man is a donkey; therefore a donkey is running'. (This is like the way we argue in a *reductio ad absurdum*. We can construct such an argument by taking something maintained by our opponent, adding to it something true, and then drawing a conclusion; and the inference itself is valid even though the conclusion may turn out to be impossible. It is like that in the present case too: the inference itself is a valid one.)

3.1.2. Things cannot be both as they were posited to be and as the premiss says they are, unless they are as the conclusion says they are. Therefore the premiss and the posited case together entail the conclusion.

3.2 *Argument for the opposite view*: It is a rule of logic that a false inference is an impossible one, and a true one is necessary. Now the mere positing of a case cannot turn an impossible proposition into a necessary one; so no matter what you care to posit or withdraw, or grant or not grant, you cannot turn a false inference into a true one.

Everyone will agree that the inference 'Every man is running, therefore a donkey is running' is false, because it is not necessary; so no case that might be posited could ever make 'Every man is running' entail 'A donkey is running'.

3.3. The solution of this sophism is easy. You can state or posit or assert any proposition you like, but you can never thereby turn a necessary inference into one that is not necessary or *vice versa*. Therefore the stated sophism is false.

3.4. Nevertheless, in view of the arguments that were advanced, I should make it clear that a proposition can be posited or admitted or stated in either of two ways: (a) It may be posited *simply*, as a proposition considered on its own; and in that case it will be irrelevant to the truth or falsity of any other propositions or inferences in the case under consideration. Or (b) it may be posited specifically *as a premiss* (or as one premiss among others) for the purpose of inferring something else; and in that case it is certainly essential to see whether the suggested conclusion does or does not follow from the posited proposition (together with any other premisses). For example, if in the present case you were to posit *simply* that every man is a donkey, the inference in the sophism would not thereby be made any more or any less valid. But if you posit *as a premiss* (i.e. for inferring a conclusion) that every man is a donkey, then I admit straight away that it does follow from this that some man is a donkey; and if you posit it as a premiss to be taken together with the other premiss that every man is running, then indeed it does follow from this that a donkey is running. And it was on that basis that the arguments proceeded.

FOURTH SOPHISM

4.0 *I say that a man is a donkey.*

The question to be asked about this sophism is whether someone who says this is saying something true or something false.

4.1 *Argument that he is saying something false*: He is saying that a man is a donkey, and that is false.

4.2 *Arguments that he is saying something true*:

4.2.1. His whole proposition was 'I say that a man is a donkey' – and that was true, since that whole thing is precisely what he was saying.

4.2.2. His proposition was an affirmative one, so the fact that its subject and predicate stood for the same thing shows that what he said was true. Now it is clear that the subject and the predicate do stand for the same thing, since if we express the copula explicitly the proposition will become 'I am someone who is saying that a man is a donkey', and obviously the terms 'I' and 'someone who is saying that a man is a donkey' stand for the same thing.

4.3. The reaction of many people to this sophism is to claim that he is both saying something true and also saying something false. Their argument is that he is saying the whole sentence 'I say that a man is a donkey', and since that is true he is saying something true; but that in the course of saying the whole sentence he is saying each part of it, and so he is saying that a man is a donkey – and in so doing he is saying something false.

4.3.1. This solution, however, seems very dubious to me, since it assumes that a part of a proposition is itself a proposition, which is something that I do not believe. The Psalmist David, when speaking under the inspiration of the Holy Spirit, never said anything false; yet he did say this whole sentence, 'The fool has said in his heart, There is no God', and therefore he said the words 'There is no God'. Now if these words had formed a proposition he would have been saying something false and heretical; so in that context they did not form a proposition at all but were only part of a proposition. (On the other hand, the fool himself, who said these words on their own, as a proposition, really did commit an error.) It is like the way in which half a worm is not an animal so long as it is still a part of an animal, but becomes an animal when it is separated from the other part. I have, however, said enough about this topic in the seventh chapter of the first tract of the *Summulae*.

4.4. It seems to me that someone who says 'I say that a man is a donkey' is quite literally speaking the truth, and I also maintain that he is not saying anything false at all.

4.5 *Reply to the opposing argument*: When it is objected that he is saying that a man is a donkey, my reply is that although he did indeed utter such an expression, he did not use it on its own so as to constitute a proposition, and that therefore it was neither true nor false.

4.6. You may, however, protest that this view would lead to the conclusion that someone who said that this proposition 'A man is an animal' is true, would be speaking falsely. Your argument would be that his whole proposition is an affirmative one but that its subject does not stand for anything; for the expression 'A man is an animal' was not a proposition but only a part of a proposition, and so the whole subject – 'this proposition "A man is an animal"' – does not stand for anything at all. It would be like my pointing to a stone and saying 'This man is a substance': the subject would not stand for anything and my proposition would be false.

4.6.1. My brief reply to that is that one needs to know what you are referring to by the demonstrative 'this'. If you are referring to the very expression 'A man is an animal' that occurs in your own proposition, then I agree that your proposition is false, as your argument showed quite clearly. If on the other hand you are referring to some other expression, equiform with it but stated on its own, then your proposition is true, and its subject does stand for something, namely for that other expression, which by itself is a true proposition. We ought therefore to interpret and accept such propositions in this latter way and not in the former. (We could perhaps take them in the former way, but conditionally: that is, we might take 'This proposition "A man is an animal" is true' to mean 'This expression "A man is an animal", if it were set down on its own, would be a true proposition'. But it seems clear that all of this simply amounts to the same point that we made above.)

FIFTH SOPHISM

The following sophism can be solved in a similar way:

5.0 *Whatever Socrates is hearing Plato is saying.*

The posited case is that Plato is saying 'No men are donkeys', and that Socrates does not hear the first word but does hear the rest (i.e. 'Men are donkeys') and nothing else.

5.1 *Argument for the sophism*: Socrates is hearing the words 'Men are donkeys', and nothing else; and Plato is saying those very words (though admittedly accompanied by another one); therefore whatever Socrates is hearing Plato is saying.

5.2 *Arguments against the sophism*:

5.2.1. What Plato is saying is not false but true; but what Socrates is hearing ('Men are donkeys') is false; therefore he is hearing something that Plato is not saying.

5.2.2. Using a *reductio ad absurdum* we can argue: Whatever Socrates is hearing Plato is saying; Socrates is hearing something false; therefore Plato is saying something false. But here the conclusion is false, since Plato's proposition ('No men are donkeys') is completely true and is not open to any imputation of falsity.

5.3. I maintain that the sophism is true.

5.4 *Refutation of the arguments for the opposite view*: I claim that Socrates is not hearing anything true or false at all, because what he is hearing is not a proposition but only a part of a (true) proposition. So I hold that Plato was not saying anything *false* – on the contrary, what he said was true and had no falsehood in it at all; nevertheless he did say something that was *not true*, though it was a part of something true.

5.5. No doubt you will raise the following objection: Any expression that produces a false mental proposition in the mind of its hearer is itself false; but the expression that Socrates is hearing does produce in him a false mental proposition, one which in the given case leads him to think that Plato has said something false; so the expression in question was false.

5.5.1. My answer to this is that someone who is speaking well and truly should not be accused of speaking badly or falsely just because someone does not hear him properly or misunderstands what he is saying. To be sure, it frequently happens that one person states a certain proposition and someone else who does not hear him properly thinks he is stating a different one; then the speaker's proposition does not produce in the hearer a mental proposition which it itself expresses, but only a mental proposition of the kind that the proposition he *thought* he was hearing *would* have expressed. In such a case it is not that the proposition actually spoken is false; it is only that a proposition of the kind that the hearer thinks he is hearing *would* be false. A proposition that is false to a hearer would be one which he heard completely, whose meaning he knew completely, and which produced in him a false mental proposition that tallied with that meaning. In our case, however, Socrates is not hearing any proposition at all, he only thinks he is hearing one. So the words he is actually hearing do not produce in him the sense that *they* express, because the sense they express is not the sense of a proposition at all; rather what they produce in him is the kind of sense that would be produced by a proposition of the kind that he *thinks* he is hearing. And all that follows from that is that what he thinks he is hearing *would* be false.

SIXTH SOPHISM

6.0 *It is true to say that a man is an animal.*

What we have to ask about this sophism is whether someone who says 'It is true to say that a man is an animal' is saying something true. The case posited is simply that he does say it.

6.0.1. I want to remark in passing that throughout our sophisms I do not intend to say anything about truth and falsity except in so far as they characterize propositions. I do not intend, for instance, to raise questions about whether God is true, or is the primary truth, or about how a man, or a coin, is false. But I do want to speak about what is true and what is false in so far as they divide up a contradiction between them, as Aristotle puts it in Book VI of the *Metaphysics*, for a logician is not concerned with truth and falsity in any other way than this.

6.1 *Argument that the speaker is not saying something true*: The predicate of the sophism – 'to say that a man is an animal' – has to be taken either significatively or materially. (a) Suppose we take it significatively. Then *to say that a man is an animal* is the same as *someone who is saying that a man is an animal* (as I maintain in my commentary on the *Physics*); someone who is saying that a man is an animal, however, is a human being, and that is not something that is true or false, since a human being is not a proposition, or an element in a contradiction, at all. (b) Suppose, on the other hand, we take it materially. Then it is clear that even then it does not stand for a proposition, for the following reason: (i) If it stands for itself, or for some other expression equiform with it, then it is obvious that 'to say that a man is an animal' (or anything equiform with it) is not a proposition, or even a complete sentence, and so is neither true nor false. And (ii) if it is suggested that it stands not for itself or for some equiform expression but for a corresponding expression in the indicative mood (in the way that, for example, '(for) a man to be running' often stands for 'A man is running', which is a proposition), then in that case it clearly does not stand for a proposition but only for part of one. We can see this as follows: Even if we were to take '(for) a man to be good' to stand for the proposition 'A man is good', still 'to be good' itself would not stand for that proposition but only for the phrase 'is good'. Analogously, in our present case we could indeed take the expression '(for) someone to say that a man is an animal' to stand for a sentence such as 'Someone is saying that a man is an animal'; but then 'to say that a man is an animal' would stand only for 'is saying that a man is an animal', which is not a proposition and is therefore neither true nor false. So we are led to the conclusion that the sophism (i.e. 'It is true to say that a man is an animal') was false.

6.2 *Arguments for the opposite view*:

6.2.1. It is true to say 'a man is an animal'; but the two expressions 'that a man is an animal' and '"a man is an animal"' are, if taken materially, equivalent, and one of them can take the place of the other; therefore it is true to say that a man is an animal.

6.2.2. To affirm a true proposition is true, just as to deny a true proposition is false; but to say that a man is an animal is to affirm a true proposition (namely, 'A man is an animal'); therefore to say that a man is an animal is true – and then by conversion we obtain the sophism itself.

6.3. In my opinion the sophism, taken literally, is false, though I admit that when we are speaking loosely propositions of this kind are sometimes taken to do duty for the ones that would really be true. This, for example, is true: 'Anyone who says that a man is an animal (i.e. anyone who says the words "A man is an animal" on their own) is saying something true'. So is this: 'To say that a man is an animal is to say something true'. And so is this: 'It is true that a man is an animal'. But the sophism, taken strictly, was false, as the argument demonstrated.

6.4 *Refutation of the opposing arguments*:

6.4.1. My reply to the first argument is that 'It is true *to say* "A man is an animal"' is just false; what is true is rather '"A man is an animal" is true'. 'It is true that a man is an animal' is also true; but 'that a man is an animal' and 'to say that a man is an animal' are two very different things.

6.4.2. Turning to the second argument, I simply deny that affirming or denying a proposition is anything that is true or false at all. For affirming or denying is nothing but a person who is affirming or denying; and that is a human being, which is not something true or false. If, on the other hand, 'affirming a proposition' is interpreted materially, then 'affirming a proposition' means the same as 'affirms a proposition', and the latter is not a proposition but only an incomplete sentence, like 'is reading Virgil'.

The seventh sophism is the following 'insoluble':

7.0 *Every proposition is false.*

The case being posited is that all true propositions have been annihilated and only false ones have survived, and that then Socrates says 'Every proposition is false', and nothing more. The question is whether his proposition is false or true.

7.1 *Argument that it is not true*: Let us assume that it is impossible for one and the same proposition to be simultaneously both true and false, provided that the person who states it and all those who hear it understand the language in the same way. That being so, if Socrates' proposition is true, it follows that not every proposition is false; for then at least one proposition will be true, and this contradicts 'Every proposition is false'. So the latter must be false; in fact it must be impossible, since every proposition that entails its own contradictory is impossible.

7.2 *Arguments that it is not false, but true*:

7.2.1. It is a universal proposition and there are no counter-instances to it: it itself is not one, and by hypothesis there are no others either. This is enough to make it true.

7.2.2. If it is false, then its subject and predicate stand for the same universally. So, since it is an affirmative proposition, it must be true.

7.2.3. If it is false, then the facts are in every respect as it says they are; for all it says is that every proposition is false, and that is how things are. Therefore it is true.

7.3. This sophism raises two grave problems. The first is whether in the stated case the proposition is true or false. The second is how to form a proposition that will contradict it or be equivalent to it.

7.4. To begin with I want to point out that even if we preserve the original case intact we can still add to it the hypothesis that the sophism is true. This should be clear from what we said in the second and third sophisms of Chapter 7. What was said there was that we can speak at one time but be referring to a different time; for example we can say truly at a certain time that Socrates is sitting, even though at that time he is not in fact sitting, since we are taking the time referred to by the verb 'is sitting' to be not the actual time of utterance of the proposition but some other time. Similarly we can suppose that during the whole of the first hour today there are no true propositions but only false ones, that after the end of the hour Socrates says that every proposition is false, and that he is speaking not with reference to the actual time of his utterance but with reference to that first hour. In that case his proposition would be true, and a complete induction on the propositions that existed during the first hour would be enough to show this.

7.4.1. Nevertheless, although this solution may be correct for such a case, it still does not remove the difficulty raised by the sophism if we consider the other possibility, namely that Socrates might be speaking with reference to the actual time of his utterance.

7.4.2. Some people who want to avoid this difficulty maintain that terms that can stand for propositions never stand for the propositions in which they themselves occur, but only for other ones. They therefore say that Socrates' proposition is true, since in it the term 'proposition' does not stand for that proposition itself but only for all the others – and all of those were false.

7.4.2.1. But this solution certainly will not do. Whatever we can think about we can also speak about. Now by means of the concept from which the word 'proposition' is derived we can think about all propositions indifferently, present ones, past ones, future ones, our own as well as those of others; and therefore we can speak about them all.

7.4.2.2. It is obvious, too, that I can say that the proposition I am now actually uttering is an affirmative one, and it can be my intention to speak about it; but the term 'proposition' that occurs in it stands for it itself.

7.4.2.3. Moreover, this way out does not succeed in removing the difficulty at all. Let us suppose that at the very moment when Socrates was saying his proposition, Plato was saying one that was equiform with it. Then any reason why what one of them was saying was true would apply to the other as well; and the same would hold for 'false'. So either both would be saying something true or both would be saying something false. Let me ask, then, whether what Socrates was saying would be true. If you say yes, then since he is at least talking about Plato's proposition (even if not about his own), it follows that Plato's proposition is false, and hence by parity of reasoning his own is false too. And if someone were to say that they are both false, it then follows that they are both true, because (a) things are as both of them assert them to be (for what they assert is that every proposition is false, and that is how things are); (b) if they are false then their subjects and predicates stand for the same, and so they are true (since they are affirmative); and (c) they are universal propositions which have no counter-instances among the relevant singular ones.

7.4.3. Others have said that a proposition such as Socrates' is both true and false at once. But this is obviously absurd, because then if its contradictory were true we should have a pair of contradictories both being true, and if its contradictory were false we should have a pair of contradictories both being false, and each of these is impossible.

7.5. The other problem was how a contradictory could be formed. Take the case in which there are now only two propositions, 'A man is a donkey' being one and Socrates' aforementioned proposition being the other. Then here is a proof that no contradictory of the latter can be formed at all: Contradictory propositions ought each to stand for precisely the same thing or things, and one of them ought not to stand for more than the other does. Now in the given case Socrates' proposition stands for only two propositions, itself and 'A man is a donkey'; but if you were to state its contradictory (namely 'Some proposition is not false') then *it* would immediately stand for three – itself and the other two – and so it would not really contradict Socrates' proposition after all.

7.5.1. This problem, however, could be solved on the basis of what was said in the second and third sophisms of Chapter 7. For the proposition contradicting Socrates' one would be formulated at a certain time but would refer not to the time of its own formulation but to the time at which Socrates' proposition was spoken. So this third proposition would stand only for the things that Socrates' proposition stood for, and thus it would not stand for itself because it did not belong to the relevant time.

7.6. Now we must look into the question of the truth or falsity of Socrates' proposition. Briefly, my view is that it is false. My argument is this: Either it is false or it is not false. If it is false, I have gained my point. If it is not false, then from this and the fact that it exists it follows that it is true; and if it is true then it follows in turn, by the argument given earlier, that it is false; so again I have gained my point that it is false.

7.7. But then it is difficult to know how to reply to the opposing arguments.

7.7.1. Some people have advanced the following view (and it was my opinion too at one time): Even if the only thing that the proposition signifies or asserts, simply in virtue of the meanings of its terms, is that every proposition is false, nevertheless every proposition, by its very form, signifies or asserts itself to be true, and as a result any proposition that either directly or indirectly asserts itself to be false, *is* false. For although the facts are as such a proposition says they are in so far as it says it is *false*, yet they are not as it says they are in so far as it says it is *true*; so the proposition is false, not true, because in order for it to be true it is necessary not merely that the facts should be as it says they are but that they should be as *in every way* it says they are.

7.7.1.1. But this reply does not now seem to me to be strictly speaking correct. I am not at present renewing my objections to expressions like 'the facts are just as the proposition says they are', for I have said enough on that score already. What I want to do is rather to show that the contention that every proposition signifies or asserts itself to be true is not correct. My reason is this: You have to take the expression 'itself to be true' either materially or significatively. (a) Suppose you take it materially. In that case even the proposition 'A man is an animal' will not signify or assert itself to be true. For that would mean that it would signify the following proposition: 'The proposition "A man is an animal" is true'; and that is incorrect, because the latter is a proposition about second intentions, and the former, since it was about first intentions only, did not signify those second intentions. (b) Suppose now that the expression 'itself to be true' is understood significatively. In that case the proposition 'A man is a donkey' will not signify itself to be true, for the following reason: Since a man cannot be a donkey, there is no such thing as *a man being a donkey*; and in just the same way, since the proposition 'A man is a donkey' cannot be true, there neither is nor can be such a thing as *that proposition being true*. Now it is not correct to say of something that does not and cannot exist that is signified or thought about or asserted – I have said enough about that in another place; in fact, if you say 'The-proposition-"A man is a donkey"-being-true is signified or thought about or asserted', then what you say is *false*, because it is an affirmative proposition whose subject does not stand for anything. Similarly, in the present case, the proposition 'Every proposition is false' cannot be true, and therefore there neither is nor can be any such thing as its being true; so this is not something that can be signified or thought about at all, and in particular the proposition in question cannot signify itself to be true.

7.7.2. So another view has been advanced, one that is quite close to the truth. According to it every proposition virtually implies a second proposition in which the subject would stand for the original proposition and the predicate 'true' would be affirmed of it. I mean 'virtually implies' in the sense in which a premiss implies whatever follows from it. As a result a propositon is not to count as true unless the subject and predicate of that implied conclusion, which is an affirmative proposition, stand for the same. For example, let Socrates' proposition 'Every proposition is false' be called 'C'; then 'Every proposition is false' entails 'C is true', and so unless the facts are as this conclusion that was virtually implied in the former proposition says they are, that former proposition is not true. The point is that for a proposition to be true it is not enough that the facts should be as it says they are by its formal meaning alone; they must also be as the conclusion virtually implied in it would say they are. This view therefore maintains that when we are dealing with a proposition that is or can be self-referential, then (as I mentioned earlier on) the condition that its terms stand for the same is not sufficient for the truth of an affirmative: it is also necessary that the terms of the implied conclusion should themselves stand for the same. But these two conditions together, it is held, do suffice for its truth. On the basis of this account the opposing arguments can easily be refuted as follows:

7.7.2.1. The reply to the first one will be that the proposition is indeed a universal one, but that it itself forms a counter-instance, not admittedly to its own formal meaning, but to the conclusion implied in it.

7.7.2.2. To the second the reply is that the subject and predicate of the conclusion referred to do not stand for the same, but it is essential for the truth of any proposition whatsoever that they should do so.

7.7.2.3. The reply to the final argument is similar: the facts are not as the implied conclusion says they are (even if such a locution is used in an acceptable sense).

7.7.3. Nevertheless this solution, though I think it is near to the truth, is still not quite accurate, since it makes the assumption that a conclusion of the kind we have mentioned follows from every proposition, and that is incorrect. For let the proposition 'A horse is running' be called 'B'; then 'B is true' does *not* follow from 'A horse is running', as was explained in the second sophism of this chapter. So to make the solution quite accurate we should rather say that from any proposition *together with a proposition to the effect that it exists*, it follows that it is true. (Thus in the above example, where the proposition 'A horse is running' is called 'B', 'A horse is running and B exists' does entail 'B is true'.) Now in our exposition of the present sophism the extra proposition is clearly supplied by the case itself, since it was posited that Socrates actually said 'Every proposition is false'. So it is posited that this proposition exists, and this means that from it and the case (or rather a proposition setting out the case) it follows that it is true. This last proposition, however, is false, and therefore either Socrates' proposition is false or else the case is false; so if the case is accepted as true we have to say that Socrates' proposition is false.

7.7.3.1. Now we have to reply to the arguments. Because of the addition we have made, the first argument has not been sufficiently refuted. When it is claimed that the proposition is a universal one with no counter-instance, what we now have to say is that although there is no counter-instance to it just as far as its formal meaning is concerned, yet there would be a counter-instance to the conclusion implied in *it and the case taken together*, and this is enough to falsify it if the statement of the case is assumed to be true. The other arguments can be dealt with in an analogous way.

7.8. Finally there is the problem of whether 'Every proposition is false' is a possible proposition. I maintain that it is (though it could not be a *true* one), because things would be as it says they are if God were to annihilate every proposition except 'A man is a donkey' and 'A horse is a goat', for in that case every proposition would in fact be false. But I should also maintain that the conjunction of it and the posited case is impossible, since it entails something impossible, namely that the proposition itself is both true and false.

EIGHTH SOPHISM

This sophism seems to me to be a more difficult one:

8.0 *What Plato is saying is false.*

Let us posit a case in which Socrates says 'What Plato is saying is false', and nothing else, and Plato on the other hand says 'What Socrates is saying is false', and nothing else. Then the question is whether Socrates' proposition (which is the sophism itself) is true or false.

8.1 *Arguments that it is true*: There is no more reason why Socrates' proposition should be true, or false, than Plato's, or *vice versa*, since they stand in an exactly similar relation to each other. So I shall assume that if either is true, so is the other, and if either is false, so is the other. Now suppose you say that Socrates' proposition is not true but false. Then by parity of reasoning what Plato is saying is false too. But then:

8.1.1. That and nothing else is what Socrates is asserting, so his assertion accords with how things are and therefore his proposition is true; and

8.1.2. His proposition is an affirmative one; its terms – 'Plato' and 'saying something false' – stand for the same, since by hypothesis what Plato is saying is false; and therefore it is true.

8.1.3. Suppose that, along with Socrates, Robert also says 'What Plato is saying is false'. Suppose too that Socrates and Robert say what they do with precisely similar things in mind, and moreover that they think that what they are saying is true, since they think that Plato is saying 'God does not exist'. Then clearly Socrates' and Robert's propositions are exactly similar both in their verbal form and in the thoughts they express, for speakers and hearers alike. But Robert's proposition is true, since by hypothesis what Plato is saying *is* false; so by the same token Socrates' proposition must be true too.

8.1.4. Suppose now that John wants to contradict Socrates, and that he does so by saying that what Plato is saying is not false. Then clearly John's proposition will be false, since by hypothesis what Plato is saying *is* false. So Socrates' proposition must have been true – unless you are prepared to say that both contradictories are false together, which is impossible.

8.2 *Argument for the opposite view*: If what Socrates is saying is true, then by parity of reasoning so is what Plato is saying. But what Plato is saying is that what Socrates is saying is false; so if what Plato is saying is true, it follows that what Socrates is saying *is* false. Thus Socrates' proposition is not true after all, but false.

8.3. My answer, in brief, is that Socrates' proposition is false, not true. The argument for this has the following form: (a) Any proposition that in conjunction with something true entails something false, is itself false; (b) Socrates' proposition, in conjunction with something true, does entail something false; therefore (c) Socrates' proposition is false. Now (a) is an infallible rule; and (b) can be proved as follows: The case we are discussing is a possible one, so let us assume that what we posited is in fact true. Now we can show that the posited case and Socrates' proposition taken together entail both (d) that Socrates' proposition is true, and also (e) that it is false. Since the conjunction of (d) and (e) is false (indeed impossible), this will establish (b). Hence all that remains is to show how Socrates' proposition and the case do entail both (d) and (e). They entail (d) because the case posits that Socrates' proposition exists and, as we said earlier on, every proposition, together with the hypothesis that it exists, entails that it itself is true. They also clearly entail (e) by the argument given above, namely that if Socrates' proposition were true then Plato's would have to be true too, and this entails that Socrates' is false. It should be noted that by just the same reasoning Plato's proposition also turns out to be false.

8.4. All that is left to do, therefore, is to reply to the arguments. These are very difficult, and the reader will have to refer back to what we said in the preceding sophism.

8.4.1. The reply to the first argument is that although the facts are as Socrates' proposition says they are, so far as its formal meaning is concerned, yet they are not as the proposition that follows from it and the case would say they are; for that proposition is to the effect that Socrates' proposition is true, and that is not so.

8.4.2. The reply to the second argument is along similar lines. Where a proposition can, directly or indirectly, have the kind of self-reference that leads to the conclusion that it is false, it is not enough for the truth of an affirmative that its subject and predicate should stand for the same; it is also necessary, as we said earlier on, that the subject and predicate of the implied proposition (i.e. that the first one is true) should stand for the same.

8.4.3. The third and fourth arguments, however, are the difficult ones. What I have to say about the third is this: It is undeniable that Socrates' and Robert's propositions are exactly similar both in verbal form and in the thoughts they express for speakers and hearers alike. Nevertheless they are not equivalent: for Plato's proposition, which they were both speaking about, contains a reference to Socrates' proposition but not to Robert's; and as a result Socrates' proposition and Plato's, together with the case, entail that Socrates' proposition is false, but we cannot draw the corresponding conclusion about Robert's proposition, which on the contrary is true.

8.4.3.1. This, however, raises the problem of how a greater degree of equivalence between propositions could be obtained than by the foregoing method. What I have to say about this is that when a proposition is capable of referring to itself because its terms stand for propositions, then a proposition that is to be equivalent to it must be capable of referring to *it*. For example, let A be the first proposition and B the second one; then if B is to be equivalent to A it is necessary that, in any circumstances in which A refers to itself, B should refer to A, in order to ensure that whenever one is true the other is true too. Now B will not succeed in referring to A in this way unless it asserts the proposition that is implied in A (namely that A is true); but if B does do this then it *will* be equivalent to A. Thus if Socrates' proposition is 'What Plato is saying is false', an equivalent proposition for Robert will be 'What Plato is saying is false and A is true' (Socrates' proposition being called 'A'). For this proposition of Robert's adds nothing that would not be indirectly implied in Socrates' proposition and a case in which Socrates' proposition actually exists; and we are in fact presupposing such a case when we suppose that the propositions are equivalent or that they contradict each other, since if they do not exist they are neither equivalent nor mutually contradictory.

8.4.3.2. Indeed, quite universally an equivalent to any proposition can be formed in this way from it and the assumption that it exists. For instance, let Socrates' proposition (which we shall call 'B') be that a man is running, and let Robert's be that a man is running and B is true; then these propositions, given that both exist, are equivalent. However, it is unnecessary to add the extra clause in the case of a proposition that cannot refer to itself; but in the case of one that can, we have to add it to ensure that if there is a reference to the first there will also be a reference to the second.

8.4.4. The fourth argument should, I think, be dealt with in the same way. Socrates' and John's propositions are both false; they do not contradict each other, for it is possible for there to be a reference to one of them which entails that it is false, but no such reference to the other, and in the posited case this situation does in fact obtain. Therefore to contradict Socrates' proposition we have to contradict the conjunction of it and the conclusion implied in it (i.e. we have to contradict the proposition that we gave as its equivalent); so what John should say is 'Either what Plato is saying is not false or A is not true', for *then* there would be no possibility of the two being either both true or both false together. It is, moreover, no objection to all this that a greater number of terms, and different ones, occur in one proposition than in the other, because all the terms that occur explicitly in one are contained in the other at least implicitly and in an equivalent way.

8.5. But someone will raise another problem here. If Socrates' and John's propositions are really contradictories, let us suppose that they are kept in being permanently by the divine power; then it is certain that no changes in other things could ever make them both false or both true together. So now let us alter the original case, so that instead of saying 'What Socrates is saying is false' Plato now says 'What John is saying is false'. The question of its truth or falsity then arises about each of the three propositions, Socrates', John's and Plato's. My answer to this is that Plato's is false, since its falsity follows directly from it itself and the case. For if we suppose that it is true it follows that John's proposition is false; and if John's proposition is false this can be only because what Plato saying is false or else because Socrates' proposition is true, and from each of these it follows that Plato's proposition is false. This in turn yields the result that John's proposition is false and Socrates' is true. For the only thing that Socrates asserts is that what Plato is saying is false, and that is so; and this time Plato does not make any reference to Socrates that might make Socrates' proposition false, and therefore the latter is true. And John's proposition, which is its contradictory, is false, since it is a disjunction whose disjuncts are both false.

NINTH SOPHISM

The ninth sophism, which is closely related to the previous one, is:

9.0 *What Socrates is saying is true.*

The posited case is that Socrates says 'What Plato is saying is false', and nothing else, and Plato on the other hand says 'What Socrates is saying is true', and nothing else. The question is then whether Plato's proposition is true or false; and the same question could be asked about Socrates' proposition.

9.1 *Argument that what Plato is saying is true*: What he is saying is either true or false. If it is true, I have gained my point; and if it is false, it still follows that it is true; so on either hypothesis it follows that what he is saying is true. I now have to prove the premiss that if what he is saying is false then it is true; and the proof is that if what he is saying is false then what Socrates is saying is not true, and if what Socrates is saying is not true then what Plato is saying *is* true. So the point has been gained again. This, then, is the proof of the sophism (i.e. that what Socrates is saying is true).

9.2 *Argument for the opposite view*: This has an exactly parallel form. What Plato is saying is either true or false. If it is false, I have gained my point; and if it is true, it still follows that it is false, so again I have gained my point. I now have to prove the premiss that if what Plato is saying is true, it follows that it is false; and the proof is that if what he is saying is true it follows that what Socrates is saying is also true, and if what Socrates is saying is true it follows that what Plato is saying is false; therefore etc.

9.3. As before, the short answer is that both propositions are false. The proof is this: Since the given case is a possible one, let us suppose that the facts are as it assumes them to be. Then the proposition expressing the case will be true, and since true propositions never entail a false one, any proposition that, in conjunction with a statement of the given case, entails something false, must itself be false. Each of our two propositions, however, in conjunction with the given case, does entail something false; therefore etc. The proof that each proposition, in conjunction with the case, entails something false, is that it entails that one and the same proposition, without any ambiguity being involved, is both true and false – for that is something false. So firstly I shall argue that Plato's proposition, together with the case, entails that a certain proposition (namely itself) is both true and false. The proof is this: The case posits that the proposition exists, and yet, as we said earlier on, every proposition, in conjunction with another one that asserts that it exists, entails that it itself is true; however, if it is true, this in turn entails that it is false. So we have obtained our conclusion that Plato's proposition is both true and false. The argument about Socrates' proposition would follow the same lines.

9.4. But now there is a problem about whether these propositions are impossible.

9.4.1 *Argument that they are impossible*: What is possible never entails anything impossible, but these propositions do entail something impossible, namely that the same proposition is both true and false; therefore etc.

9.4.2 *Argument for the opposite view*: A proposition that is in fact false is nevertheless a possible one if it can be made true by some alteration in the things it refers to. Now Plato's proposition (that what Socrates is saying is true) can be made true in this way, for example if we suppose that what Socrates is saying is 'God exists'; so it is possible, i.e. not impossible. It is also clear that Socrates' proposition is a possible one because it would be true if Plato were saying that a man is a donkey.

9.4.3. The reply to the previous argument is that neither proposition by itself entails anything impossible, but that each *together with the posited case* yields the impossible result referred to. So I grant that the conjunction of each and the case is impossible. And indeed it frequently happens that a conjunction is impossible though each conjunct by itself is possible. For example, 'Everything that is running is a horse and a man is running' entails something impossible, namely that a man is a horse; and 'Socrates is running and Socrates is not running' is also impossible, even though each conjunct is possible.

9.5. Finally we have to reply to the original argument for the view that Plato's proposition is true. It was claimed first of all that it is either true or false. Now that is something I accept, since in fact the proposition is a false one. What I deny is the validity of the inference from its being false to its being true. The proof offered for this begins by claiming that if what Plato is saying is false then it follows that what Socrates is saying is not true. That step I also accept. But the further step is that if what Socrates is saying is false it follows that what Plato is saying is true; and that inference I reject. For what makes Socrates' proposition false is not that the facts are different from what by its formal meaning it says they are (for in that respect it simply says that what Plato is saying is false – and indeed it is); rather what makes it false is the falsity of the conclusion implied in it and the (true) case: for that conclusion is that A is true (Socrates' proposition being called 'A'), and that is not so, since in fact A is not true.

9.5.1. If it is argued that Socrates' proposition (which says that what Plato is saying is false) is true because its terms stand for the same, or because the facts are as it says they are, or because its equivalent stated by Robert would be true, or because its contradictory stated by John would be false, then all these arguments can be dealt with as they were in the preceding sophism.

The tenth sophism makes a similar point. It is:

10.0 *There are the same number of true and false propositions.*

Let us posit that there are only four propositions: (1) 'God exists', (2) 'A man is an animal', (3) 'A horse is a goat', and (4) the above sophism. Given that situation, the question is whether the sophism is true or false.

10.1 *Argument that it is not true*: If it were true the facts would not be as it says they are, since then there would be three true propositions and only one false one, and so there would be more true ones than false ones.

10.2 *Argument that it is not false*: If it were false the facts would be as it says they are, since there would then be two true propositions and two false ones. Therefore it is true.

10.3. I maintain, briefly, that the sophism is false, because from it and the given case we can deduce both that it is true and also that it is false.

10.4 *Refutation of the argument for the opposite view*: What makes the sophism false is not that the facts are different from what by its formal meaning it says they are. What makes it false is that the facts are not as they would be said to be by the proposition that is virtually implied in it and the case (in the way that a conclusion is implied in its premisses). For what is thus implied in them is 'A is true' (the sophism being called 'A'), and the facts are not as 'A is true' would say they are.

10.5. It can also be asked whether the sophism is possible, and whether it could be true.

10.5.1. We can say at once that it is possible, since it could be the case that there were just the same number of true and false propositions. This would be so, for instance, if there were only these four: 'God exists', 'God is good', 'A man is a donkey' and 'God does not exist'.

10.5.2. I also maintain that it could be *true*, provided we have a case in which we are taking the time to which the verb refers, not as the actual time when the sophism was formulated, but as the time when there were only the four propositions just listed. In fact, even 'Every proposition is negative' could be true in that way; but it cannot be true if the time referred to by the verb is taken to be the time at which it was being stated, nor can the present sophism be either. Nevertheless, even assuming that the case posited in the sophism is exactly as we stated it, some other person arriving on the scene can quite truly say, speaking of the time of the case itself, 'There *were* exactly the same number of true and false propositions'. But if the verb is in the present tense no one can say it truly, except in the way just explained, i.e. by using the tense of the verb to refer to a different time from the precise time of utterance of his proposition.

ELEVENTH SOPHISM

The eleventh sophism, which again makes a similar point, is:

11.0 *What I am saying is false.*

The posited case is that I say 'What I am saying is false', and nothing else. Then the question is whether this proposition of mine is true or false.

11.1. If you say it is true, then the facts are not as it says they are, so it is not true after all but false.

11.2. If, however, you say it is false, then the facts *are* as it says they are, since it is an affirmative proposition whose terms stand for the same; so it is true. So clearly if it is false it must be true.

11.3. From this it follows in turn that we have to say that it is both true and false. The proof is this: Anyone who grants the antecedent of a true conditional ought to grant the consequent too. Now we have to grant either that the sophism is true or else that it is false. But then, if it is true it is false, and if it is false it is true. So we have to say it is both.

11.3.1. But now this result is absurd. For if the contradictory of the sophism were true, then two contradictories would be true together; and if its contradictory were false, then two contradictories would be false together; and all this is impossible.

11.4. Then there are the problems of how the contradictory of the sophism is to be formed, and of whether the sophism itself is possible or imposible.

11.5. I maintain, briefly, that the sophism is false, because from it and a proposition expressing the case there follows something false, and yet the proposition expressing the case is taken to be true. (The 'something false' that follows is that the sophism is both true and false at once.) Now any proposition which, together with something true, entails something false, is itself false.

11.6. The arguments for the contrary view can be refuted in the same way as before. It was claimed that if the proposition is false it follows that it is true. I reject that inference. You may try to defend it on the ground that if the proposition is false then the facts are as it says they are. That I admit, as far as its formal meaning is concerned. But this is not enough to make it true, because it is self-referential. And in fact it is *not* true, since the facts are not as the conclusion implied in it and the case would say they are: for that conclusion is that A is true (my proposition being called 'A'), and the facts are not as 'A is true' would say they are. The argument about the terms standing for the same can be dealt with in the same way.

11.7. You might, however, still want to argue that its falsity entails its truth, in this way: If it is false, it follows that it exists; but then from it and the fact that it exists, it follows that it is true; so if it is false it does follow that it is true. And, you may add, anyone who grants the antecedent ought to grant the consequent too; so we ought to admit that the proposition is true.

11.7.1. In reply to this I still maintain that from its being false it does not follow that it is true. I entirely agree that from its being false it follows that it exists. I admit, too, that from the proposition itself and the fact that it exists it follows that it is true. But I do not admit the premiss of this inference – indeed I deny it, for it consisted of the original proposition together with the fact that it exists, and I deny the original proposition. So I also deny the conclusion, i.e. that the proposition is true.

11.8. There is still, however, the problem of how you could contradict me. The problem is this. If you simply produce a negative proposition with a verbally identical subject (i.e. if you say 'What I am saying is not false'), then you are not contradicting me; for in a pair of contradictories a term in one ought to stand for the same things as the corresponding term in the other, and that is not so in the present case because in my proposition the term 'I' stands for me but in yours it stands for you. If, on the other hand, you produce a negative proposition in which the term 'I' is replaced by 'you' (i.e. if you say to me 'What you are saying is false'), then it seems you are not contradicting me in the proper way; for contradictories ought to have the same subjects and predicates, and having different subjects standing for the same thing is not enough. Besides, my proposition and yours are both false, so they do not contradict each other.

11.8.1. My solution is this. Contradictories do not have to be constructed from exactly similar verbal expressions. The first point is that they must differ in respect of being affirmative or negative. The second point is that they may differ in their signs of quantity or in their modalities. For example, 'Every man is running' and 'Some man is not running' are contradictories, and so are 'It is possible that Socrates is running' and 'It is necessary that Socrates is not running'. Sometimes, too, when relative terms are involved, we can change the verbal form of the predicate as well. For instance, if we say 'Every man who has a horse sees it', and we have to contradict this by some other method than prefixing a negation to the whole proposition, then we must make a change in the predicate. For 'Some man who has a horse does not see it' is not its contradictory, since both of these would be true if every man had one horse that he saw and another one that he did not see. The contradictory would seem rather to be 'Some man who has a horse does not see any horse that he has'. But this topic will be dealt with specifically elsewhere.

11.8.2. Furthermore, as we said in the eighth sophism, if we are dealing with a proposition that is or could be self-referential, then in forming its contradictory we have to add an extra clause in order to mention the conclusion implied in the original proposition.

11.8.3. In the present case there is the additional point that if someone speaks about himself in the first person then anyone else who wants to contradict him will have to speak in the second person, not the first. Thus if Socrates says 'I am running', Plato would contradict him by saying not 'I am not running' but 'You are not running'. We have to direct our attention primarily to people's thoughts, since we use words only to express thoughts; so if we cannot express the mental contradictory of a proposition without changing the words, then we have to change them.

11.8.4. It seems therefore that to contradict me you should say 'What you are saying is not false', but with the addition mentioned in earlier sophisms. For if you want to say something equivalent to my proposition, then (assuming that my proposition is called 'A') you should say 'What you are saying is false and A is true'; and then the contradictory will be 'Either what you are saying is not false or A is not true' – and that disjunction is true.

TWELFTH SOPHISM

We can deal in a similar fashion with the next sophism, which is:

12.0 *God exists and some conjunction is false.*

Let us posit that this is written on a wall, and that it and its conjuncts are the only propositions there are. The question is whether it is true or false.

12.1. The arguments go just as before. If it is true it follows that it is false; and if it is false then at least it seems to follow that it is true, firstly because the facts are then as it says they are, and secondly because its contradictory – 'Either God does not exist or no conjunction is false' – is false.

12.2. The correct view is that the sophism is false, and we can refute the objections in the same way as before. That is, the facts are admittedly as it says they are as far as its formal meaning is concerned, but they are not as the conclusion implied in it and the posited case would say they are. Moreover, given that the sophism is called 'A', its contradictory would be 'Either God does not exist or no conjunction is false or A is not true'.

12.3. It is possible to devise analogous sophisms about disjunctive propositions (e.g. 'Either a man is a donkey or some disjunction is false' – assuming that this is the only disjunction there is); about exceptive propositions (e.g. 'Every proposition except an exceptive one is true' – assuming that there are no propositions apart from the exceptive one just mentioned and two others, namely 'God exists' and 'A man is an animal'); and about exclusive propositions (e.g. suppose that Socrates says 'God exists', Plato says 'Only Socrates is saying something true', and no one else says anything). We can also construct sophisms on the themes of whether a proposition is doubtful or not doubtful, or known or not known, or believed or not believed.

THIRTEENTH SOPHISM

13.0 *Socrates knows the proposition written on the wall to be doubtful to him.*

The posited case is that this proposition and no other is written on a wall, that Socrates looks at it, considers it, is in a state of doubt about whether it is true or false, and knows perfectly well that he is in such a state of doubt. The question then is whether it is true or false.

13.1 *Arguments that it is true:*

13.1.1. It was posited that Socrates does in fact know the proposition to be doubtful to him. Now this is just what the proposition itself says, so it is true.

13.1.2. If one of a pair of equiform propositions is true, so is the other. But if anyone were to say something equiform with the present proposition, what he said would be true; so it must be true too.

13.1.3. If anyone were to state the contradictory of the proposition, what he said would be false, so it itself must be true.

13.2 *Argument for the opposite view*: Any proposition that entails something impossible is false; but the sophism entails something impossible, namely that Socrates both knows and doubts the very same proposition. For on the one hand the case itself states that he doubts the sophism. But on the other hand the following argument shows that he also knows it: He knows it is doubtful to him; it is in fact also possible that he *knows* that he knows it is doubtful to him, and the proposition says no more than that; so he knows that things are as it says they are. Now to know that things are as a proposition says they are is to know that proposition (you know the proposition 'A man is an animal', for instance, just by knowing that things are as it says).

13.3. A further proof that if he thinks about the matter he will know that the sophism is true lies in the fact that if you say something equiform with it he will know what you are saying is true, and so for the same reason he will know that it too is true.

13.3.1. Analogously, if you state the contradictory of the sophism he will know that what you are saying is false; but anyone who knows one contradictory to be false must know the other one to be true if he reflects on the matter and knows that they are contradictories; therefore etc.

13.4. The reaction of some people to this sophism is to say that in the case described the proposition written on the wall is a double one, in the sense that there is one *complete* proposition, namely that Socrates knows that the proposition written on the wall is doubtful to him, and also a *partial* one – i.e. one which is a part of the complete one – namely that the proposition written on the wall is doubtful to him. Then what they maintain is that Socrates does know the partial one (that the proposition written on the wall is doubtful to him), but that he does not know the complete one – in fact he finds that one doubtful; and, they say, there is nothing impossible about this. So their position is that the whole proposition is true.

13.4.1. But that solution does not seem to me to get rid of the problem entirely:

13.4.1.1. In the first place it is not true that in the case described there is a twofold proposition written on the wall: as we remarked elsewhere, no part of a proposition is itself a proposition so long as it remains a part of a proposition.

13.4.1.2. Moreover, the proposition that was originally posited as written on the wall is not the one cited in the suggested solution, but rather this: 'Socrates knows *the proposition written on the wall to be doubtful to him*'. Now the infinitive phrase 'the proposition written...'

is not itself a proposition. It could of course *stand for* a proposition, but the only one it could stand for is the complete one, since there is no other one written on the wall. So if Socrates knows any proposition written on the wall, the one he knows is the complete one.

13.4.1.3. Thirdly, it has been posited that Socrates not only knows that the proposition is doubtful to him but also knows that he knows this. So since this is possible, let us now posit it. Then Socrates not only knows that the proposition is doubtful to him, he in fact knows that *Socrates knows the proposition to be doubtful to him*. So it seems to follow that in such a case he does know the complete proposition, and not merely the partial one.

13.4.2. My own position therefore is a different one. I agree that the proposition written on the wall is doubful to Socrates, and moreover that he knows quite certainly that it is doubtful to him, and indeed knows that he knows this. But whether he knows the proposition itself is a further problem.

13.5. To reach a solution of this problem we should first note that conceiving covers more than knowing does. For there can be a conceiving without any mental synthesis, and mental synthesis without assertion; but we do not have *knowledge* unless we have knowledge of some assertion. Now a necessary condition for knowledge is that someone should assent with conviction to a true assertion. When we assent with conviction and good reason to such an assertion, we say that *it* is *known* and that *we* have *knowledge* of it. But we not only say that we have knowledge of the assertion itself, we also say we have knowledge of the things that are signified by its terms. We have therefore to distinguish between two sorts of objects of knowledge: firstly there is a *primary* or *immediate* object of knowledge, which is the assertion itself to which we assent in the way described; and secondly there are *remote* object(s) of knowledge, which consist of the things that are signified by the terms of the assertion that is known in the first way.

13.5.1. Now it is impossible for a proposition that you are doubtful about to be a primary object of knowledge for you; for if you are doubtful about it you cannot be assenting to it with conviction and good reason, as you do to a proposition that you know in the primary way. So obviously the proposition written on the wall is not a *primary* object of knowledge for Socrates, since he is doubtful about it and does not know whether it is true or false. I do claim, however that it is a *remote* object of knowledge for him, on the following grounds: He forms in his mind some such mental proposition as 'The proposition written on the wall is doubtful to me'; to this mental proposition he does assent with conviction and good reason, and so *it* is a primary object of knowledge for him; thus, since the subject of this mental proposition stands for the proposition actually written on the wall, the latter must be a remote object of knowledge for him.

13.5.2. Moreover, I maintain that if Plato says 'Socrates knows the proposition written on the wall to be doubtful to him', then if Socrates hears and understands Plato properly he will straight away know Plato's proposition in the primary way, for he will assent to it with conviction and good reason as true and not at all doubtful. Similarly, if a proposition exactly like the one written on the wall is written on a sheet of paper, then if Socrates sees and reads it he will know it is true and will not find it doubtful.

13.6. There is, however, a problem about how this could be possible, i.e. how there can be two equiform propositions and yet someone be certain about one of them but doubtful about the other, even though he is paying attention to them and knows that they are equiform.

13.6.1. In my opinion such a thing is perfectly possible. For Socrates is well aware that the proposition written on the wall is self-referential, and so he is wondering whether on that account it may be false, as turned out to be the case in the previous sophisms. But he also notices that Plato's proposition, or the one written on paper, is not self-referential, so he has no doubt that it is true.

13.6.2. It was argued that if Plato states the contradictory of the sophism (i.e. 'Socrates does not know the proposition written on the wall to be doubtful to him') then Socrates will know straight away that this proposition is false. I agree with this so far. But when you then go on to infer that he must therefore know that the proposition written on the wall is true because it is its contradictory, then I reply that that does not follow at all. For Socrates does not know that they are genuine contradictories, since he may wonder whether the self-referential character of the proposition on the wall spoils the contradiction.

13.7. We come at last to the problem of whether the proposition written on the wall is true or false. I maintain that it is true: its self-referential character does not make it false, it only makes it doubtful, and from that it does not follow that it is false.

13.8. *Refutation of the argument for the contrary view*: The argument was that the proposition entails something impossible. But I deny that, since it does not follow that Socrates knows the proposition, except merely as a remote object of knowledge. The argument proceeds by claiming that Socrates knows that the facts are as the proposition says they are. I agree so far; but if from this you draw the conclusion that if he pays attention to it he will not doubt that it is true, then I reply that that does not follow at all. For Socrates notices that in earlier sophisms many propositions were false because of their self-referential character, even though the facts were as they said they were, and therefore his lack of skill in these matters may make him think that this one too is false because he sees it is self-referential – or at least he may have some doubts about it.

13.9. A different problem arises about the sophism if we add to the original case the further condition that Socrates is a perfect reasoner, and then ask whether the proposition is true or false. My comment on that is that the case itself is then impossible. For if Socrates has a complete mastery of logic and gives his full attention to the proposition, then if it is true it follows that he knows it to be true and if it is false it follows that he knows it to be false; but neither of these is compatible with his finding it doubtful.

13.9.1. Suppose, however, that we were then to delete from the case the clause stating that he finds the proposition doubtful, and ask again whether it is true or false. In that case I should say that it is false, and that Socrates knows that it is false and not at all doubtful to him.

14.0 *Either Socrates is sitting or the disjunction written on the wall is doubtful to Plato.*

Let us posit a case in which this proposition and no other is written on a wall and in which Plato sees it and considers to the best of his ability whether it is true or false. Let us also posit that Plato has a complete mastery of all relevant intellectual skills and disciplines, but that he cannot see Socrates and does not in fact know whether he is standing or sitting, with the result that he is in a state of doubt about the proposition 'Socrates is sitting'. The question then is: how is Plato related to the whole disjunctive proposition – does he know it to be true, know it to be false, or find it doubtful?

14.1 *Argument that he does not know it to be true:* To do so he would have to know one of the two disjuncts to be true, since for a disjunction to be true one or other of the disjuncts must be true. But (a) by the given case he does not know the first disjunct (that Socrates is sitting) to be true; and (b) he does not know the second disjunct to be true either, because if he did it would follow that that second disjunct was both true and false, which is impossible. The proof that that would follow is this: (i) It would follow that the disjunct was *true* because only what is true can be known to be true. (ii) It would follow that the disjunct was *false* for this reason: The truth of one disjunct is enough to make a disjunction true. So if Plato knew that the second disjunct was true he would know that the whole disjunction was true. Therefore the whole disjunction would not be doubtful to him, and so the second disjunct would be false, since what it says is just that the whole disjunction *is* doubtful to Plato.

14.2 *Arguments that Plato does not know the disjunction to be false:*

14.2.1. To know a disjunction to be false one has to know each disjunct to be false; but it was posited that Plato does not know whether the first disjunct is true or false.

14.2.2. By hypothesis Plato has a complete mastery of all the relevant skills, so if he knew that the disjunction was false he would also, if he were to attend to it, know that its contradictory was true. But he does not know this; for the contradictory is 'Socrates is not sitting and no disjunction written on the wall is doubtful to Plato', and he does not know that this conjunction is true, since he does not know whether the first conjunct is true or false.

14.3 *Argument that Plato does not find the disjunction doubtful:* If he finds it doubtful he certainly knows that this is so – indeed even a person with very little education, if he were to turn his mind to some proposition, would know very well whether he doubted it or not. But if Plato knows that the disjunction is doubtful to him then he knows that the second disjunct, which says just this, is true; and if he knows that the second disjunct is true then he knows that the whole disjunction is true, and therefore it is *not* doubtful to him.

14.4. My own answer is that Plato does not know the disjunction to be true and does not know it to be false, for the reasons stated above. So by elimination he finds it doubtful, and moreover he knows he does.

14.4.1. Here is a proof of the last point. As we shall show in a moment, the second disjunct is false; and Plato must know this since by hypothesis he is fully expert in such matters. As a result he knows that the whole disjunction is false if the first disjunct is false and true if the first disjunct is true. Therefore since he knows he is doubtful about the first disjunct, he knows he is doubtful about the whole. So what we now have to do is to show that the second disjunct *is* false. The proof has the following form: (a) Any proposition which, in conjunction with something true, entails something false, is itself false; (b) the second disjunct satisfies this condition; therefore (c) it is false. The proof of (b) is this: Since the whole case is a possible one, I shall assume that the proposition stating it is true; yet from the case and the second disjunct there follows something that is false – indeed impossible. This is so because it follows that the whole disjunction is both doubtful to Plato and also not doubtful to him: doubtful because that is what the second disjunct itself asserts, and not doubtful for the reasons already given.

14.4.1.1. A further proof of (b) is that from the second disjunct and the case it follows that that disjunct is both true and false. For (i) it follows that it is true because the case posits that it exists and, as we have repeatedly said, from any proposition and another one to the effect that it exists, it follows that the first one is true. But (ii) it follows from this in turn that it is false, for this reason: If it is true then Plato knows this, since by hypothesis he is a complete expert and knows whether he doubts the disjunction or not. But if he knows that the disjunct is true then he knows that the whole disjunction is true; so he is not in a state of doubt about this, and as a result the second disjunct is false.

14.5 *Refutation of the argument for the opposite view*: Although Plato knows that the facts are as the second disjunct says they are as far as its formal meaning is concerned, yet he does not know that it is *true*. In fact he knows that it is false, since he knows it has a self-reference that, in conjunction with the case (which is assumed to be true), entails its falsity, and he also knows that every such proposition is false.

14.6. The following argument may, however, be urged against my view: If Plato finds the disjunction doubtful he should find its contradictory doubtful too. Yet this cannot be so; for its contradictory is 'Socrates is not sitting and no disjunction written on the wall is doubtful to Plato', and Plato is not doubtful about that at all – he knows it is false because it is a conjunction whose second conjunct is known to be false. So it follows that Plato should not doubt the proposition written on the wall but rather should know it to be true.

14.6.1. The solution lies in the fact that the contradiction was not formulated accurately, because the original proposition is self-referential. We therefore have to make explicit the proposition implied in it and the case. So if the disjunction written on the wall is called 'A', an equivalent to it will be 'Either Socrates is sitting or the disjunction written on the wall is doubtful to Plato, and A is true'; and then its contradictory will be 'Socrates is not sitting and no disjunction written on the wall is doubtful to Plato, or A is not true'. And then I maintain that this *is* doubtful to Plato; for it is a disjunction of a conjunction which is known to be false and a categorical proposition which is doubtful, and this means that the whole is doubtful.

FIFTEENTH SOPHISM

15.0 *Someone is doubting a proposition.*

I posit the case that this proposition, and no other, is put to you, and you do not know whether any other proposition is being put to anyone else. It is also posited that you are thoroughly expert in logic, and that to the best of your ability you try to decide whether the proposition is true or false. Then the question is whether you know it to be true, know it to be false, or are doubtful about it.

15.1 *Arguments that you do not know it to be false:*

15.1.1. To know it to be false you would have to know that no one was doubting any proposition at all (it would clearly be true if, for instance, Robert was doubting some proposition in Rome); and since you cannot tell whether that is the case, you cannot know that the sophism is false.

15.1.2. Alternatively, if you knew that the sophism was false you would also know that its contradictory was true, if it were put to you, since you are an expert in these matters. But it is impossible for you to know that 'No one is doubting any proposition' is true. Therefore etc.

15.2 *Argument that you do not know it to be true:*

You do not know whether anyone other than yourself is doubting any proposition or not, so the only way you could know that *someone* is doubting a proposition is by knowing that you are doubting the proposition that is now being put to you. But it is quite impossible for you both to know this proposition to be true and also to know that you are doubting it, since this would entail that you were both doubting it and not doubting it: not doubting it because you knew it to be true, and doubting it because you knew you were doubting it.

15.3 *Argument that you are not doubtful about it:*

If you were doubtful about it you would certainly know that you were, and therefore you would certainly know that *someone* was doubting a proposition – namely yourself. So you would know that the facts were as the proposition says they are, and hence you would know it was true, with the result that you would *not* after all be doubtful about it.

15.4. From all this it follows that you would neither know the proposition to be true nor know it to be false nor be doubtful about it. But this is impossible, given the posited case – i.e. that you were thinking about it to the best of your ability and were skilful enough for this task.

15.5. My view is that you would be doubtful about the proposition and also know you were doubtful about it. The arguments given above proved quite adequately that you could neither know it to be true nor know it to be false, so by elimination you must be doubtful about it.

15.5.1. The explanation of this is as follows: Firstly, if anyone else is doubting some other proposition, the sophism is straightforwardly true. Next, I shall prove that if, on the other hand, no one else is doubting any proposition, then the sophism is false.

15.5.1.1. My proof of this starts from the principle (a) that if a proposition, together with something true, entails something false, then it is itself false, and then shows (b) that in the present case this condition is fulfilled. To prove (b) I shall, since the case is a possible one, assume that it is true, and then show that from the proposition under consideration and the case it would follow that that proposition itself was both true and false, which is impossible.

15.5.1.2. The proof that from it and the case it follows that it is *true* is that the case posits that it exists, and, as I have repeatedly pointed out, from any proposition and another one saying that it exists, it follows that the first one is true.

15.5.1.3. Next I shall show that from the proposition and the case it follows that the proposition is *false*. To begin with, you know you are doubting the proposition; you know too that this is what it itself asserts by its formal meaning; so you know that the facts are as it says they are as far as its formal meaning is concerned. However, since you are a trained logician, you ought to know that if the facts are as a proposition says they are by its formal meaning, then that proposition is true, *unless* it has the kind of self-reference that makes it false. And from all this you should be able to infer (and hence also know) the following disjunctive conclusion: *either the sophism is true, or else it is self-referential in a way that makes it false*. Furthermore, again since you are a trained logician, you ought to know whether or not there can be a case in which the proposition is self-referential in this way; and if you know there cannot be such a case, then you know it is true. However, as we said before, you do *not* know that the sophism is true; so you do know that in some case it can be self-referential in the relevant way. But you also know that it would not be self-referential in this way if anyone other than yourself was doubting a proposition, since you know that in those circumstances it would in fact be true. So by elimination you know that if no one other than yourself were doubting any proposition, then the sophism *would* have the kind of self-reference that would make it false, and therefore *would* be false.

15.5.1.4. So it is clear that from the sophism and the case we were positing (namely that no one else is doubting any proposition) it does follow that the sophism is false. And that is what we set out to prove.

15.5.2. To resume: It has now been demonstrated that the sophism is true if anyone else is doubting any other proposition, and false if no one else is doubting any other proposition. But you do not know whether anyone else is doubting any other proposition or not, and that is why you are bound to be in doubt about whether the sophism is true or false.

15.6 *Refutation of the argument for the opposite view*: You do indeed know that you are doubting the sophism, and that the facts are as it says they are as far as its formal meaning is concerned. But it does not follow from this that you know it is true, or even that it *is* true; for it is capable of having the kind of self-reference that makes it false, and you are not in a position to know whether in fact it does have it or not.

15.7 *Some further objections to our thesis*:

15.7.1. If you are presented with a pair of contradictory propositions and you know one of them to be false, then you are bound to know that the other one is true (assuming that you are paying attention to them and that you are skilled in such matters). But if the contradictory of the sophism (i.e. 'No one is doubting any proposition') is put to you, you will certainly know that that is false, because you know that your own case forms a counter-example to it – for you know that you are doubting a proposition that has just been put to you. So it follows that you know that the sophism itself is true.

15.7.2. Another argument that has been strongly urged to show that you do not doubt the sophism but know it to be true, runs like this: Suppose I argue: *You are doubting a proposition; you are someone; therefore someone is doubting a proposition.* Then that syllogism is formally valid because it is an expository one. But you know that the premisses are true; so (since you are an expert and are paying attention) you also know that the conclusion is true, for you know that true premisses never entail a false conclusion. The conclusion, however, is just the sophism itself; therefore you do know that the sophism is true, and so it was a mistake to say that you were doubting it.

15.8 *Refutation of these objections*:

15.8.1. The reply to the first is that the contradictory was not adequately formulated. Since the proposition is capable of having the kind of self-reference that makes it false, what we have to take is the contradictory of the conjunction of it itself and the proposition implied in it and the case (i.e. the proposition that it is true). Thus, if the proposition itself is called 'A', its equivalent will be 'Someone is doubting a proposition and A is true', and so its contradictory will be 'Either no one is doubting a proposition or A is not true'. Now you will certainly find *this* doubtful, just like the original proposition, since you know that the first disjunct is false and you do not know whether the second is true or false.

15.8.2. In reply to the second objection, I agree that the inference mentioned (*You are doubting a proposition; you are someone; therefore someone is doubting a proposition*) was a valid one. I agree too that you know it is valid, that you know its premisses are true, and that as a result you know that its conclusion is true. But that conclusion is *not* the sophism itself: it is equiform with the sophism, but it is a distinct proposition, and one which you know to be *true* because its terms stand for the sophism and you know that the sophism is something you are doubting. Nor is it even equivalent to the sophism that was originally posited to exist. To form a proposition equivalent to the sophism we have to say that someone is doubting a proposition *and A is true* (the sophism, as before, being called 'A'); but then *that* does not follow from these known premisses.

15.8.2.1. In this connection it is worth noting carefully that if someone first of all says this doubtful thing to you, 'Someone is doubting something', then when you have considered whether this is true or false, you will be in a state of doubt about the matter. But if, while that situation still obtains, someone else arrives on the scene and says to you that someone is doubting something, you will know that what *he* is saying is true, that *his* proposition is true, not however with reference to itself but with reference to the earlier proposition.

15.9.1. Now, however, you may posit a different case, one in which Socrates and Plato come to you simultaneously, and each of them says 'Someone is doubting something'. Suppose moreover that neither speaks before the other, and you pay equal attention to them both. The question then is whether you will doubt both propositions or whether you will doubt one of them and know the other to be true.

15.9.1.1. I maintain that you will doubt them both, because in this case you could not know that either of them was true with reference to the other. The proof of this is as follows: If you did know that one of them was true with reference to the other, any reasons you might have for this would apply in the reverse direction too, and so you would know that both were true. That, however, cannot be so, since as far as you can tell they may both be false: in fact they would both be false in a situation in which no other proposition was being doubted by anybody. The reason for this is that in such a case, if you were to know them to be true you would not doubt them and so no one would be doubting anything at all; but that is just the opposite of what these propositions themselves would be asserting, and so they would be false.

15.9.1.2. Nevertheless, given that a doubt does exist in your mind, if any other proposition to the effect that someone is doubting something were to be put to you while you are in that state of doubt, you would then know that *it* was true, though not with reference to itself but with reference to what you are already doubting.

15.9.2. Finally in connection with this sophism, someone might raise the problem of what the position would be if it were not laid down in the posited case that you were an expert reasoner. My answer to that is that you might very well then not be in a state of doubt, just because of your lack of expertise. Perhaps for some reason you might think that the proposition was true, and entertain no doubt about this, even though in fact it was false; or perhaps for some other reason you might think it was false, again without having any doubt about this: it often happens that people hold false opinions but have no doubts about them. As Aristotle remarks in Book VII of the *Ethics*, some people who merely hold opinions hold them with complete conviction and with no doubt in their minds; for some people believe no less strongly in what they only have opinions about than others do in what they really know.

SIXTEENTH SOPHISM

The sixteenth sophism is concerned with the relation between an answer and a question. It is this:

16.0 *You are going to answer in the negative.*

Let us suppose that this proposition is put to you, and that you are under an obligation to respond directly to any proposition put to you by saying either 'Yes' or 'No'. Now this is an obligation that you should be willing to undertake: after all, any proposition that may be put to you is either true or not true, and by 'Yes' we simply mean that it is true and by 'No' that it is not true; so we can always respond correctly to a proposition by saying 'Yes' or 'No', and therefore you ought to be prepared to undertake the obligation of replying in this way. So now I request you to make your response to the proposition under consideration, i.e. 'You are going to answer in the negative'.

16.1. If you say 'Yes' I shall complain that you are giving a wrong answer, on the ground that you are claiming to be answering in the negative, and yet you are not doing so – you are in fact answering in the affirmative.

16.2. On the other hand, if you say 'No' I shall again complain that you are giving a wrong answer, on the ground that you are denying that you are answering in the negative, and yet in fact you *are* answering in the negative.

16.3. I maintain that in terms of the obligation in question it is impossible for you to give a correct reply at all. In the absence of such an obligation, however, you could easily do so: you could, for example, tell your interlocutor that what he was saying was false, or that his proposition was a false one; or you could give a correct reply by saying that what he was saying was not false. So I maintain that you should not have undertaken the obligation unless it was subject to the condition that no proposition would be submitted to you whose meaning, together with that of your answer, would give your answer a self-reference that would inevitably make it false.

16.4. It was argued that you should have undertaken the obligation because any proposition submitted to you would be either true or false. Now I agree that the proposition that was put to you was either true or false, but the reason for this is as follows: (a) If you make no reply at all, it was false; (b) if you answer 'Yes' then again it was false – and your answer was false too, since it asserted that something that was false was true; (c) if you answer 'No' then the proposition itself was true, but your answer was false because it denied something that was true. So when it is contended that we ought to answer 'Yes' to every true proposition and 'No' to every false one, then I agree except when the reply would have a self-reference that would automatically make it false. In such a case the form of the reply has to be altered.

16.5. We have a similar situation if someone wants to put you under an obligation to respond to every proposition he is going to put to you by saying definitely either that it is true or that it is not true. You should not undertake such an obligation. In the first place you cannot tell whether he will then present you with a proposition that you find doubtful. But even if he merely wants you to undertake to say either that it is true or that it is not true or that you find it doubtful, you should still not accept such an obligation except with the qualification previously stated. So to the proposition 'You are going to answer in the negative' you should not reply either that it is true or that it is not true or that you find it doubtful; but you could correctly reply that it is false.

16.6. Someone will, however, raise the following objection: 'What you have just said is true' and 'What you have just said is not true' are contradictories. Yet no matter which of these you give as your reply to the person who is putting the sophism to you, your reply will be false. But this means that two contradictories are both false, and that is impossible.

16.6.1. My answer is this: If you give either of these replies without the other, then the one you give will be false; but it does not follow from this that two contradictories are simultaneously false, since they are not simultaneous. If, on the other hand, you were to make both replies simultaneously, then you would be answering both in the negative and in the affirmative at the same time; hence your negative answer would make the sophism true, with the result that your affirmative answer would be true and your negative one false; so we still should not have two contradictories being false together.

16.7. The same situation arises if we lay it down that 'A' is to signify everyone who either is answering or is going to answer in the negative, and nothing else (in the way that the word 'man' signifies every man and nothing else), and then the 'opponent' puts it to you that you are an A and asks you whether that is so or not so. For this is exactly as if someone were to say 'You are either answering or going to answer in the negative' and then ask you whether that is so or not so; and therefore self-reference would again prevent you from giving a correct answer by saying directly either that it is so or that it is not, though you could reply truly by saying that what he said was false, or for that matter that it was not false but true.

SEVENTEENTH SOPHISM

The seventeenth sophism will deal with a conditional proposition that expresses a promise or a vow. The sophism is:

17.0 *You are going to throw me into the water.*

I posit the following case: Plato is a powerful lord who is guarding a bridge with a strong band of helpers, so that no one can go across it without his permission. Then Socrates arrives on the scene and pleads urgently with Plato to let him cross. But Plato flies into a rage and swears an oath in these terms: 'I give you my word, Socrates, that if the next proposition you utter is a true one, then I shall allow you to cross; but just as surely, if what you say is false I shall throw you into the water'. Now suppose that Socrates replies to Plato by uttering the above sophism, i.e. 'You are going to throw me into the water'. The question then is, what should Plato do in order to keep his promise?

17.1. The problem is that if he throws Socrates into the water this will violate his promise, for then what Socrates said was true and so he should have let him cross, but that if he lets him cross this too will clearly violate his promise and his oath, for then what Socrates said was false and so Plato should have thrown him into the water.

17.2. This sophism raises several questions: (a) Is Socrates' proposition (the sophism itself in the posited case) true or false? (b) Was Plato's proposition (his promise or vow) true or false? (c) What ought Plato to do to fulfil his promise or vow?

17.3. My answer to (a) is that Socrates' proposition is one about a future contingency, and as a result I cannot know whether it is true or false until I see how the future event will turn out. It is therefore in Plato's own power whether it is true or false, for if he throws him into the water it is true and if he lets him cross it is false.

17.4. My reply to (b) is this: Plato's proposition was a conditional one, and in the strict sense it could not have been true at all, since its antecedent could have been true without its consequent's being true: it was possible, after all, for Socrates to have uttered some great truth (e.g. that God exists) and for Plato nevertheless not to have allowed him to cross. However, propositions that express promises are, in a less strict sense, counted as true in cases where, on the fulfilment of the stated condition, the promise is also fulfilled. For example, suppose I say 'If you come to me I shall give you a horse'; then if on your arrival I do give you a horse, everyone would reckon that what I said was true. But even using words in this way, I maintain that what Plato said was not true. For Socrates fulfilled the required condition, since he did utter a proposition that was bound to be either true or false (even though it would not be determinately true or determinately false until some future event occurred – on this topic see the *De Interpretatione*); yet when he had done so, Plato was not able to fulfil his promise because Socrates' proposition gave that promise a self-reference that made it inevitably false.

17.5. My reply to (c) – what Plato ought to do to keep his

promise – is that he has no obligation to keep it at all, simply because he cannot do so. Moreover he ought not to make such a promise in the first place except with the proviso that Socrates should not utter any proposition whose meaning would be related to the promise itself in such a way as to ensure that the promise was incapable of being made true.

EIGHTEENTH SOPHISM

18.0 *Socrates wants to eat.*

Let us posit that Socrates want to eat if Plato wants to eat, but not otherwise; for people often have such a strong desire for company at a meal that without company they would not want to eat at all. Let us also posit that Plato, by contrast, does not want to eat if Socrates wants to eat, but does want to eat if Socrates does not want to; for he bears Socrates a grudge about something, and that makes him not want to eat with him. The question then is whether the sophism is true or false; for 'Socrates want to eat' and 'Socrates does not want to eat' are contradictories, and so one must be true and the other false no matter what case is posited.

18.1. The problem is this: If you say that Socrates does want to eat, then the opposite of this follows; for it follows that Plato does not want to eat, and from this in turn it follows that Socrates does not want to eat. On the other hand, if you say that Socrates does not want to eat, then again the opposite follows; for it follows that Plato wants to eat, and from this in turn it follows that Socrates too wants to eat.

18.2. My first comment is that on a strict interpretation the case as posited in an impossible one. For 'Socrates wants to eat if Plato wants to eat' is a conditional proposition, but the inference from the antecedent to the consequent is invalid, since it is quite possible for Socrates not to want to eat even though Plato does. On the other hand, if we understand conditional propositions in the way they are usually understood when they express our promises or vows or wishes, the case is then a possible one: for Socrates would like to make the following proposition true (or would like the facts to be as it says they are), 'If Plato eats here and now I shall eat with him, but if he does not neither shall I'; and Plato by contrast would like to make this one true, 'If Socrates eats here and now I shall not, but if he does not then I shall'. But I maintain that it is impossible for both of them to *fulfil* these wishes.

18.3. You may, however, raise the question whether Socrates does or does not want to eat here and now. My answer is that unless Socrates and Plato have some other wishes than the ones we have mentioned, neither of them wants to eat here and now. For a wish has to be a wish for a certain object, and in neither case was the wish a wish specifically *to eat here and now*. (For this reason, too, 'I want to go to Rome if Socrates goes' does not entail 'I want to go to Rome'.)

18.3.1. You may object that if Socrates does not want to eat here and now, then it follows that Plato does want to. But that is just what I deny: that conditional was false and unacceptable. What *is* acceptable is the *categorical* proposition that Socrates would like things to be as the proposition 'If Plato eats here and now I shall eat with him' says they are; and Plato hates this idea and wants to bring about the contrary. But nothing impossible follows from all that.

NINETEENTH SOPHISM

19.0 *Socrates is cursing Plato.*

The posited case is that Socrates says 'May Plato be cursed if he is cursing me, but not otherwise', and Plato for his part says 'May Socrates be cursed if he is *not* cursing me, but not otherwise'. The question concerns the truth of the sophism, whether Socrates is in fact cursing Plato.

19.1. If you say he is, then it follows that Plato both is and is not cursing Socrates, which is self-contradictory. And if you say he is not, then the opposite of this follows, since it follows that Plato is cursing Socrates and consequently that Socrates is cursing Plato.

19.2. My view is this: You can take the following proposition to express the posited case: 'Socrates is saying that Plato is to be cursed if he is cursing Socrates'. Now this proposition can be understood in either of two ways. (a) It can be understood as a conditional, i.e. as meaning 'If Plato is cursing Socrates then Socrates is saying that Plato is to be cursed'. But that proposition is false, impossible and quite unacceptable, because 'Plato is cursing Socrates' does not entail 'Socrates is saying etc.'. In fact, whether Plato is cursing Socrates or not, Socrates is saying just whatever he happens to be saying and not saying just whatever he happens not to be saying. Alternatively, (b) the proposition can be understood as a categorical one meaning 'Socrates is saying the words "May Plato be cursed if etc."'; and this *is* acceptable, since it is quite possible for Socrates to be saying that. An analogous distinction has to be made for the second proposition posited by the case, 'Plato is saying etc.'

19.2.1. In that case what the question amounts to is whether Socrates and Plato in saying these things are cursing each other. My answer is this: To curse someone is to say that some harm should befall him, using a verb in the optative mood; thus I take 'Plato be cursed' to mean the same as 'May some harm befall Plato'. Next, sometimes such cursing expressions are *absolute* curses, with no conditions attached, like the plain 'Plato be cursed', but at other times they are *conditioned* curses, like 'Plato be cursed if he goes to the fields'. Now words have their meanings only by convention, so if you want to call both kinds 'curses' *simpliciter* then I shall say that each of them was cursing the other, though not with an absolute curse.

19.2.1.1. You may object to this on the ground that if Socrates is cursing Plato then it follows that Plato is *not* cursing Socrates. But I reject that inference, since I have not accepted the proposition expressing the case as a conditional. What I have accepted is that Plato was uttering the proposition in question, and it is true that he was uttering it; so he was cursing Socrates, with a conditioned curse, irrespective of whether Socrates was saying anything at all or not.

19.2.2. If, however, you do not want to call a conditioned curse a curse at all, then I shall say that neither of them is cursing the other. And from the fact that Socrates is not cursing Plato it does not follow that Plato is cursing him: the only thing that follows is that Plato is saying whatever he was saying, and that was only a conditioned curse.

TWENTIETH SOPHISM

A verbal curse seems to represent a wish that some harm should befall someone, so to amplify our discussion of the preceding sophism I shall add one more:

20.0 *Socrates wishes Plato harm.*

The posited case is that Socrates wishes Plato harm conditionally, in the sense that he wishes Plato harm if Plato wishes him harm, and that Plato on the other hand wishes Socrates harm if Socrates does *not* wish him harm. The question about this sophism is whether Socrates does wish Plato harm or not.

20.1. The arguments could proceed exactly as in the case of cursing.

20.2. My view is, as before, that the propositions that express the case can be taken in either of two ways. (a) They can be interpreted as conditionals, and in that case they should not be admitted, since 'Plato wishes Socrates harm' does not entail 'Socrates wishes Plato harm'.

Or (b) they can be accepted as categorical propositions to the effect that Socrates would like things to be as is expressed in the sentence 'Plato is to come to harm if he wishes Socrates harm'. In that case if it is asked whether Socrates wishes Plato harm I shall say that he does, though only with a conditioned wish, not an absolute one.

NOW LET US TURN AWAY FROM CURSES
AND MAY GOD GIVE US HIS BLESSING
WHO IS BLESSED FROM ALL ETERNITY
AMEN

COMMENTARY

SOPHISM 1

The discussion of this sophism follows the orthodox pattern described on p.
4, with two modifications. (a) After stating the second argument against
the sophism (1.2.2), Buridan immediately presents a reply to this argument
(1.2.2.1) and then an objection to that reply (1.2.2.2), the arguments against
the sophism being resumed at 1.2.3. (b) Between the statement of his own
view and the replies to the opposing arguments he interposes a sequence of
five 'conclusions' (1.4.1–1.4.5). Although these 'conclusions' are formally an
interruption of the standard pattern, they contain the heart of what Buridan
has to say here.

The sophism itself is an inference. The question to be asked about it is not
explicitly stated, but it clearly is 'Is the inference valid?' No special situation
is needed to raise this question, so no case is posited.

Sophisms 1–3 are concerned with the problem: what makes an inference
a valid one? i.e., under what conditions are we to say that the conclusion of
an inference follows logically from its premiss or premisses? (Nearly all of
Buridan's examples of inferences have only a single premiss, but there is no
difficulty in adapting his comments to apply to those that have two or more.)
Now one answer to this question, frequently advanced both in his day and
in our own, can be stated as follows:

> An inference is valid if and only if it is impossible for the premiss(es) to be true
> without the conclusion's also being true.

Let us call this *Theory A*. It appears also to have been formulated by some
of Buridan's contemporaries in a less precise form, with the phrase 'without
the conclusion' replacing 'without the conclusion's being true', and both
formulations are mentioned together at 1.2.2.1; but we need not pay much
attention to the difference between the two versions here. Buridan's strategy
in this first sophism is to use the example given in the sophism itself to refute
Theory A, and then to advance an alternative theory of his own. The example
refutes the theory, he argues, because it is a clearly valid inference which the
theory would force us to pronounce invalid.

The *arguments in favour of the sophism* (which Buridan clearly accepts) are
straightforward, but some comments on matters of detail seem to be called
for.

1.1.1. By 'contraries' we are to understand not contrary *propositions* but
contrary *terms*, in the sense of terms that cannot apply simultaneously to the

same object. The principle appealed to is that if B and C are contrary terms, then 'Every A is B' entails 'No A is C'.

1.1.2. An *enthymeme* is often described in logic text-books as an inference in which one or more premisses are omitted or 'suppressed'. In his work, the *Consequentiae* (Book III, ch. 1) Buridan tells us that in the strict sense (the sense he obviously favours, and in which he is clearly using the word in the present passage), an enthymeme is a 'truncated syllogism', i.e. an inference that could be made into a syllogism by the addition of one extra premiss; though he adds that in a broader sense the word is sometimes applied to any inference from one categorical proposition to another. The general principle appealed to in this paragraph, and from which there seems no reason to dissent, is that if two propositions, *p* and *q*, jointly entail *r*, then if *p* is a necessary proposition, *q* by itself entails *r*. In other words, deleting a necessary proposition from the premisses of a valid inference still leaves us with a valid inference. We do not have to accept Buridan's claim that 'Everything that flies has wings' *is* a necessary proposition in order to see the point of his example.

A syllogism in *Darii* (literally, the third mood of the first figure) is an inference of the form 'Every B is (a) C, Some A is (a) B, *therefore* Some A is (a) C'. A syllogism in *Celarent* (literally, the second mood of the first figure) is one of the form 'No B is (a) C, Every A is (a) B, *therefore* No A is (a) C'. Both are standard valid inference-forms in traditional syllogistic logic.

Note the distinction drawn in this paragraph between a valid inference in general and a *formally* valid inference. A formally valid inference is one whose validity depends solely on its structure and not at all on the meanings of its categorematic terms. Any syllogism in *Celarent*, for example, is formally valid, since we can replace 'A', 'B' and 'C' in the schema for *Celarent* by any terms we please that are capable of functioning as subjects and predicates in categorical propositions, and the resulting inference will always be valid. Clearly the present sophism is not *formally* valid: the inference 'Every dog is four-legged, therefore no dog is black' has the same structure as it does, but is patently not valid. The argument of 1.1.2 is that the sophism is nevertheless (non-formally) valid because it can be obtained from the formally valid inference (in *Celarent*) 'No affirmative is negative, Every proposition is affirmative, *therefore* No proposition is negative' by deleting a premiss that is a necessary proposition. (We could of course analogously turn the example about dogs into a formally valid inference by adding the premiss 'No four-legged creature is black', but this proposition is obviously not a necessary one, and in fact there is no necessary proposition that could serve the purpose.)

1.1.3. The principle here is that of *contraposition*, *viz.* that in order to show that *p* entails *q* it is sufficient to show that *not-q* entails *not-p*. Note that Buridan tacitly assumes the standard principle of syllogistic logic that the negation (or contradictory) of 'No A is (a) B' can be expressed as 'Some A is (a) B'.

The *arguments against the sophism* Buridan will of course in the end wish to refute. In the mean time he states them as fairly and persuasively as he can.

1.2.1. That an impossible proposition never follows from a possible one is a standard principle of modal logic, which Buridan does not challenge. An alternative formulation is: If *p* entails *q*, then if *p* is possible so is *q*. Nor will he wish to dispute the claim that the premiss of the sophism ('Every proposition is affirmative') is a possible proposition. As was pointed out in the Introduction (pp. 5–6), a proposition for Buridan is a certain kind of individual inscription or utterance, and it is therefore entirely conceivable that at a certain time the only propositions that happen to exist should be affirmative ones; the picture of God's destoying all negative propositions is simply a dramatic way of making this point. The remaining step in the proof is the argument that the conclusion of the sophism ('No proposition is negative') is an impossible proposition, and *this* is what Buridan will challenge, on the ground that it confuses 'impossible' and 'not possibly true' (see 1.4.3 and 1.5).

1.2.2. Here the argument is based explicitly on what I have called Theory A. The sophism, it is claimed, is invalid because it fails to satisfy the condition stated in this theory; for (a) the premiss can be true but the conclusion (as was argued in 1.2.1) could not be true in any circumstances, and (b) if the premiss is true the conclusion does not exist, and so is not true. Buridan will reverse the argument and use the established validity of the sophism as a reason for rejecting Theory A (1.4.1, 1.4.2).

1.2.2.1. Some of Buridan's contemporaries held a more sophisticated theory of the conditions of validity, obtained by adding to Theory A the clause 'when the premiss(es) and the conclusion are formulated at the same time' (*ipsis simul formatis*). Let us call this, *Theory B*. In 1.2.2.1 Buridan envisages an adherent of Theory B pointing out that even if Theory A can be accused of invalidating the sophism, Theory B cannot. For if we suppose that the premiss and the conclusion of the sophism both actually exist, then at least one proposition (the conclusion) will not be affirmative, and so in these circumstances it will be impossible for the premiss to be true; hence *a fortiori* it will be impossible for the premiss to be true and the conclusion not true, and therefore the sophism does satisfy the conditions for validity laid down in Theory B.

(The unknown author commonly called Pseudo-Scotus, who was probably a near contemporary of Buridan, mentions Theory B and gives as an argument in its favour precisely the fact that it validates the inference that Buridan uses as Sophism 1. See Kneale [1962], p. 287.)

In 1.2.2.2 Buridan implicitly concedes that Theory B would rescue the sophism from the clutches of the argument in 1.2.2, but raises the objection that it would validate too much. It would mean, for instance, that the proposition 'No proposition is affirmative' would entail any and every affirmative proposition, and he takes it as obvious that it does not. 'There is a stick standing in the corner' is of course intended only as an arbitrary example of an affirmative proposition.

1.2.3. The principle stated at the beginning ('If the premiss...not valid') may read as if it applies only to inferences with premisses that are actually true, but what is meant, I believe, is that in any valid inference in which the premiss(es) *can* be true, premiss(es) and conclusion must be compatible and hence capable of being true together. The argument is that in the sophism the premiss and the conclusion are not compatible because the very existence of the latter makes the former false, though on its own it could be true. Buridan will agree that premiss and conclusion must be compatible, but will deny that this means that they must be able to be true together (1.5).

In 1.3 Buridan not merely states that in his view the sophism is valid, but also endorses the arguments already given for this (1.1.1–1.1.3). It is worth noting that it is unsafe to assume that he approves of the arguments he lists in support of views that he agrees with, unless, as he does here, he explicitly says so.

1.4.1–1.4.5 are labelled 'conclusions', but this is not to be taken to mean that the views expressed in them can be inferred from the foregoing paragraphs. As the word is being used here, a 'conclusion' is a proposition for which a proof can and should be given, as contrasted with a fundamental principle which is self-evident and stands in no need of proof.

1.4.1. Theory A cannot be correct. Take any valid inference in which the premiss(es) can be true (and there are obviously many such inferences). Now it is *always* possible for the conclusion not to exist, and therefore not to be true. So in such an inference it is *not* impossible for the premiss(es) to be true but the conclusion not to be true.

1.4.2 makes a stronger point. Not merely can we have a valid inference in which it is possible for the premiss(es) to be true but the conclusion not true, we can even have one in which the premiss(es) can be true but the conclusion cannot possibly be true at all. In adducing the present sophism as a case in point Buridan is not begging the question: he has already claimed that he has demonstrated its validity, and he will present refutations of the counter-arguments at 1.5. The proof that 'No proposition is negative' cannot be true is given at 1.2.1, in a part of the argument of which he obviously approves.

In the example at the end of 1.4.2 the reason why the conclusion cannot be true is presumably that no matter how we divide the Latin word *unica* into syllables, at least one of them must consist of a single letter. The example would perhaps read more naturally in English if we replaced 'syllable' by 'word'.

1.4.3 draws the important distinction, which we shall encounter many times in later sophisms, between a proposition's being *possible* and its being *possibly true*. This distinction is a development of the one explained in the Introduction on pp. 20–1 between *the facts being as a certain proposition says they are* and *that proposition's being true*. For the latter, it may be recalled, though not for the former, Buridan requires the existence of the proposition in question; and clearly, given his concept of a proposition, it may happen that the facts are as a certain proposition says they are even though that proposition does not exist, or does not exist at the relevant time. Two questions about possibility therefore arise in connection with any given proposition: (a) is it possible for the facts to be as it says they are? and (b) is it possible, consistently with their being so, for it itself to exist? If the answer to (a) is Yes, Buridan will say that the proposition is a *possible* one; but only if the answer to (b) is also Yes will he say that it is *possibly true*. Normally, of course, if a proposition is possible it is also possibly true. What the proposition 'There are horses', for example, says is simply that animals of a certain kind exist; and clearly it is perfectly possible that at one and the same time there should be such animals and also someone who is asserting that there are. But in certain special cases the existence of the proposition is incompatible with things being as it says they are. In particular, in the present case it is quite possible that at a certain time no proposition should be negative – but this can be so only if the proposition 'No proposition is negative' does not itself exist at that time; for it is a negative proposition, and so its existence is incompatible with no proposition's being negative. It therefore counts as possible, but not as possibly true.

Buridan will use this distinction (at 1.5) to refute the argument of 1.2.1. He does not challenge the principle that whatever follows from a possible proposition is itself possible, but it seems clear that he would not accept a principle to the effect that whatever follows from a possibly true proposition is possibly true. He maintains that the argument of 1.2.1 shows quite correctly that the conclusion of the sophism is not possibly true, but that it argues illegitimately from this to the incorrect conclusion that it is not a possible proposition.

For the 'good sense explained in Chapter 2', see the Introduction, pp. 20–1.

In 1.4.3 Buridan refers to Aristotle's *Prior Analytics* in connection with the principle that the impossible never follows from the possible, but there is a problem about what passage he had in mind. Scott locates it as 32ᵃ, 17–27, where the most relevant sentence reads (in Jenkinson's Oxford translation): 'I use the terms "to be possible" and "the possible" of that which is not necessary but, being assumed, results in nothing impossible'. I do not think, however, that this can be correct. There are two senses of the word 'possible', a wider and a narrower, to be found in Aristotle. In the narrower sense, which is clearly intended in the passage just quoted, it covers only what is neither necessary nor impossible; in the wider sense it is equivalent to 'not impossible' and therefore covers what is necessary as well. Now Buridan (like most modern logicians) regularly uses 'possible' only in the second, wider, sense, and uses 'contingent' for 'possible' in Aristotle's narrower sense. So, although it is true that the principle that what is possible never entails anything impossible holds good for both senses of 'possible', it seems unlikely that Buridan would appeal to a passage in which Aristotle was using the term in a different sense from his own. Another possible reference is 34^a, 22–24, which (again in Jenkinson's translation) reads: 'If then, for example, one should indicate the premisses by A and the conclusion by B, it would not only result that if A is necessary B is necessary, but also that if A is possible, B is possible.' This, however, does not state the principle Buridan has in mind quite as directly as one would wish. A further possibility is that Buridan is referring not to the *Prior Analytics* at all but to his own commentary on it; but I have been unable to explore this possibility for lack of access to a text of that work.

1.4.4. In the first part of this paragraph Buridan is saying that Theory B is at least an improvement on Theory A in that it does state a *necessary* condition of validity (though not, as we shall see, a *sufficient* one). The point of the second part seems to be to insist that, even if we construe the condition as only a necessary one, the impossibility required must be that of the *simultaneous* truth of the premiss(es) and non-truth of the conclusion, for there are valid inferences in which premiss(es) and conclusion coexist but the premiss(es) are true at one time and the conclusion is false at another time. Buridan uses the present sophism to contruct an example. Suppose 'Every proposition is affirmative' is formulated at t_1, is true at that time, and goes on existing until t_2. Now suppose that 'No proposition is negative' is formulated at t_2. Then the two propositions exist at the same time (t_2), as Theory B requires; but since 'No proposition is negative' is false whenever it exists, it is false at t_2. Nevertheless the inference from the former proposition to the latter is a valid one, as has already been proved. Buridan's point, however, is that although the premiss is true at t_1, it is not true at t_2, and so there is no moment at which the propositions coexist and at which the first is true but the second is not.

The Aristotelian reference in 1.4.4 is presumably to the *Prior Analytics* 53^b, 7–8.

1.4.5. Theory B does not give us a *sufficient* condition of validity, since there are inferences that satisfy the condition it states and yet are not valid: Buridan recalls the example given in 1.2.2.2 and adds another. So a further necessary condition is needed, and this, he maintains, is that it should be impossible for the facts to be as the premiss(es) say they are but not as the conclusion says they are. The important feature of this condition is that it makes no reference to the truth or the existence of the propositions themselves, but is concerned only with what they assert to be the case (or what they would assert to be the case if they were actually formulated). Buridan does not explicitly claim that if we add these two conditions together we obtain a necessary-and-sufficient condition of validity, but I think that is probably his view nevertheless. For more on this topic see the next sophism, especially 2.4.2 and the commentary thereon.

The reference at the end of 1.4.5 is again to the passage in Chapter 2 discussed in the Introduction on pp. 17–21.

1.5 consists of the formal replies to the arguments stated in 1.2.1, 1.2.2.

and 1.2.3. The material contained in 1.4.1–1.4.5 enables Buridan to be very brief here. The reply to 1.2.2 is indeed not even stated: we are simply referred back to what was said earlier. The reference is to the criticisms of Theory A in 1.4.1 and 1.4.2.

SOPHISM 2

Sophism 1 was a valid inference which an initially plausible theory would make invalid. In Sophism 2 Buridan offers us an invalid inference which some *prima facie* plausible views would force us to count as valid. The aim, of course, is to criticize these views and thus gain a better insight into the conditions of validity. The upshot will be a refinement and clarification of the account given towards the end of the first sophism.

As before, Buridan states the arguments in favour of the validity of the sophism first, but this time these will be the ones he sets out to refute. It may therefore be better to begin with the arguments on the other side.

2.2.1. The argument is simply that the sophism is invalid because it fails to satisfy what was laid down as a necessary condition of validity in 1.4.5.

2.2.2. Note that the principle appealed to is not that no proposition whatsoever can entail its own contradictory, but only that no *possible* proposition can do so. This is a standard principle of modal logic; an alternative formulation is, 'Any proposition that entails its own contradictory is impossible'. The argument assumes that 'No proposition is negative' is a possible proposition, but Buridan claims to have shown this at 1.4.3.

I turn now to the arguments for the sophism.

2.1.1. This argument is based on (a) a principle, quoted from Aristotle (*Categories* 14^b, 10–22), to the effect that every proposition entails its own truth, and (b) the view, held by Buridan himself, that only an actually existing proposition can be true. In reply (2.4.1) Buridan maintains that (a) is not correct as it stands. Using Aristotle's own example, he argues that the proposition 'A man exists' does not entail '"A man exists" is true'. Suppose, as is conceivable, that there were men but no propositions. Then things would be as the former proposition says they are, but they would not be as the second one says they are, since this second one makes an assertion about a proposition. So the inference fails to satisfy the condition stated in 1.4.5, and is therefore invalid.

This refutation of (a) is enough to demolish the argument of 2.1.1. Buridan goes on to say, however, (2.4.1.1) that the principle quoted from Aristotle, though incorrect as it stands, is only an over-simplified version of a principle which is perfectly sound, and that is that if we take any proposition and add to it the further proposition that it exists, then from these two premisses together we can validly infer that the original proposition is true. This principle is not subject to the criticism brought against the earlier version, for now the existence of the proposition is explicitly asserted in the premisses. It will play an important part in the discussion of some of the later sophisms, and seems to deserve a name of its own. In the Introduction I called it *the principle of truth-entailment*, and I shall go on doing so.

2.1.2. The second argument for the validity of the sophism starts by quoting the condition that Buridan himself formulated in 1.4.5 and then tries to show that the sophism satisfies it. The crucial step is the contention that for things to be as the premiss says they are the premiss must exist, since a non-existent proposition cannot say anything at all. But of course, in the case of the present sophism, if the premiss exists then things automatically are as the conclusion says they are.

Buridan's reply in 2.4.2 makes it clear that he regards this argument as one that he has to take very seriously. The main point of 1.4.5 was to formulate the impossibility required for validity in terms that did not involve the existence of premiss(es) or conclusion, and the argument of 2.1.2 is suggesting that this cannot be done. Moreover, the suggestion that it cannot be done is based on a principle that he himself cannot very well reject; for the very reasons that lead him to hold that the existence of a proposition is necessary for its truth must also force him to maintain that the existence of an inference (and therefore of the propositions that occur in it) is necessary for its validity. If an inference does not exist there is just nothing to *be* valid – or invalid either.

He is therefore faced with the task of re-formulating, or at least clarifying, the validity-criterion stated in 1.4.5, in such a way that it will incorporate a reference to the existence of premiss(es) and conclusion but not allow the argument of 2.1.2 to be constructed. And it seems clear that he is looking for a condition that will be both necessary and sufficient; for although the condition stated in 1.4.5 was at that point claimed only to be a necessary one, yet near the beginning of 2.4.2 it is claimed to be sufficient, given that premiss(es) and conclusion exist.

The overall argument of 2.4.2 is this. Buridan entirely agrees with the principle that seems to underlie the argument of 2.1.2, that the existence of an inference is necessary for it to be valid. He agrees, too, that an adequate statement of the criteria of validity must make this explicit. But, he says, there are two quite different ways in which the condition stated in 1.4.5 could be expanded in order to do so. Firstly, we might say that an inference is valid if and only if

(1) The following conjunction is impossible: the premiss(es) and the conclusion exist, the facts are as the premiss(es) say they are, and the facts are not as the conclusion says they are.

This, he says, is the criterion being implicitly appealed to in 2.1.2, and he agrees that the sophism satisfies it. What this shows, however, he maintains, is that (1) cannot be an accurate account of validity, since the sophism is patently invalid; and as an alternative and, he thinks, correct formulation he offers us this: An inference is valid if and only if

(2) The premiss(es) and the conclusion exist; and in addition the following

conjunction is impossible: the facts are as the premiss(es) say they are, and they are not as the conclusion says they are.

The sophism, he claims, is invalid because it fails to satisfy the second clause in (2).

The difference between (1) and (2) lies in the fact that in the former, though not in the latter, the assertion of the existence of the premiss(es) and the conclusion is made to come within the scope of the 'impossibility-operator'. Buridan's use of the terms 'composite' and 'divided' seems to be intended to indicate this difference of scope. He is, in effect, complaining that the argument of 2.1.2 mislocates the impossibility that is required for the validity of an inference. His own view, to put it in other words, is this: The existence of premiss(es) and conclusion is indeed necessary for the validity of an inference, in that without it there would be no inference to be valid at all; but, given their existence, the impossibility that is necessary and sufficient for the validity of the inference is simply the impossibility of things being as the premiss(es) say they are but not as the conclusion says they are, and *not* the joint impossibility of this together with the existence of premiss(es) and conclusion.

The main positive results of Sophism 2, then, are firstly the explicit statement of the principle of truth-entailment at 2.4.1.1, and secondly the final shaping-up of the validity-criterion towards which Buridan was working in Sophism 1.

SOPHISM 3

The opening sentence of this sophism is somewhat obscure. In it Buridan is telling us that the sophism will be concerned with *sequentia*, but it is not at all clear what these are supposed to be. The interpretation that seems to me most plausible, and on which I have based my translation, is that the term is drawn from the technical vocabulary of the mediaeval 'obligation' exercise. This exercise was certainly very familiar to him and to his original readers, and Sophism 16 later on is explicitly set in the context of it. Brief accounts of what it involved will be found in the commentary on that sophism (p. 155) and in the texts referred to there. If this interpretation is correct, then 'Every man is a donkey' is here not an ordinary 'posited case' of the kind that we find in most of Buridan's other sophisms, but a proposition which a 'respondent' has undertaken to maintain consistently for the duration of an obligation exercise, and the question at issue is whether 'Every man is running, therefore a donkey is running' is a *sequens* – i.e. a logical consequence – of that proposition. The rules of the exercise required a respondent to assent to any consequence of the originally posited proposition, and it was therefore important to be able to determine whether something was such a consequence or not.

The mediaeval obligation-literature has not yet been at all exhaustively investigated, and I cannot feel completely confident about the correctness of this interpretation; nevertheless the following points in Buridan's treatment of the sophism seem to lend some support to it. (a) Usually he takes great care to ensure that his posited cases are possible ones (see 13.9 for his rejection of a suggested posited case on the grounds of its impossibility). Now he would certainly have regarded 'Every man is a donkey' as an impossible proposition, yet he raises no objection to its being posited here. The rules of the obligation exercise, however, did permit the positing of impossible propositions, subject to certain conditions which are in fact met in the present instance. (b) Like most other mediaeval logicians, Buridan subscribed to the principle that from an impossible proposition anything whatsoever follows, yet he makes no use of it here, in spite of the fact that the posited proposition is an impossible one. There is, however, reason to believe that the rules of the obligation exercise did not permit an appeal to this principle in determining whether one proposition was a consequence of another (it would indeed have made nonsense of the practice of positing impossible propositions had they done so). (See, e.g., De Rijk [1974], especially p. 118.)

Fortunately, the main point of Sophism 3 can readily be disentangled from such problems of interpretation. This point is a straightforward one but, as Buridan rightly thinks, it is easy to become confused about it. The question is this. Suppose a proposition r follows from a pair of propositions p and q taken together. Suppose then that we are given that p is the case. Does this entitle us to say that r follows from q? Buridan is emphatic that it does not. The question whether r follows from q, or in general whether any (existing) inference is valid, is purely a question of logic; and this means that if one proposition follows from another, then the proposition that it does so is not merely true but necessary, and if it does not so follow then the proposition that it does is not merely false but impossible. So if r does not follow from q alone, it is impossible that it should so follow; and the assumption, or even the discovery, that p is true cannot make r follow from q, since that would involve turning an impossible proposition into a necessary one, which is absurd. In other words, we have to be careful to distinguish between (a) simply assuming or positing p and then asking whether r follows from q alone, and (b) adding p to q as an extra premiss and asking whether r follows from both of them taken together. (Buridan in 3.4 calls (a) 'positing *simply*' and (b) 'positing *as a premiss*'.) Irrespective of whether p is true or false, assumed or denied, 'q, therefore r' and 'p, q, therefore r' are different inferences, and the latter may well be valid even if the former is not.

Buridan may have placed this sophism immediately after Sophism 2 in order to clarify further the distinction between the correct and the incorrect versions of the rule discussed in 2.4.2 (numbered (2) and (1) respectively on p. 87). For another way of looking at this distinction is by saying that in the correct version the existence of premiss(es) and conclusion is posited simply, while in the incorrect version it is posited as a premiss. To apply this to Sophism 2 itself: according to the correct version of the rule, we have to posit simply that the inference that forms the sophism exists, in order for there to be anything whose validity we can enquire into; but when we have done that, the question is just whether 'Some proposition is negative' follows from 'No proposition is negative' *alone*, and the answer is that it does not. According to the incorrect version, the question is whether 'Some proposition is negative' follows from 'No proposition is negative' together with the additional premiss that the two propositions in question exist; and the answer is that it does.

Similar considerations apply to the principle of truth-entailment. In order to raise the question whether 'A man exists' entails '"A man exists" is true', we have to posit simply that the proposition 'A man exists' exists. But merely positing that 'A man exists' exists is not the same as using it as a premiss, and we have to do the latter in order to be able to draw the conclusion that 'A man exists' is true.

The only other comments that seem called for are on points of detail.

3.1.1. A syllogism in *Darapti* (literally, the first mood of the third figure) is an inference of the form 'Every B is (a) C, Every B is (an) A, *therefore* Some A is (a) C'.

The expression that I have translated '*reductio ad absurdum*' means literally 'syllogism to the impossible'. In mediaeval logic this term covered not only syllogisms whose conclusions are impossible propositions but also those with conclusions that are given as, or known to be, false. The chief use in practice of such inferences is, of course, to demonstrate the falsity of a premiss (see, for example, 5.2.2 below). This, however, does not appear to be the point being made here. If I interpret correctly the passage I have enclosed in brackets, its main aim is rather to emphasize the fact that the validity or otherwise of an inference is purely a matter of whether the conclusion follows from the premisses, and does not depend either on the truth of the conclusion or on whether we are using the inference to make deductions from known truths; and this point is then applied to the syllogism at the beginning of the paragraph. I am not fully confident, however, that this interpretation is the correct one, since the text is obscure and as a result the exact drift of the argument is unclear. The readings of some of the Mss. would make the passage appear to claim that the syllogism under discussion is itself a 'syllogism to the impossible'; but I do not think this can be correct, since 'A donkey is running' is often used by Buridan as a standard example of a *contingent* proposition, and there is no suggestion that in this context it is even to be assumed to be false.

Buridan's criticism of both 3.1.1 and 3.1.2 is that they treat the posited proposition as a premiss, and that as a result the inference whose validity they correctly maintain is not the one mentioned in the sophism itself.

It might appear that the discussion of this sophism is structurally defective in that it lacks a formal reply to the opposing arguments. We can, however, take the 'arguments' referred to in the very last sentence of 3.4 as the arguments of 3.1.1 and 3.1.2, and in that case this sentence, brief though it is, will constitute the formal reply to them.

SOPHISM 4

Structurally, 4.3, 4.3.1, 4.6 and 4.6.1 are deviations from the standard pattern. After stating the arguments for and against the sophism, and before giving us his own view, Buridan interpolates what he considers to be an incorrect solution (4.3) and then criticizes it (4.3.1). And after his reply to the opposing argument he expounds an objection that might be raised against his own view (4.6) and then replies to that objection (4.6.1). As often happens, the most interesting material is found in these additions to the main structure.

Sophisms 1–3 were concerned with the validity of inferences. Sophisms 4–6 deal principally with the nature of propositions. As was pointed out in the Introduction (pp. 5–6), a proposition for Buridan is a particular inscription or utterance (sentence-token) of an assertive type. Not every sentence-token that is capable of being a proposition, however, actually is one, and in Sophism 4 Buridan's main contention is that a 'part of a proposition' is never itself a proposition, even though it has the structure appropriate to a proposition and could be a proposition if it were not embedded in a larger one. His reasons for holding this at first sight surprising view cast considerable light on what he understands by the term 'proposition'. Some of these reasons are given in the present sophism, but for a fuller discussion of the topic he refers us to a chapter in his general work on logic, the *Summulae de Dialectica* (Tractatus I, chapter 7).

It is perhaps easiest to begin by considering the example he discusses in 4.3.1. This is the verse from the Psalms, familiar to most students of philosophy from the use that Anselm makes of it in his formulation of the Ontological Argument: *The fool has said in his heart, There is no God.* For simplicity let us suppose that the fool says vocally, rather than 'in his heart',

(1) There is no God

and that the Psalmist then comments

(2) The fool has said, There is no God.

Now both (1) and (2) are propositions, but Buridan insists that the last four words of (2) do not form a proposition at all. His reason is that if they did form a proposition then the proposition they formed would be a false one ('God does not exist' is frequently used by mediaeval logicians as a standard false proposition), and hence the Psalmist in saying (2) would be saying something false, which he is not. One does not have to share either Buridan's theism or his attitude to the Bible to take the point that even if (1) is assumed to be false, someone who says (2) is not saying anything false at all.

The crucial difference between (1) and the equiform (i.e. verbally identical) sentence embedded in (2) is that the former is being used assertively but the latter is not, and it is this that prevents the latter from counting as a proposition in Buridan's eyes. So he insists that the Psalmist speaks only a single proposition – the whole of (2) – and that in enunciating its last four words he is not saying anything that is true or false at all. These last four words have the function not of *being* a proposition but of *referring to* or *standing for* one, but the proposition they refer to is not any part of (2), but (1).

It appears, then, that what Buridan understands by a 'proposition' is a sentence-token of an appropriate kind *used assertively*, and that it is this that leads him to the view that a part (i.e. a proper part) of a proposition is not itself a proposition. Certainly if one declarative sentence, S_1, is embedded in another, S_2, we do not on that acount want to say that anyone who asserts S_2 thereby asserts S_1 as well.

Buridan carries through consistently this doctrine that a part of a proposition is not a proposition. In 4.6 and 4.6.1 he considers an apparent exception to it. It seems reasonable to suppose that the following proposition,

(3) The proposition 'A man is an animal' is true

is itself true, and yet its truth appears to presuppose that the expression 'A man is an animal' embedded in it is itself a proposition. Buridan, however, holds fast to the view that it is no such thing. (3) can indeed, he says, be true, but only on condition that there exists some other, genuinely propositional, occurrence of 'A man is an animal', to which the subject of (3) ('The proposition "A man is an animal"') refers; otherwise the subject of (3) lacks a referent and (3) is in consequence false.

In other passages Buridan speaks in a way that seems inconsistent with his own doctrine; for he refers to the conjuncts in a conjunctive proposition and the disjuncts in a disjunctive proposition both as parts of the propositions in question and also as propositions themselves (see, e.g., Sophisms 12 and 14 below), and with great frequency he speaks of the antecedent and the consequent of a conditional proposition as true or false, and hence by implication as propositions. The passage in the *Summulae* to which he refers us in 4.3.1 shows, however, that the inconsistency here is only apparent. In that passage he discusses a wide range of complex propositions commonly described as consisting of a pair of propositions joined by a conjunction or an adverb, and he criticizes this characterization of them precisely on the ground that their constituents are not strictly speaking propositions at all, but only expressions that *would* be propositions if they were spoken or written on their own. His reason is this. It is possible for a disjunction to be true but to contain a disjunct which, if it were a proposition, would have to be regarded as false; it is equally possible to have a true conditional in which both antecedent and consequent, if they were propositions, would be false. Now it is, he says, absurd to suppose that a true proposition can have any parts that are false; so the embedded expressions in question cannot be propositions. Nevertheless, he adds, for the sake of convenience and brevity he is willing to acquiesce in the common but strictly inaccurate practice of referring to them as propositions; and that is what we must understand him to be doing throughout our present text.

The argument I have quoted from the *Summulae* will be apt to strike a modern reader as strange, but its strangeness may grow less if we bear in mind that in Buridan's preferred or 'strict' sense of 'proposition' nothing counts as a proposition unless it is being asserted. Now in asserting a proposition of the form '*p* or *q*' or 'if *p*, *q*' I am neither asserting *p* nor asserting *q*, so my saying of them cannot count as 'saying a proposition' (*dicere propositionem*), but only as 'saying an expression' (*dicere vocem*, or *orationem*) that might have been a proposition but is not. And a true proposition cannot have false parts, because that would mean that in asserting something true I am asserting something false, which is not so. Buridan does indeed say that the necessary and sufficient condition for the truth of a disjunction is that at least one of its disjuncts should be true, but it seems clear that he regards this as merely a convenient but loose way of saying that at least one of the disjuncts must be such that it *would* be true if it were asserted on its own.

Buridan's argument does not perhaps apply so obviously to conjunctive propositions as to the others he discusses, since it is less clear that someone who asserts a conjunction does not thereby assert each conjunct. Nevertheless he maintains that even the conjuncts in a conjunctive proposition are not strictly speaking propositions any more than the disjuncts in a disjunction are. He may well have thought it would be anomalous not to treat disjunctions and conjunctions in parallel ways.

It may be worth noting that to say that a proposition must express an assertion is not at all the same as to say that it must express a belief held by the speaker. There is no suggestion in Buridan that for my words to count as a proposition I must *believe* what I am saying. A debater who argues for a certain thesis is certainly stating a proposition in Buridan's sense, but it need not be assumed that he himself believes the proposition he is defending; and the person who tells a lie consciously asserts what he does not believe. Moreover, certain propositions, such as 'A man is a donkey', are regularly used by Buridan as sample false propositions; but while he certainly envisages people asserting them, he does not suggest that those who do so actually believe them.

Sophism 4 raises other issues as well as the ones I have just mentioned, and it is difficult to be sure precisely what Buridan wants to say about them, though certain things are clear enough. We are to envisage someone saying

(4) I say that a man is a donkey

and the question is whether in saying this he is saying something true or something false. ('A man is a donkey' is of course a 'standard false proposition' – or at least it would be if uttered assertively on its own.) Now on the face of it (4) is ambiguous. It might be construed as an alternative way of saying 'A man is, I say (*or* I maintain), a donkey', where 'I say' (*or* 'I maintain') is employed as what is sometimes called a 'parenthetical verb' and the whole remark is understood as an emphatic way of asserting that a man is a donkey. Taken in this way, of course, (4) presents no problem: it counts as straightforwardly false. Alternatively, we might understand (4) as an assertion that the speaker is making about himself, just as we would naturally take someone who says 'I have a broken leg' to be making an assertion about himself, or the Psalmist to be making an assertion about the fool when he says (2). It is clear that Buridan interprets (4) in this second way. But then the question arises of what exactly the speaker is supposed to be asserting about himself. For 'to say that a man is a donkey' can mean either (a) *to assert the proposition that a man is a donkey*, or (b) *to speak the words 'a man is a donkey'*. Now Buridan says emphatically that the words 'a man is a donkey' in (4) do not constitute a proposition, and so if we were to understand 'to say that a man is a donkey' in sense (a), then by his own principles (4) would be false. He says quite clearly, however, that he regards it as true (4.4), and I think we have to draw the conclusion that he wants us to understand 'to say that a man is a donkey' in sense (b). This interpretation seems also to be borne out by the wording of 4.5; and certainly it will make (4) true, since it is manifest that anyone who says (4) thereby speaks the words 'a man is a donkey'.

With this interpretation, however, it is difficult to know what to make of 4.2.1. It is in any case hard to reconcile 4.2.1 and 4.2.2, the two arguments that Buridan lists in the exposition in favour of his own answer to the original question. The argument of 4.2.2 is straightforward. It consists in spelling out the sophism in the conventional logical form (subject – copula – predicate) and then applying the relevant correspondence truth-conditions explained in the Introduction on pp. 17–18. Since the subject ('I') stands for the speaker, and the predicate is 'someone who is saying that a man is a donkey', it is clear that if we take 'to say that a man is a donkey' in sense (b), then the subject and the predicate do 'stand for the same', as the relevant truth-condition requires. But the problem about 4.2.1 is this. We have made sense both of Buridan's overall argument and of 4.2.2 by taking the sophism to mean that the speaker is asserting of himself that he is speaking the words 'a man is a donkey'; but 4.2.1 seems to maintain that what he is asserting about himself is that he is uttering the sophism in its entirety, i.e. the whole expression 'I say that a man is a donkey'. Now no doubt he is uttering that whole expression; but it is very difficult to see how he could be interpreted as asserting that he is doing so, at least if we understand the sophism in the way that 4.2.2 seems to require us to.

To be fair to Buridan, he never in this sophism explicitly claims that the initial arguments for the answer he agrees with are sound ones, and as I remarked in the commentary on 1.3 it is unsafe to assume that he endorses an argument in the exposition of a sophism unless he says so. All that the sophism technique demands is that *some* arguments on each side be stated at the outset, not that all the arguments on one side should be good ones. It may in fact be that Buridan, while he approved of 4.2.2, did not approve of 4.2.1, but included it just because he had come across it somewhere and thought it deserved a mention. At any rate, it seems to me that on his own principles he ought to reject it.

SOPHISM 5

In the light of the discussion of Sophism 4 this next sophism is easy to follow. We are again to take 'saying something' in the sense of *speaking certain words* rather than in the sense of *asserting a proposition*. It is then clear that in the posited case Plato does say 'men are donkeys'; and this is all that Socrates hears, so the sophism is true. The contrary arguments (5.2.1 and 5.2.2) both depend on regarding the verbal expression 'men are donkeys' as a proposition, but in Buridan's view it is not: it is something that Plato spoke, but not something that he asserted.

In 5.2.2 the *reductio ad absurdum* (literally, as at 3.1.1, a 'syllogism to the impossible' – see the commentary on that paragraph) consists of a valid syllogism with a conclusion that both Buridan and the proponent of the argument agree is false. From the falsity of the conclusion it follows that at least one premiss is false; but whereas the proponent of the argument takes it that the second premiss ('Socrates is hearing something false') is true and concludes that the first premiss, which is the sophism itself, must therefore be false, Buridan rejects the second premiss (see 5.4) and is thus able to regard the first as true.

The standard formal pattern ends at 5.4, and the argument is plain sailing up to this point. The main interest lies in the new material Buridan introduces in the form of an objection and a reply as a kind of appendix at 5.5 and 5.5.1. Here he is concerned with the relation between verbal and mental propositions. Mental propositions were referred to briefly in the Introduction (p. 11) where they were described as thoughts that something or other is the case. Mental propositions, according to Buridan, are, like verbal ones, either true or false; indeed they are in a certain way more fundamental than verbal ones, for in his view the main point of propositional language is for a speaker to express in words the mental propositions that he has in his mind, with the intention of producing similar mental propositions in the minds of his hearers. In 5.5 the objector appears to be proposing a certain causal theory of the nature and truth-value of (verbal) propositions, to the effect that any linguistic expression that produces a mental proposition in the mind of a hearer is to count as a proposition, and as one that is true or false according as that mental proposition is true or false. This is indeed not at all a plausible theory, and it is not surprising to find Buridan rejecting it outright; but he is able to use his refutation of it to set out his own ideas more fully.

Suppose that a speaker has a definite mental proposition in mind that he wants to express, and that he uses words in a conventionally established way that is appropriate to the expression of it; in that case, Buridan wants to maintain, his spoken words form a proposition that expresses that mental proposition and no other, and that has the same truth-value as the mental proposition has. None of this, he says, can be affected by any mishearings or misunderstandings on the part of the audience. As far as the present posited case is concerned, he thinks the position is as follows:

(a) Plato is speaking one proposition only, and that a true one.

(b) Plato is saying the words 'men are donkeys', but these words that he speaks do not constitute a proposition, either a true one or a false one.

(c) The words 'men are donkeys' *would* constitute a proposition (a false one) if spoken on their own with the appropriate intention.

(d) Socrates genuinely hears the words 'men are donkeys' spoken by Plato and believes that what he is hearing is a proposition; but this belief of his is incorrect.

(e) The words 'men are donkeys' that Plato speaks and Socrates hears do produce in Socrates a mental proposition that is false.

It is quite wrong, however, he thinks, to infer from all this that Socrates is hearing a false proposition; in fact in the posited case there is no false (spoken) proposition for Socrates to hear at all. All we are entitled to conclude is that if the words that Socrates heard had formed a proposition (as he mistakenly thought they did), then such a proposition *would have been* a false one.

Note the care with which Buridan expresses himself in 5.5.1. Speaking of the general case in which A states a certain (true) proposition but B thinks he is stating a different (false) one, he says that 'a proposition *of the kind* that [B] thinks he is hearing *would be* false', not that 'the proposition that B thinks he is hearing is (*or even* would be) false' (*talis...qualem*, not *ista...quam*), for in the case envisaged there is in fact no actual proposition that B even *thinks* he is hearing. He also warns us against describing A's proposition as 'false to B'; that expression (which is not one that he uses much himself) would, he thinks, be best reserved for cases in which A's proposition really is false and there is no misunderstanding of it on B's part; but obviously the case under discussion is not like that.

SOPHISM 6

The main point being made in this sophism is that what is true or false, in the only sense of 'true' and 'false' with which a logician as such is concerned, is *what is said*, not the saying of it. Buridan recognizes that we commonly use idioms such as 'It is true to say that...' to mean no more than 'It is true that...', and indeed he sometimes uses them himself; but such usages are, he thinks, loose ones and misleading if taken literally. The present sophism is a case in point: taken literally, it attributes truth to the saying (or even to the sayer) rather than to what is said, and so it is strictly speaking false. Buridan deals explicitly only with spoken propositions, but presumably he would hold an analogous view about written ones.

6.0.1 is a prefatory paragraph designed to make it clear that 'throughout our sophisms' (i.e. not merely in this one) Buridan intends us to understand the words 'true' and 'false' only in the sense which he regards as peculiarly the concern of the logician as such, and which he contrasts with, e.g., the use of 'a true X' to mean 'a genuine X' or 'a good X'. His first step in making explicit the sense he has in mind is to say that it is the sense in which *propositions* are true or false. But he does not appear to regard this as a sufficient characterization, perhaps because we can speak of something as a 'true proposition' and mean thereby that it is a genuine proposition and not merely something that superficially appears to be one. So he pinpoints the relevant sense more exactly as that in which we say of a pair of mutually contradictory propositions that one must be true and the other false. Certainly we do not say that one must be genuinely a proposition and the other not.

The Aristotelian reference appears to be to *Metaphysics* E, 1027^b, 18–20, which may be translated: 'Truth and falsity...taken together depend on the dividing up of a contradiction.'

6.1 contains the main argument given for Buridan's own view that the sophism is false, and he explicitly says at the end of 6.3 that he approves of it. The argument involves the distinction between significative and material supposition, of which some account was given in the Introduction on pp. 14ff. In particular we have to consider what it is that infinitive phrases stand for in propositions of various kinds; and according to Buridan such phrases sometimes have to be taken significatively, sometimes have to be taken materially, and sometimes can be taken in either way. Infinitive phrases are much commoner in Latin than in English. To adapt an example given in the Introduction, the English sentence

(1) It is true John to be a scoundrel,

though no doubt it is intelligible enough, sounds barbaric; but its literal Latin equivalent is quite idiomatic. Now in order to assess the truth-value of (1) we have first to ask what the infinitive phrase 'John to be a scoundrel' stands for. Buridan would say that it stands (materially) for a corresponding expression in the indicative mood, viz. 'John is a scoundrel', that that indicative expression is a proposition, and that (1) is to be understood as asserting that that proposition is a true one. On the other hand he holds that infinitive phrases cannot always reasonably be taken in this kind of way. An example he discusses in Chapter 2 of the *Sophismata* is

(2) To cut is to act.

We want to say that (2) is true; but if we treat 'to cut' and 'to act' in the way we treated 'John to be a scoundrel', we shall be taking (2) to assert that the expression 'cuts' is the expression 'acts', which it clearly is not. So he says that in (2) we have to take 'to cut' and 'to act' significatively, i.e. as standing not for linguistic expressions but for things in the world. Now 'to cut' *signifies* activities of a certain kind; so in accordance with the pattern explained on p. 15 it will *stand for* people who are performing such activities. And if we deal with 'to act' analogously, the result will be that we shall construe (2) as asserting that people who are cutting are people who are acting – which of course is true.

Now let us look at the arguments of 6.1 in the light of all this. In the sophism the infinitive phrase to be considered is 'to say that a man is an animal'.

Buridan's aim is to show that no matter whether we take this phrase significatively or materially, the sophism will be false.

(a) Suppose we take the phrase significatively. Then by analogy with what we said about 'to cut', it will stand for people who are saying that a man is an animal, and so the sophism will be asserting of such *people* that they are true. But in the logician's sense of 'true' a person cannot be true (here the warning of 6.0.1 is relevant), and so the sophism must be rejected. (When Buridan writes, 'to say that a man is an animal is the same as someone who is saying that a man is an animal', he is not claiming that the two expressions 'to say that a man is an animal' and 'someone who is saying that a man is an animal' have the same meaning. He would in fact insist that they do not, since the concepts they signify in the mind belong to different categories: one is a concept of an *activity* of a certain kind and the other is a concept of a *substance* of a certain kind. What he is claiming, perhaps somewhat obscurely, is that the things the two expressions *significatively stand for* are the same. Or we can put the point this way. I can form the concept of *speaking* or *cutting*, and this will be a concept of an activity; but if I am asked to point to something in the world that falls under that concept, all I can point to is a person who is speaking or a person who is cutting. There are not in the world activities distinct from people or things that perform these activities. Similar comments apply to the remark in 6.4.2 that 'affirming or denying is nothing but a person who is affirming or denying'.)

(b) The alternative is to take the infinitive phrase 'to say that a man is an animal' materially, as standing for the corresponding indicative expression. But this will not make the sophism true either, for the corresponding indicative expression is merely 'is saying that a man is an animal', which is not a proposition since it lacks a subject. In the example discussed earlier, the infinitive phrase 'John to be a scoundrel' provided us with a word ('John') to slot into the subject-position in the corresponding indicative expression, which thus formed a complete sentence. 'To say that a man is an animal', however, provides us with no such word or phrase, and so what it materially stands for is not a proposition at all, and hence is not something to which we can attribute truth. So with this interpretation too the sophism must be rejected as false.

6.2.1 and 6.2.2 contain the arguments for the sophism's truth.

6.2.1 poses a special problem of translation. In mediaeval (though not in classical) Latin an accusative and infinitive construction and a noun clause beginning with *quod* are equally idiomatic with *dicere* ('to say'), so that Buridan can just as naturally write (a) *dicere hominem esse animal* (literally, 'to say a man to be an animal') or (b) *dicere quod homo est animal* (literally, 'to say that a man is an animal'). English idiom, however, offers us no such choice with 'say', but insists on the noun clause construction. The result is that the almost unavoidable natural translation of (a) is 'to say that a man is an animal', which coincides with the literal (and also natural) translation of (b). The translator's problem at 6.2.1 is that the argument turns explicitly on the distinction between (a) and (b), and – correctly – identifies the former, not the latter, with the phrase used in the sophism itself. So some way has to be found of translating the two phrases differently. The solution I have adopted is to use the normal translation ('to say that a man is an animal') for (a), but to use the direct speech form ('to say "A man is an animal"') for (b). I do not want to claim that this captures exactly the difference between the two Latin phrases (though I think there is reason to suppose that Buridan sometimes uses the *quod*-construction to express direct speech); but it at least provides an idiomatic rendering of each, and I believe it allows the essential point of both the argument and Buridan's reply to it to be made without distortion.

With this way of representing (a) and (b), the argument of 6.2.1 can be expressed as follows. It is first of all assumed that we are prepared to grant

(3) It is true to say 'A man is an animal'.

Now the sophism itself, of course, is not (3) but

(4) It is true to say that a man is an animal.

(3) and (4), however, differ only in respect of the phrases that come after 'say', *viz.* (i) '"A man is an animal"' in (3) and (ii) 'that a man is an animal' in (4). Now clearly these phrases, in these contexts, have to be taken in material supposition, as standing for propositions. But then each of them will stand for precisely the same proposition. For (i) is a quotation-name of, and therefore stands (materially) for

(5) A man is an animal.

And (ii) represents an accusative and infinitive phrase in Latin that literally runs 'a man to be an animal', and, as we saw earlier on, such a phrase stands materially for a corresponding indicative sentence, which in this case is precisely (5) again. Therefore, the argument runs, since (i) and (ii) stand for precisely the same thing, either can be substituted for the other without altering the truth-value of the proposition in which it occurs. Hence if we grant (3) we have to grant (4) – the original sophism – as well.

Buridan's reply (6.4.1) is simply to reject (3), and to accuse the proponent of the argument of confusing it with

(6) 'A man is an animal' is true

which correctly attributes truth to a proposition, not to the saying of it or to the speaker, as (3) does. He does not deny the legitimacy of replacing (i) by (ii) or *vice versa*, but what such a replacement in (6) gives us is not the original sophism but only the unobjectionable

(7) That a man is an animal is true

– or, in more natural English, 'It is true that a man is an animal'.

6.2.2 argues that since 'A man is an animal' is true, to affirm it is true; but to say that a man is an animal is just to affirm this, and hence it must itself be true. In reply (6.4.2) Buridan in effect repeats briefly the argument of 6.1, with 'affirm' in place of 'say'.

Note the step of *conversion* at the end of 6.2.2. The immediate conclusion of the argument is

(8) To say that a man is an animal is true

– but this is not regarded as the sophism itself, since the terms are in the wrong order. At the beginning of 6.1, indeed, Buridan himself refers to 'to say that a man is an animal' as the *predicate* of the sophism, not its subject. He must therefore regard 'true' (*verum*) as the subject, and I think he would take the sophism as a particular affirmative proposition which could be spelled out as

(9) Some true thing is a saying that a man is an animal.

I think too that he would take (8) as a universal affirmative, meaning

(10) Every saying that a man is an animal is a true thing.

The relevant conversion principle would then be the one that allows us to infer from 'Every A is (a) B' to 'Some B is (an) A'. By this means we can derive (9) from (10), and therefore the original sophism from (8).

SOPHISM 7

With this sophism we reach the insolubles proper. The first batch of these, which runs to Sophism 12 inclusive, deals with propositions that directly or indirectly assert their own falsity. They are therefore variants on what is often called the *Liar Paradox*, which itself forms the topic of Sophism 11.

The structure of Sophism 7 is quite complex, and the following analysis is intended to help the reader to follow it. The exposition, which takes us down to 7.2.3, follows the regular pattern. But then at 7.3, instead of announcing his own view, Buridan remarks that the sophism raises not one problem but two: (A) the originally stated problem of whether the sophism is true or false; and (B) the problem of how to form a contradictory or equivalent proposition.

Next he considers three unsatisfactory solutions to (A). The first is stated at 7.4 and criticized at 7.4.1; the second is stated at 7.4.2 and criticized at 7.4.2.1–7.4.2.3; the third is stated and summarily dismissed at 7.4.3.

He now drops problem (A) temporarily and turns to problem (B); this is elaborated at 7.5 and a solution is suggested at 7.5.1.

At 7.6 he returns to (A), the original question, and states his own answer with a brief argument for it.

All that remains to complete the standard pattern is to reply to the opposing arguments. This proves, however, to raise difficult issues, and he considers three theories on which the replies might be based. (a) The first is stated at 7.7.1

but rejected at 7.7.1.1. (b) The second is stated at 7.7.2; he says it is close to the truth and he thinks it is worthwhile to spell out what the answers based on it would be (7.7.2.1–7.7.2.3). (c) The third, which he thinks is correct, is stated at 7.7.3, and the replies to the opposing arguments are then modified in the light of it (7.7.3.1).

Finally there is an appendix (7.8) in which he raises and answers yet a third problem about the sophism.

The standard structure can therefore be discerned by following through 7.0–7.2.3, 7.6, 7.7.3 and 7.7.3.1, though the last two of these paragraphs would not be easily intelligible without those that immediately precede them.

It is characteristic of a paradoxical proposition of the *Liar* type that not merely can we present plausible arguments for its truth and plausible arguments for its falsity, but *prima facie* if we assume it to be true we can rigorously deduce that it is false, and if we assume it to be false we can in turn deduce from this that it is true. We thus seem to be driven inexorably to the intolerable conclusion that it is true if and only if it is false.

The problems posed by these paradoxes are by common consent extremely difficult ones. A great many solutions or resolutions of them have been proposed both in mediaeval and in modern times, but none has won anything like general acceptance. Buridan does not attempt to survey the rival solutions current in his day, though he refers to one or two of them, but instead concentrates on expounding his own solution. What is most distinctive about this is that he maintains that the paradoxical propositions are *false*. He accepts without objection some at least of the standard arguments to show that if they are true they are false, but he offers reasons for rejecting the converse arguments that purport to prove that if they are false they are true. The success of his solution must be judged largely by the consistency with which he can reject these latter arguments. I have tried to sketch the main lines of his solution in the Introduction on pp. 23ff; I shall consider the details in the commentary on the next few sophisms.

The problem of their truth-value is not the only problem that Buridan thinks the paradoxes raise. One other problem is that of how their contradictories should be formulated. Yet another concerns their modal status: are they possible propositions, and if so are they possibly true? His fullest discussion of the problem of their truth-value occurs in Sophism 7, and the main conclusions he reaches there are taken for granted in later sophisms. On the other hand, the problem of formulating a contradictory is dealt with only in a preliminary way in Sophism 7; a much fuller discussion occurs in Sophism 8, and its conclusions should be read back, *mutatis mutandis*, into Sophism 7 itself. Indeed it is hardly too much to say that we shall not fully understand what Buridan has to say about any of Sophisms 7–11 unless we work through them all.

I turn now to the details of Sophism 7.

7.0. The posited case is essential to the formulation of the problem, since if at the time when Socrates speaks there are any true propositions in existence at all, then what Socrates says is straightforwardly false and no paradox is even *prima facie* generated.

7.1. The reasoning here is condensed and needs unravelling. In fact two arguments can be distinguished in it: there is firstly (a) an argument designed to show that if the sophism is true then it is false, and then (b) an argument to show that it *is* false.

(a) runs as follows: Let us first assume that

(1) Socrates' proposition is true.

Now from (1), by a process that modern logicians often call 'existential generalization', we can infer

(2) Some proposition is true.

Since no proposition can be both true and false, (2) in turn entails

(3) Not every proposition is false.

But (3) is the contradictory of Socrates' proposition itself, so from it we can infer

(4) Socrates' proposition is false.

The last step, from (3) to (4) is only implicit in 7.1; I think, however, that Buridan would accept it, and in fact later on, in a remark in 7.6 that can only refer to the present argument, he claims that it has already been proved that if Socrates' proposition is true it is false. Note that the step from (2) to (3) requires the principle that no proposition can be both true and false, for if 'true' and 'false' were compatible predicates, like 'white' and 'square', the inference from (2) to (3) would be obviously invalid. This accounts for the first sentence in 7.1. Buridan formulates the principle in question with great care. There is no difficulty in supposing that a proposition might be true at one time and false at another; moreover, one and the same written or spoken proposition might be true under one interpretation but false under another. What is impossible is only that a proposition, given a constant interpretation, should be both true and false at the same time. It is of course being assumed that in the case of the present sophism only one time is under consideration and that no questions of variations in interpretation arise.

(b) The second argument assumes that it has just been proved in (a) that Socrates' proposition entails its own contradictory, and then appeals to a quite standard principle of modal logic to the effect that any proposition that entails its own contradictory is impossible and therefore false.

Since 7.1 is explicitly stated to be an argument to show that Socrates' proposition is not true (the heading is in the Latin), it is the conclusion of (b) that must be regarded as the main conclusion of the whole paragraph. It does not seem, however, that (b) succeeds in establishing its conclusion (that

Socrates' proposition is false); not because of any defect in the modal principle it appeals to, but because (a) did not in fact prove what (b) begins by claiming it did, *viz.* that Socrates' proposition entails its own contradictory. For even if we accept that (3) is the proper contradictory of Socrates' proposition (and Buridan will present reasons in the next sophism for doubting this), what was shown to entail it was not Socrates' proposition itself but *the proposition that Socrates' proposition is true* (i.e. (1)), and for Buridan that is a different and stronger proposition than Socrates' proposition itself.

In fact I do not think that Buridan himself believed that argument (b) proved its point. For (b) argues that Socrates' proposition is an impossible one, and he explicitly denies this at 7.8. Moreover, when he states his own opinion, at 7.6, he refrains from endorsing 7.1 and instead produces a quite different argument to prove that Socrates' proposition is false. In the course of this argument he does indeed refer us back to 7.1, but only to argument (a), not to (b).

The contrary arguments 7.2.1–7.2.3 appeal to certain widely-accepted criteria of truth and argue that Socrates' proposition satisfies them. It is taken for granted in each case that Socrates' proposition is a false one (this presumably being assumed to have been established in 7.1), so that in effect what is being claimed in each argument is that if it is false it is true.

The phrase 'stand for the same universally' used in 7.2.2 was explained on p. 17. The only other point that seems to call for elucidation in these paragraphs is the reference to *counter-instances* in 7.2.1. Many mediaeval logicians held that the truth-conditions of universal affirmative propositions could be stated in terms of conjunctions of singular propositions, in the sense that 'Every A is (a) B' was true if and only if

(X) This A is (a) B and that A is (a) B and...(and so for the rest of the A's)

was true. A *counter-instance* to the universal would be someting that was an A but was not (a) B, and which would therefore falsify one of the conjuncts in (X) and thereby falsify the universal itself.

7.3 merely mentions that there is a second problem in addition to the original one, and gives a sketchy indication of what it is. The nature of this second problem is explained in more detail at 7.5.

7.4–7.4.3 survey some solutions of the truth-value problem that Buridan thinks are inadequate or incorrect.

In 7.4 we are referred to Sophisms 2 and 3 of Chapter 7. The most relevant passage is in Sophism 3, where the following case is considered. Suppose that at a certain time Socrates is sitting and that at that time you say 'Socrates is not sitting'. Then clearly what you say is false. Now it must be possible for me to contradict you by saying 'Socrates is sitting', for that is the proper contradictory of your proposition; and if I do so then since your proposition is false mine must be true. By the time I have spoken, however, Socrates may have stood up and therefore not be sitting at all. But this does not mean,

Buridan maintains, that my proposition as well as yours must be regarded as false. For my proposition must be understood in the sense in which I intended it, and my intention was to contradict you, i.e. to deny precisely what you affirmed or affirm precisely what you denied. So since, by hypothesis, you were speaking about what Socrates was doing at the time you spoke, I too must be understood to be speaking about what he was doing at that same time and not about what he was doing at the time at which I myself spoke, in spite of the fact that I used the present tense in what I said. From this Buridan draws the conclusion that in general it is possible for a present-tense proposition to be spoken at one time but to be referring to a different time (to be spoken *in aliquo tempore pro alio tempore*); whether or not this happens in a particular case is to be determined by the intention of the speaker, i.e. by the thought he intends his proposition to express.

In 7.4 Buridan applies all this to the present sophism. It is possible, and quite consistent with the originally posited case, to interpret Socrates' proposition as referring not to the time at which he actually spoke it but to the immediately preceding time, at which by hypothesis all propositions were false. In that case it would not include itself among the things it talks about, and it would be simply and unproblematically true.

(In this paragraph I have used 'complete induction' rather than simply 'induction' to translate *inductio*, since this word does not mean what 'induction' usually does in modern philosophy. It refers rather to the process of establishing the truth of a universal proposition by running through all the cases that fall under it.)

Now there is nothing absurd or inconsistent, Buridan thinks, in interpreting the sophism in the way suggested in 7.4. The only trouble is that it avoids the problem instead of solving it. For it is equally possible for Socrates' proposition to be referring to the time of its own utterance – that in fact is the natural way to take a present-tense statement – and if so the original problem remains (7.4.1).

In 7.4.2 Buridan mentions a view, well-known both in his day and in our own, which would rule out self-referential propositions in principle. According to this view it is senseless to suppose that any proposition can make an assertion about itself, and any proposition that ostensibly does so has to be interpreted as making an assertion only about some other proposition or propositions. This theory, if it were correct, would provide a solution to the sophism, since if 'Every proposition is false' refers only to propositions other than itself, then the posited case will make it unproblematically true.

Buridan, however, is contemptuous of any such theory, and in 7.4.2.1–7.4.2.3 he gives three arguments against it.

The argument of 7.4.2.1 is simply that since we have a concept that covers all propositions, and a word ('proposition') that expresses this concept, there is nothing to prevent us from speaking about the totality of propositions if we choose to do so.

7.4.2.2 argues that the theory would rule out too much, since there are many self-referential propositions that clearly do make sense, and are indeed true. 'This proposition is an affirmative one' is his example, and it is easy to think of others.

7.4.2.3 is an ingenious attempt to show that even if we were to accept the theory, the paradox could be reconstructed by a slight variation in the posited case. The new case is that, as before, only false propositions exist, that Socrates then says 'Every proposition is false', and that at that same moment Plato too says 'Every proposition is false'. Let us call the original false propositions, $F_1, \ldots, F_n$, Socrates' proposition S, and Plato's proposition P. It is, Buridan argues, absurd to suppose that S and P have different truth-values, since there is no difference between them that could be relevant to whether they are true or false. We now ask the original question, 'Is S true or false?' This time we assume that no proposition can be self-referential, and therefore that what Socrates is attributing falsity to is each of $F_1, \ldots, F_n$ and P, but not S, and what Plato is attributing falsity to is each of $F_1, \ldots, F_n$ and S, but not P. Then the paradox can be reconstructed as follows: (i) Suppose S is true. Then P must be false, since this is one of the things that S asserts. But S and P have the same true-value. Therefore S is false. (ii) Suppose now that S is false. Then since S and P have the same truth-value, P is also false. By hypothesis $F_1, \ldots, F_n$ are all false; so the arguments of 7.2.1–7.2.3 can be repeated to show that S is true. ((a)–(c) in 7.4.2.3 are simply these arguments in the reverse order.) It is not, of course, that Buridan thinks these arguments are good ones – he will later on give reasons for rejecting them. His point is only that the theory that rules out self-reference allows them to be repeated in the newly-constructed case, and so the problem remains unsolved.

7.4.3 mentions a third way of dealing with the sophism, *viz.* maintaining that Socrates' proposition is both true and false at the same time. Not surprisingly, Buridan rejects this immediately as inconsistent. What is perhaps a little more surprising is that he thinks it necessary to produce an argument for its inconsistency. The argument is based on the following principle:

(C) If p and q are a pair of mutually contradictory propositions, then exactly one of them is true and the other is false.

Now suppose that Socrates' proposition (S) is both true and false. Let S' be the contradictory of S. If S' is true, then since S is true, S and S' are both true, which contravenes (C); and if S' is false, then since S is false, S and S' are both false, which again contravenes (C). So given (C), it is impossible for S to be both true and false. This argument of course presupposes that S' is either true or false; but the most interesting thing about it is that Buridan seems to have regarded (C) as in some way more basic or more evident than the principle that no proposition can be simultaneously true and false.

For the sake of continuity I shall postpone consideration of 7.5 and 7.5.1, which form an interpolation dealing with the second problem mentioned at 7.3, and pass directly to 7.6. Here Buridan gives his own argument for his view that Socrates' proposition (S) is false. As I remarked earlier, it makes use of the argument I numbered (a) in commenting on 7.1, but not of (b), which I believe he ought to reject in any case. The present argument can be analysed as follows:

Either (5) S is false or else (6) S is not false. (Law of Excluded Middle.) Suppose (5) holds, i.e. that S is false. Then this is itself the desired result. Suppose on the other hand that (6) holds, i.e. that S is not false. Now by the posited case we are given

(7) S exists.

We therefore have, from (6) and (7):

(8) S is true.

But by argument (a) of 7.1, (8) entails

(9) S is false

– and this again is the desired result.

The principle behind the step from (6) and (7) to (8) is that every *existent* proposition is either true or false. Something was said about this in the Introduction on p. 21.

The remaining task in dealing with the truth-value problem is to refute the arguments stated at 7.2.1–7.2.3. Such a refutation, however, requires, Buridan believes, an account of the relation between a proposition and its own truth, or more exactly between a proposition *p* and a proposition to the effect that *p* is true. At 7.7.1, 7.7.2 and 7.7.3 he formulates three theories about this relation, which I shall call the *meaning-theory* (7.7.1), the *simple entailment-theory* (7.7.2) and the *sophisticated entailment-theory* (7.7.3) respectively. The third of these represents his own view, and he gives reasons for rejecting the other two.

7.7.1 *The meaning-theory.* According to this, every proposition 'signifies or asserts itself to be true'. I take this to mean that, for any proposition *p*, the truth of *p* is part of the very meaning of *p* itself, or that anyone who asserts *p* is in so doing asserting *p*'s truth. Buridan indicates briefly how this theory could be used to reply at least to the argument of 7.2.3: a proposition, such as the present sophism, that even indirectly asserts itself to be false, must by the theory be asserting itself to be both false and true; and so, although the facts are in some respects as it says they are, it is impossible for them to be *in every way* as it says they are, and hence it must count as false.

Buridan says that he once held the meaning-theory himself, but in 7.7.1.1 he gives his reasons for having abandoned it. A modern reader of English may find his argument here difficult to follow, partly because of its use of mediaeval terminology and partly because of the occurrence of Latin idioms (especially the accusative and infinitive construction) which are almost impossible to translate into English that is both accurate and natural; I shall, however, try to make it as intelligible as I can. Let *p* be any proposition. According to the meaning-theory, at least part of what p 'signifies or asserts' is *itself* (p) *to be true*. But how are we to understand this last expression, 'p to be true'? As we saw earlier (in the commentary on 6.1), two interpretations of such infinitive phrases are in general possible: we can take them either (a) materially or (b) significatively. Let us examine each of these possibilities in the present case.

(a) Suppose we take 'p to be true' materially. This will mean that it will stand for a corresponding expression in the indicative mood, *viz.* 'p is true'. In that case the meaning-theory will hold that 'p is true' is part of the meaning of, or part of what is asserted by, p itself. But this cannot be so, even in a case in which p happens in fact to be a true proposition, such as 'A man is an animal'; for the sense of 'p is true' contains the concept *true*, and the sense of p itself does not (except in special cases) contain this concept. Roughly speaking, 'A man is an animal' is only about men and animals, but '"A man is an animal" is true' is about a proposition.

(In the terminology that Buridan uses, if the things that fall under a concept C are not themselves concepts, C is said to be a *first intention*, and if at least some of the things that fall under C are themselves concepts, C is said to be a *second intention*. The concept that corresponds to the word 'horse' is a first intention, since the only things that fall under it are animals of a certain kind. The concept that corresponds to the word 'true' is a second intention, since at least some of the things that fall under it are mental propositions, which are themselves concepts.)

So much for taking 'p to be true' materially. The alternative is (b) to take it significatively, i.e. as standing for some object or objects that it signifies. But the only object that it could conceivably be taken to stand for would be *the true proposition p*. And then the theory will break down at least in cases where p is a proposition that cannot be true; for in such cases there cannot be anything that answers to the description 'the true proposition p', and so the claim that p 'signifies of asserts' p to be true will be false because the last phrase is bound to lack a referent.

The upshot, therefore, is that no matter how we interpret the phrase 'itself to be true', the meaning-theory of 7.7.1 has to be rejected.

Some comment may be needed on the at first sight surprising remark in 7.7.1.1 that what does not and cannot exist cannot be thought about either. (The Latin phrase is *non potest intelligi*. In most contexts 'understand' is the natural translation of *intelligere*, but 'think about' seems nearer the mark here.) Chimeras, for example, according to Buridan, not merely do not but could not exist; he would therefore maintain that a chimera cannot be thought about. But in saying this he does not mean that the *word* 'chimera' cannot be thought about (or understood, for that matter), for he certainly thinks it can. Nor does he mean that we do not have a *concept* corresponding to the word 'chimera', for he says explicitly that we do. To understand his contention we have to realise that in 'A chimera cannot be thought about' he intends us to take the word 'chimera' *significatively*, and that he regards *thinking about* as a relation between a person and an object or objects. As a result, since there can be nothing for which the word 'chimera' stands, there is in this case nothing for us to stand in the required relation to. To be sure, he does not insist that for something to be thought about it must be an *actually existing* object; it is enough that it should be one that *could* exist. Roses, he says, can be thought about in winter, even if there are no roses then, since there at least *could* be roses in winter. In his terminology, the term 'thought about' in 'X is thought about' ampliates the supposition of 'X' to include possible though non-existent X's as well as actual ones. But even this extension of what 'X' can stand for will not let in things that could not possibly exist at all.

    7.7.2 *The simple entailment-theory.* This paragraph is one of the most important in the whole of Chapter 8. Although Buridan finds fault with the view expressed in it, he thinks it is along the right lines and he formulates what he believes to be the correct theory (7.7.3) merely by introducing a single modification into it.

    According to the simple entailment-theory, '*p* is true', although it is not part of what *p* itself means, is entailed by (i.e. logically follows from) *p*. More exactly, it *would* be entailed by *p* if it were actually formulated – this seems to be the point of the word 'virtually' in the phrase 'virtually implies'. (As was pointed out at 2.4.2, an inference is not valid unless its premiss(es) and conclusion exist; and it is always possible for *p* to exist but '*p* is true' not to be formulated at all.) The theory holds, then, that the relation between *p* and '*p* is true' is that of premiss to conclusion in a valid inference, but only in the sense that if an inference *were* to be formed with *p* as premiss and '*p* is true' as conclusion, then that inference *would* be a valid one.

    The notation that Buridan uses here is, however, more exact than the one I have just been employing. He wants to make it perfectly clear that in the inferences he is discussing the subject of the conclusion stands precisely for the proposition that forms the premiss, and his way of ensuring that it does so is to take an arbitrary letter, say 'A', and lay it down that this is to be taken as a name of that proposition and of nothing else. It would therefore be closer to his own mode of expression to formulate the principle as follows: If *p* is any proposition and 'A' is a name of *p*, then *p* entails 'A is true'. The point is that in order to assert something about a proposition we need to *mention* that proposition, the most convenient way of doing so being by using its name. In modern philosophical writing the name of a linguistic expression is commonly formed by using inverted commas. Thus an example of the kind of inference we have been discussing might be written as

(10) A man is an animal
Therefore (11) 'A man is an animal' is true.

This notation has, however, the disadvantage that, as the conventions for the use of inverted commas are usually explained, it is unclear whether the expression '"A man is an animal"' that occurs in (11) is a name of (10), or of the expression that lies within the inverted commas in (11) itself, or indeed of some other expression equiform with these. Buridan, who had in any case no inverted commas at his disposal, would prefer to stipulate that, say, 'A' is to be a name of (10), and then write the conclusion as

(12) A is true.

And here there is no danger of ambiguity of reference. In this example, such ambiguity might have no serious results, but in cases where two equiform propositions have different truth-conditions the consequences could be disastrous.

The next point in the simple entailment-theory is this. If a proposition p is to be true, then not merely must its own correspondence truth-conditions be satisfied, but the correspondence truth-conditions of the 'virtually implied' proposition 'A is true' (where 'A' names p) must also be satisfied; and therefore if the latter are not satisfied, p is not true but false. Now it does seem entirely reasonable to maintain that if a proposition is true then any other proposition that, if formulated, would follow from it must have its own truth-conditions satisfied; nevertheless there is *prima facie* an appearance of vacuousness about the principle we have just mentioned. For by hypothesis 'A' stands for p and for nothing else, and since 'A is true' is a singular affirmative proposition, its correspondence truth-conditions are simply that 'A' and 'true' should stand for the same, i.e. that p should be one of the things that are true; and so it looks as if the theory is maintaining that one of the necessary conditions of the truth of a proposition is that it should be true. I have suggested in the Introduction (pp. 22–3) that this appearance of vacuousness is dispelled if we recognize that there are other ways of showing that p is false (and therefore that the correspondence truth-conditions of 'A is true' are not satisfied) than by showing that the correspondence truth-conditions of p itself are not satisfied, and I refer the reader to what was said there. In the present case of Socrates' proposition, one of these other ways of demonstrating its falsehood, Buridan would hold, is provided by the argument of 7.6; for what was shown there was, in the terminology introduced on p. 18, that it is contextually inconsistent, but not that its correspondence truth-conditions fail to be satisfied.

Note the expression 'by its formal meaning' (*secundum formalem significationem*), which occurs in 7.7.2 and frequently, with minor variations, in later sophisms. When Buridan says that the facts are as a proposition *by its formal meaning* says they are, he means that the correspondence truth-conditions of that proposition itself are satisfied, irrespective of whether those of the 'virtually implied' proposition that asserts its truth are satisfied or not.

Buridan believes that the theory of 7.7.2 is so nearly correct that he thinks it worthwhile to spell out what the replies to 7.2.1–7.2.3 based on it would be. His own final replies at 7.7.3.1 will be given merely as modifications of the ones stated here.

These replies (7.7.2.1–7.7.2.3) all take the form of conceding that Socrates' proposition does fulfil the conditions mentioned in the original arguments, but denying that the entailed proposition 'A is true' (where 'A' names Socrates' proposition) fulfils these conditions. Hence by the simple entailment-theory Socrates' proposition does not satisfy all the conditions necessary for its truth, and so, contrary to what the arguments claim, we cannot deduce its truth from the assumption of its falsity.

7.7.3. *The sophisticated entailment-theory.* This is Buridan's own view. The only fault, he thinks, in the theory of 7.7.2 is that it presents an over-simple account of the relation between p and 'A is true' (where 'A' names p). For reasons that were given at 2.4.1 and 2.4.1.1, it is not correct to say that the former entails the latter. The correct principle is that p and 'A exists' together entail 'A is true'. (This is what I earlier called the *principle of truth-entailment.*)

If we now modify the theory of 7.7.2 in the light of this, the position will be that if the entailed proposition turns out to be false, what we can conclude is that at least one of the premises must be false. In the present sophism this means that either Socrates' proposition itself is false or 'A exists' is false (where 'A' names Socrates' proposition). 'A exists', however, is given as true by the posited case itself. So, granted the posited case – and the question all along was whether Socrates' proposition was true or false in the situation posited in the case – we have to say that Socrates' proposition is false.

Note that towards the end of 7.7.3 Buridan is careful to say '...from it and the case (*or rather a proposition setting out the case*) it follows that...' Strictly speaking, of course, it is only propositions that entail anything, and a posited case is not itself a proposition. When Buridan speaks, as he frequently does in subsequent passages, of a proposition following from a case, we must always take 'case' in the sense explained here, i.e. as an abbreviation for 'proposition setting out, or expressing, the case'.

7.7.3.1 details the changes that will have to be made in 7.7.2.1 if it is to form a reply to 7.2.1 in terms of the revised theory, and leaves the reader to work out the analogous modifications required in 7.7.2.2 and 7.7.2.3.

The theory expounded in 7.7.2 and modified in 7.7.3 is used extensively by Buridan in his discussion of the remaining sophisms in the present group, and forms indeed the main key to his solution of them. I have discussed it in a general way in the Introduction and tried to defend it against charges of arbitrariness and inconsistency.

I turn now to the second problem mentioned in 7.3, which I postponed in order not to interrupt the discussion of the truth-value problem. This second problem was described in 7.3 as that of how to form a contradictory or equivalent of Socrates' proposition, but when he comes to expound it in 7.5 he deals only with contradictories. The contradictory of a proposition must deny precisely what the original asserts, and in order to do so its terms must refer to just the same things as those in the original refer to. Now the standard contradictory of 'Every A is B' is 'Some A is not B', and so the standard contradictory of Socrates' proposition will be 'Some proposition is not false'.

Buridan asks us to imagine someone trying to use such a proposition, just after Socrates has spoken, in order to contradict what Socrates has said. The difficulty is that by so doing he brings an additional proposition into being, so that what he says refers to more things than Socrates' proposition did, and therefore cannot act as its strict contradictory.

In reply (7.5.1) Buridan appeals, as he did at 7.4, to the results of Chapter 7 in order to show that the second speaker could be understood as referring only to the time at which Socrates spoke. In that case the second proposition, 'Some proposition is not false', would be non-self-referential, and so the propositions it refers to would be just those referred to by Socrates, and the stated objection to its being the contradictory of Socrates' proposition would thereby be overcome.

That is all that Buridan has to say about this problem here. It is, however, highly unsatisfactory. Suppose we do take 'Some proposition is not false' in the way suggested, i.e. as asserting that some proposition existing at the time when Socrates spoke was not false. Now according to Buridan Socrates' proposition was itself false, and by hypothesis all others that existed at that time were also false. So if 'Some proposition is not false' is interpreted in the way suggested, than what it asserts is not the case, and so it is false. And the trouble is that in that case both it and Socrates' proposition turn out to have the same truth-value, and so they cannot be contradictories after all since contradictories must have opposite truth-values. Thus the very manoeuvre that was intended to make them genuine contradictories by ensuring that they referred to the same things turns out to prevent them from being contradictories by giving them identical truth-values.

Now Buridan is in fact very well aware of all this, for in Sophism 8 he raises difficulties of the kind I have just mentioned and attempts to meet them by a much more detailed and subtle discussion of the problem of contradictories. I think we must therefore regard 7.5 and 7.5.1 as only a preliminary skirmish with the problem, and for a more adequate solution read back into Sophism 7 the results obtained in Sophism 8. Possibly Buridan thought that the elaborate discussion of the truth-value problem made Sophism 7 long and complicated enough already; if so, his readers will no doubt agree with him.

The final paragraph of this sophism (7.8) raises three questions concerned with possibility. (a) Is Socrates' proposition ('Every proposition is false'), considered by itself – i.e. independently of the posited case – a possible one? (b) Is it a *possibly true* proposition? (c) Is the conjunction of it and the statements that express the posited case possible? The distinction between a proposition's being possible and its being possibly true was explained at 1.4.3.

Buridan's answer to (a) is Yes, and the reason he gives is straightforward. His answer to (b) is No. He does not give a reason for this answer, but presumably his argument would be this. For Socrates' proposition to be true it has to exist, but if it exists it must be false for the following reason: if some other proposition is true, it will be false because it denies this, and if every other proposition is false, it will be false for the reason given in 7.6. Finally, his answer to (c) is again *No*, because the conjunction in question entails something impossible, and whatever entails something impossible is itself impossible and therefore false. The 'something impossible' that is entailed is said to be that A is both true and false (where 'A', as before, names Socrates' proposition). He omits to say just how this is entailed by the conjunction, but I think he would argue as follows: (i) The posited case asserts that A exists, so 'A is true' follows by the principle of truth-entailment. (ii) Socrates' proposition is 'Every proposition is false'; the case gives us the information that A is a proposition; so 'A is false' follows by ordinary syllogistic reasoning.

The three problems raised in connection with Sophism 7 – the problem of the truth-value of the stated sophism itself, the problem of how to formulate an equivalent or a contradictory, and the problem, or cluster of problems, about possibility – run through all the sophisms in the present group, though the prominence given to each varies from case to case.

SOPHISM 8

The overall structure of this sophism is straightforward – the orthodox pattern followed by an appendix at 8.5 – but some of the arguments in it are complex and difficult. Although the question posed at the outset is, as with Sophism 7, that of the truth-value of the sophism, Buridan largely takes for granted the main results of Sophism 7 in answering it, and concentrates most of his attention on the problem of how to formulate an equivalent or a contradictory of a self-referential proposition, a problem that was discussed briefly in the previous sophism but receives its fullest treatment in this one.

One illustration of a paradox of self-reference that is often given in modern discussions of the topic consists of a card which bears on one side the inscription 'The sentence written on the other side of this card is false' and on the other side the inscription 'The sentence written on the other side of this card is true'. It is easy to see how, starting from either side of the card, we can apparently reach the conclusion that if the sentence written on it is true it is false, and if it is false it is true. Such a paradox may be called an *indirect* paradox of self-reference, for neither sentence explicitly refers to itself but only to a second sentence which in turn refers back to it. Moreover, neither sentence would have generated any paradox if the other sentence had been, say, 'Paris is in France' or '$2 + 3 = 7$'. Now this paradox is formally analogous not to Sophism 8 but to Sophism 9, in which Socrates says 'What Plato is saying is false' and Plato says 'What Socrates is saying is true'. The analogue of Sophism 8 would be a card on *each* side of which was written 'The sentence written on the other side of this card is false'. This, however, does not generate a paradox in the same straightforward way; for if we suppose the sentence written on one side to be true, we do indeed have the result that the sentence written on the other side is false, but that in turn merely yields the conclusion that the sentence written on the first side is true, as we originally supposed. In fact, provided that we are prepared to assign opposite truth-values to the two sentences, no inconsistent assignment of truth-values will arise. It is clear, then, that in order to generate even a *prima facie* paradox from this example we need some additional premiss, and clear enough, too, that one premiss that would do the job is that the two sentences have the same truth-value, i.e. that they are either both true or both false. This premiss is in fact extremely plausible, at least if any truth-values are to be assigned to the sentences at all, for there seems to be nothing in the case described that could act as any basis for discriminating between them in respect of their truth or falsity.

Buridan sees quite clearly the need for such a premiss in the formally analogous Sophism 8, for he says at 8.1 that he is assuming that Socrates' and Plato's propositions are either both true or both false, and he repeats this at 8.3, where we can be sure that he is stating his own views.

8.1 is a preamble to four arguments (8.1.1–8.1.4) for the truth of the sophism. In fact each argument consists of an attempted deduction of the truth of the sophism from the hypothesis, stated in 8.1, of its falsity, so what each would prove, if it were successful, is strictly speaking only that if the sophism is false then it is true.

8.1.1 and 8.1.2 need not detain us. They follow, *mutatis mutandis*, the lines of 7.2.3 and 7.2.2 respectively, and at 8.4.1 and 8.4.2 Buridan replies to them precisely on the basis of the theory formulated in 7.7.3. 8.1.3 and 8.1.4 however, are new, and lead us straight into the problem of equivalents and contradictories.

In 8.1.3 we are asked to imagine a third person, Robert, who says something precisely equiform with what Socrates is saying, *viz*. 'What Plato is saying is false'. So that there may be no loopholes, we are even assured that the thought that Robert expresses in the words he says is precisely similar to the thought that Socrates expresses in the words *he* says. It then seems clear, the argument proceeds, that Socrates' and Robert's propositions are equivalent in the sense of necessarily having the same truth-value. But by hypothesis (8.1) what Plato is saying is false, so since that is just what Robert is asserting, Robert's proposition is true. Therefore Socrates' (equivalent) proposition must be true too.

It may be wondered why this argument proceeds in such a roundabout fashion. Why not argue directly from the falsity of Plato's proposition to the truth of Socrates'? Why bring Robert in at all? Part of the answer, I think, lies in the fact that Robert's proposition is not even indirectly self-referential (it refers to Plato but Plato makes no reference to Robert), and so in considering it we need not fear the sorts of complications we encounter in dealing with self-referential propositions. Another part of the answer is that the argument provides a convenient peg for Buridan to hang his discussion of equivalent propositions on.

8.1.4 gives us a corresponding argument about contradiction. John produces the standard contradictory of Socrates' proposition, *viz.*, 'What Plato is saying is not false'. Socrates' and John's propositions, the argument runs, must have opposite truth-values. But, again on the hypothesis of 8.1 that Plato's proposition is false, John's proposition will be false and so Socrates' must be true.

The main interest in Sophism 8 lies in the theory that Buridan develops in order to refute 8.1.3 and 8.1.4.

8.2. We are given only one argument on the other side at this point. It is also an argument only for a hypothetical conclusion, *viz.* that if Socrates' proposition is true then it is false. The reasoning is easy to follow and, as becomes clear in the course of 8.3, Buridan accepts it as sound.

In 8.3 Buridan couples his announcement of his own opinion with a detailed argument for the categorical conclusion that Socrates' proposition is false (not merely the hypothetical conclusion that if it is true it is false). Structurally this argument is a typical example of the type described in the Introduction on pp. 32–3. In the translation I have tried to help the reader by lettering the propositions embedded in it and by translating a little more freely than usual, but I have kept the order of the steps exactly as Buridan has it.

Let us use 'S' for Socrates' proposition, 'PC' for the proposition that expresses the posited case, and '(a)', '(b)' etc. for the propositions so lettered in the translation. Then the form of the argument can be analysed as follows:

(1) (a) and (b) together entail the desired conclusion (c) (by ordinary syllogistic logic).

(2) (a) is a reliable logical principle.

(3) Proof of (b) – i.e. that the conjunction of S and some true proposition entails some false proposition:

    (i) PC is true.   (Assumption.)

    (ii) S and PC together entail (d). (To be proved later.)

    (iii) S and PC together entail (e). (To be proved later.)

    (iv) The conjunction of (d) and (e) is impossible and therefore false.

Therefore:

    (v) (b).

(4) Proof of (3)(ii).

(5) Proof of (3)(iii).

All the necessary premisses are there and the connections between them are clearly indicated. It is only the order of assembly that is unfamiliar to most modern readers.

Here are some notes on the details of the argument.

(a) may be restated as: If p and q together entail r, and q is true, and r is false, then p is false. This is a principle to which Buridan appeals several times in later sophisms. It is easily derived from two simpler ones: that a true proposition cannot entail a false one, and that if a conjunction is false then at least one of its conjuncts is false.

(3)(i). That PC is true is of course merely an assumption, but it is one that we can consistently make because the posited case is a possible one, and that it is legitimate to make because the question at issue is whether Socrates' proposition is true or false *given the case as stated*.

The proof of (3)(ii) is by the principle of truth-entailment: since part of what the posited case states is that S actually exists, S and the posited case together entail that S is true. The proof of (3)(iii) consists in appealing to the argument of 8.2 to show that this last proposition in turn entails that S is false.

At the end of 8.3 Buridan remarks that an analogous argument would give the conclusion that Plato's proposition too is false. We have only to read 'Plato' for 'Socrates' and *vice versa* throughout 8.3 and 8.2.

As I mentioned earlier, 8.4.1 and 8.4.2 are replies to 8.1.1 and 8.1.2 made on the basis of the theory of 7.7.3, and involve no points we have not considered already. 8.4.3–8.4.4, however, contain the most important new material in this sophism. 8.4.3 replies directly to 8.1.3. 8.4.3.1 and 8.4.3.2 formulate a general theory of the equivalence of propositions, designed in particular to solve problems raised by self-referential propositions. 8.4.4 extends this theory to apply to mutually contradictory propositions and so to refute the argument of 8.1.4.

It was argued in 8.1.3 that since Socrates' and Robert's propositions are identical in wording and express exactly similar thoughts, they must be equivalent and therefore have the same truth-value. Buridan's counter to this is that they can be proved to have different truth-values, and that therefore being identical in wording and expressing exactly similar thoughts cannot be a sufficient guarantee of equivalence. The argument for regarding the two propositions as equivalent stressed their similarities, but overlooked an important difference between them, *viz.* that Socrates' proposition is self-referential (even if only indirectly) but Robert's is not. It was the self-referential nature of Socrates' proposition that enabled us to prove that, although its correspondence truth-conditions were satisfied, it was nevertheless false because together with the posited case it entailed a self-contradiction. But since Robert's proposition is not self-referential no parallel proof of its falsity can be given, and its truth-value has to depend solely on whether or not its correspondence truth-conditions are satisfied. If we accept Buridan's argument that Plato's proposition is a false one, then these conditions plainly are satisfied, and so Robert's proposition must count as true.

As I see it, Buridan is here grappling with part of the problem of the conditions under which equiform sentences can have different truth-values. Manifestly they sometimes can. The most familiar cases are those that contain 'token-reflexive' words such as 'I', 'you', 'now' and 'here'. 'I'm an Irishman' can be true if spoken by one person and false if spoken by another, and the obvious explanation is that in the two cases the word 'I' refers to or stands for different people. Sentences containing 'I', we might say, are semantically sensitive to the identity of the speaker. Buridan would want to add self-reference to the list of things to which sentences can be semantically sensitive, and the arguments in the present sophism give his reasons for doing so.

It is unsatisfactory, however, simply to say, or even to prove, that Socrates' and Robert's propositions are not equivalent. It must, Buridan thinks, be possible for Robert to say *something* that will be equivalent to what Socrates has said. So the question arises: if repeating Socrates' proposition word for word would not, on Robert's lips, produce an equivalent proposition, what would? What *is* the (or even a) proper equivalent of Socrates' proposition? Buridan maintains (8.4.3.1) that it is

(R) What Plato is saying is false and A is true

(where 'A' names Socrates' proposition). Now (R) is certainly more complex than Socrates' own proposition, since the first conjunct is equiform with what Socrates is saying and a second conjunct ('A is true') is added. But Buridan maintains that this does not matter: for by the principle of truth-entailment this second conjunct is entailed by Socrates' proposition itself (together with its existence, which is, however, presupposed by the fact that we are trying to formulate an equivalent for it), and therefore, he argues, the addition of this conjunct does nothing to upset the equivalence of (R) to Socrates' proposition. Moreover, we now no longer run into the problem of differing truth-values; for although the first conjunct of (R) is true, the second is false, and so (R) itself is false, just as Socrates' proposition is.

Buridan is not, it seems to me, maintaining that Socrates' proposition and (R) have precisely the same meaning. His remarks in 7.7.1.1 would, I think, debar him from saying that. What I think he is claiming is that there is a relation of mutual entailment between them, or more accurately that there is a relation of mutual entailment between Socrates' proposition plus that element in the posited case that asserts its existence on the one hand, and (R) on the other. For (a) the former entails the second conjunct in (R) by the principle of truth-entailment, and Socrates' proposition itself entails the first conjunct. And (b) as far as the reverse entailment is concerned, Buridan holds in general that, where 'B' names a proposition, 'B is true' entails both 'B exists' and the proposition that 'B' names; so the second conjunct of (R), and therefore (R) itself, entails both Socrates' proposition and the relevant element in the posited case.

The justification that Buridan offers for his formulation of (R) as the proper equivalent of Socrates' proposition is this: Socrates' proposition, irrespective of the particular case in which it occurs, is of a kind that is at least *capable* of referring to itself; indeed, any proposition that contains terms such as 'proposition' or 'what X is saying' *could* be self-referential given a suitable case, though of course it need not be. Now, he argues, any genuine equivalent of such a proposition must make reference to *it*, since otherwise there will always be the danger that the two propositions do not refer to precisely the same things and so might come in certain circumstances to differ in truth-value, which it must be logically impossible for equivalent propositions to do in any circumstances whatsoever. And that is the point of the second conjunct in (R), which contains an explicit reference to Socrates' proposition.

It is worth emphasizing that the equivalence of Socrates' proposition and (R) does not at all depend on the fact that in the posited case Socrates' proposition actually is self-referential. Suppose we modify the case in such a way as to make it not self-referential, and in fact true, e.g. by supposing that what Plato is saying is '$2 + 3 = 7$'. Then both conjuncts in (R) will be true, and so (R) will again have the same truth-value as Socrates' proposition. Indeed, at 8.4.3.2 Buridan maintains that the method of forming an equivalent that is illustrated by (R) is of completely general applicability. That is, if p is any proposition whatever, and 'A' is a name of p, then p is always equivalent to the conjunction of (i) a proposition equiform with p and (ii) 'A is true'. However, he adds, the second conjunct is redundant, and adding it solves no problems, if p is not the kind of proposition that could possibly be self-referential. (It will emerge later on, at 11.8.3 – 11.8.4, that this prescription for forming equivalents has to be modified in cases that involve token-reflexive terms, but this point need not concern us at present.)

8.4.4 advances an analogous theory about contradictories in reply to 8.1.4. The fact that Socrates' and John's propositions are both false proves that in spite of appearances they do not form a pair of contradictories, and again the relevant difference between them is that in the posited case Socrates' proposition is self-referential but John's is not. Even setting the posited case aside, it would be *possible* for both of them to be false, and no such possibility should exist for genuine contradictories. Buridan's contention is that we should form a proper contradictory of Socrates' proposition by first of all forming its equivalent by the method described above, and then negating that. By the de Morgan Law which transforms 'not both p and q' into 'either not-p or not-q', this gives us as the contradictory of Socrates' proposition:

(J) Either what Plato is saying is not false or A is not true

('A' naming Socrates' proposition as before). Socrates' proposition and (J) will then be bound to have opposite truth-values: for in the posited case the second disjunct in (J) will be true and therefore the whole disjunction will be true; and if we change the posited case to make Socrates' proposition non-self-referential and true, then each disjunct in (J), and therefore (J) itself, will be false.

8.5. If a pair of propositions, p and q, are genuine contradictories, then it ought to be logically impossible for them to have the same truth-value in any circumstances. A change in the circumstances may indeed change p from, say, being true to being false, but it must then automatically change q from being false to being true (assuming, that is, that q remains in existence). The purpose of this paragraph seems to be to submit the claim that Socrates' proposition and (J) are contradictories to a further test by imagining a variation in the posited case which may affect the truth-values of some of the propositions involved, and then checking whether Socrates' proposition and (J) still have opposite truth-values as they ought to have. The point of stipulating that these two propositions are 'kept in being permanently by the divine power' is perhaps twofold: we want to be sure it is the very same propositions that we are considering, not some other pair equiform with them; and, as was remarked in 8.4.3.1, if propositions do not exist they are neither equivalent nor mutually contradictory.

In the new posited case Plato says 'What John is saying is false', Socrates' proposition as before is 'What Plato is saying is false', and it is clear that John's proposition is intended to be (J), not the one attributed to him in 8.1.4. In (J), of course, 'A' still names Socrates' proposition. Buridan argues that in this case (a) Plato's proposition is false, (b) Socrates' is true, (c) John's is false, and that therefore the opposition of truth-values required for contradiction is preserved.

His argument for (a) I find a perplexing one. It appears to consist of a *reductio ad absurdum* of the hypothesis that Plato's proposition is true, effected by deducing from this hypothesis the conclusion that Plato's proposition is false. As I understand it the argument is this:

(6) Plato's proposition is true. (Hypothesis.)

Since what Plato says is simply that (J) is false, (6) entails

(7) (J) is false.

This in turn entails

(8) Either (i) what Plato is saying is false, or (ii) A is true

(since (i) and (ii) are the negations of the disjuncts in (J)). But since A asserts that Plato's proposition is false, each disjunct in (8), and therefore (8) itself, entails

(9) Plato's proposition is false.

There seem to me to be two odd features of the step in this argument from (7) to (8). One is that if a disjunction is false *both* disjuncts, and not merely at least one of them, must be false: Buridan, like most of his contemporaries, used 'either...or...' in the 'weak disjunction' sense, and he makes this quite explicit on several occasions. One wonders, therefore, why he did not argue directly from (7) to (i) in (8), which gives him his result immediately. The other, and more serious, misgiving one may have is this: the claim made by (8) is that at least one disjunct in (J) fails to have its correspondence truth-conditions satisfied. But by Buridan's own principles it seems that (J) might be false for quite a different reason, *viz.* that each of its disjuncts is contextually inconsistent; and if (J) were false for that reason, (8) would not appear to follow from (7) at all. I confess I do not know how Buridan might reply to these criticisms.

The argument for (b) is that in the new posited case Socrates' proposition is not even indirectly self-referential, since although it refers to Plato's proposition the latter does not refer to it; so it will count as true if its correspondence truth-conditions are satisfied, and in the light of (a) they plainly are. One may again have qualms about this. Admittedly Plato's proposition does not refer directly to Socrates', but it does refer to John's, and the second disjunct in John's proposition does refer to Socrates'. One may well wonder whether this does not make Socrates' proposition self-referential at two steps' remove.

Finally, the argument for (c) is that John's proposition is false because each of its disjuncts is false. Presumably the first is false because, by (a), Plato's proposition is false, and the second is false because, by (b), Socrates' proposition (i.e. A) is true. Given (a) and (b), this argument at least does seem to be a sound one.

SOPHISM 9

This sophism has obvious affinities with Sophism 8, but is simpler in one respect. In order to generate the paradox in Sophism 8 we needed a premiss to the effect that Socrates' and Plato's propositions have the same truth-value. Here, however, we need make no initial assumption about the truth-values of the two propositions – either that they are the same or that they are different.

I remarked at the end of the commentary on Sophism 7 that three main problems run through the present batch of sophisms: (a) the problem of whether the stated sophisms are true or false; (b) the problem of how to formulate their equivalents and contradictories; (c) the problem of whether they are possible, or possibly true. Sophism 7 concentrated on (a) and Sophism 8 on (b); Sophisms 9 and 10 deal mainly with (c).

The arguments for and against the sophism at 9.1 and 9.2 parallel one another exactly. If in 9.1 we replace 'true' by 'false' and vice versa, then with a few minor verbal changes we have 9.2. The structure of each of these arguments is the same as that of the argument in 7.6; it seems to have been a style of presentation of which Buridan was fond. In spite of their parallelism he will find a way of accepting 9.2 but rejecting 9.1.

In 9.3 Buridan gives it as his opinion – which will not surprise any reader by now – that Plato's and Socrates' propositions are both false; that is, of course, false given the posited case. He then produces an elaborate argument to prove this. I can see no reason to think that he would find fault with the argument of 9.2 for the falsity of Plato's proposition, though he does not explicitly endorse it. Perhaps he preferred the argument of 9.3 for some reason that he does not mention; or perhaps he thought that both arguments were worth stating, and placed 9.2 where it is because of its parallelism with 9.1. The argument of 9.3 does, however, if the analysis given below is correct, make use of part of 9.2, so the two are not entirely independent.

The argument in 9.3 claims to prove that both Plato's and Socrates' propositions are false, but I shall first of all follow it through only as far as Plato's is concerned, and then make some comments on its applicability to Socrates'.

The argument is set out in the style described on pp. 32–3, and is strongly reminiscent of the one found in 8.3. It uses the following general principles, all of which we have encountered before:

(A) If p and q together entail r, and q is true, and r is false, then p is false. (Cf. 8.3.)

(B) If 'A' names p, then p and 'A exists' together entail 'A is true'. (The principle of truth-entailment.)

(C) For any proposition p, 'p is both true and false' is false.

The argument begins by remarking that the situation described in the positing of the case (that Plato and Socrates say the things ascribed to them and nothing else) is a perfectly possible one, and that therefore we can consistently suppose that the proposition that describes this situation is true. (This in fact does not strictly follow, since, as we saw at 1.4.3, a proposition can be possible without being possibly true; but the present case does not have any features that might give rise to this complication.) Suppose then that we do assume the proposition describing the case, which I shall call 'PC', to be true, since it is only on that basis that the question whether Plato's proposition is true or false is asked; and let us call Plato's and Socrates' propositions 'P' and 'S' respectively. Then the argument, with some re-ordering of the steps, runs as follows:

(1) PC is true.   (Hypothesis.)
(2) P exists.   (From (1).)
(3) P and (2) together entail 'P is true'.   (By (B).)
(4) 'P is true' entails 'P is false'.   (By 9.2?)
(5) P and (2) together entail 'P is both true and false'.   (From (3) and (4).)
(6) P and PC together entail 'P is both true and false'.   (From (5) and the derivability of (2) from (1).)
(7) 'P is both true and false' is false.   (By (C).)
(8) P is false.   (From (6), (1) and (7), by (A).)

In Buridan's exposition line (4), which in his ordering comes almost at the end of 9.3, is stated without any proof, but clearly some reason for it is needed. I have assumed that he takes it to have been established by the second half of 9.2, since I do not see what other passage he could be referring to.

That, then, is the argument for the falsity of Plato's proposition. At the end of 9.3 it is claimed that Socrates' proposition can be proved false in a similar way. There is, however, a difficulty here. The crucial step in such an argument would be obtaining the analogue of (4), viz. that 'S is true' entails 'S is false' (for all the rest seems straightforward). Now this has not been explicitly argued for in 9.2, so let us see if we can recast the second half of that paragraph in terms of Socrates' proposition instead of Plato's. The argument would have to run thus: '(a) If what Socrates is saying is true it follows that what Plato is saying is false, and (b) if what Plato is saying is false it follows that what Socrates is saying is false'. Now there seems no possibility of querying (a), but on Buridan's own principles it is difficult to see how he could maintain (b). For according to him there are two distinct grounds on which a self-referential proposition might be false: (i) its correspondence truth-conditions might not be satisfied, or (ii) it might (together with some truth) entail a self-contradiction. Now (b), in deriving the falsity of S from the falsity of P, seems to assume that P is false because of (i) rather than (ii), but this ignores the possibility that it might be false only because of (ii). And in fact Buridan has already argued that (ii) does hold in the case of P, so he would not seem entitled to assume that (i) holds as well.

If this criticism is correct, neither 9.2 nor 9.3 could be recast to prove the falsity of S, and in that case the possibility is left open of saying that in the posited case P is false but S is true. I have to admit that this possibility feels counter-intuitive to me, and clearly Buridan would want to reject it, but I do not see what argument available to him would enable him to rule it out.

9.4–9.4.3 contain the main new material in this sophism, though they can be dealt with more briefly. These paragraphs themselves have the structure of a sophism, so that we have here a small-scale sophism embedded in a larger one. The posited case is assumed to be the same as that of the main sophism (9.0), but the question now being asked about each of the two propositions (Plato's and Socrates') is not whether it is true or false but whether it is possible or impossible.

9.4.1 argues that both propositions are impossible. It takes its stand on the principle that we first encountered in 1.2.1, and which Buridan does not question, that whatever entails an impossible proposition is itself impossible, and argues that it has already been proved (presumably in 9.3) that each of the propositions in question does entail something impossible.

The argument in 9.4.2 against their impossibility harks back to a principle that is at least implicit in the discussion of Sophism 3 (see 3.2–3.3). To be impossible, a proposition must be incapable of ever being true at all, no matter what the circumstances may be. So if we have a proposition which is admittedly false as things stand but would have been true had the situation been different, then it is not an impossible one. In the present case, if we were to suppose that Socrates was saying not what the posited case portrays him as saying but something that was uncontroversially true, then Plato's proposition would clearly be true; and similarly, if Plato were saying something uncontroversially false, Socrates' proposition would be true. So each is a possible proposition by the test we have mentioned.

9.4.3 contains implicitly Buridan's own view, viz. that both propositions are possible ones, and explicitly a reply to 9.4.1. In 9.3 a self-contradiction was deduced from Plato's proposition in conjunction with the posited case, but 9.4.1 portrays this incorrectly as the deduction of a self-contradiction from Plato's proposition alone. The conjunction of Plato's proposition and the posited case is indeed shown to be impossible by the argument of 9.3, but to show that the conjunction of two propositions is impossible is not to show that either proposition by itself is impossible. A couple of simple examples are given to illustrate this point.

9.5 picks up the thread of the main discussion of the sophism by replying to 9.1. Buridan takes us step by step through 9.1 and tells us exactly what he accepts and what he rejects. The crucial step he objects to is the inference from 'what Socrates is saying is not true (or, is false)' to 'what Plato is saying is true'. Adverting to the theory of 7.7.3, he points out that what makes Socrates' proposition false is not at all that its correspondence truth-conditions are not satisfied; rather it is that the proposition (implied in it and the posited case) that asserts its truth has been shown not to be true (by the deduction of a self-contradiction from Socrates' proposition and the posited case). The falsity of Socrates' proposition therefore does not guarantee that its correspondence truth-conditions are not satisfied, and so leaves open the possibility that Plato's proposition may not be true after all. (This is in fact just the objection that I brought a few paragraphs back against the attempt to recast 9.2 to apply to Socrates' proposition.)

Finally, 9.5.1 remarks that an attempt might be made to adapt the arguments of 8.1.1–8.1.4 to apply to Sophism 9, and simply refers us back to the refutations of them in Sophism 8.

SOPHISM 10

This is probably the most entertaining variant of the *Liar* paradox that Buridan discusses. All that is essential to the example, of course, is that there should be precisely *n* non-self-referential true propositions, precisely *n*-1 non-self-referential false ones, the sophism itself, and no other propositions at all.

The standard sophism structure is followed till 10.4, but the arguments are only lightly sketched in and we are expected to fill them out for ourselves by making use of the material in earlier sophisms, especially Sophism 7. The new material occurs in 10.5–10.5.2, where the discussion of possibility is taken further than in any of the previous sophisms.

In 10.3 it is claimed that from the sophism and the posited case we can deduce both that the sophism is true and that it is false. In the light of earlier discussions the deduction would presumably go as follows. From the sophism and the posited case (which asserts among other things that the sophism exists) we deduce by the principle of truth-entailment that the sophism is true. But given that the sophism is true, we then have three true propositions and only one false one; so the correspondence truth-conditions of the sophism are not satisfied, and therefore it follows in turn that it is also false.

In the discussion of possibility in Sophism 9 no attention was paid to the question of whether the sophism was *possibly true* as distinct from being merely *possible*. (For this distinction see again 1.4.3 and the commentary thereon.) In the present sophism both questions are taken up.

10.5.1 maintains, as we might have expected, that the sophism is a possible proposition. A situation could arise in which the only propositions that existed comprised precisely *n* true ones and precisely *n* false ones, none of them capable of being self-referential. In such a situation things would be just as the sophism says they are, and the possibility of such a situation is enough to show that the sophism is a possible proposition. (In such a situation, of course, the sophism itself would not exist.)

10.5.2 discusses the question of whether the sophism is possibly true. Since in order to be true at a certain time a proposition has to exist at that time, the question is whether the existence of the sophism is consistent with the existence of a situation in which things are as it asserts them to be. Buridan distinguishes three cases in this connection.

(a) There is first the straightforward case in which the sophism genuinely makes an assertion about the actual time at which it is stated. In such a case, he claims, it will be bound to be false, and therefore cannot possibly be true. It is, however, difficult to see why he should maintain this so confidently. For suppose we have a case in which the only propositions that exist in addition to the sophism are one non-self-referential true one and two non-self-referential false ones. Then no inconsistency seems to be involved in saying that the sophism is true, since in that case there will be two true propositions and two false ones, which is entirely consonant with what it asserts. It is true that by analogous reasoning we can argue that there is no inconsistency involved in regarding the sophism as false either, since that would give us three false propositions and only one false one, which is entirely consonant with its being false. And there is indeed a problem here, though one that Buridan does not discuss, for it is at least perplexing to be faced with a proposition and to have no basis whatsoever for deciding whether it is true or false *even though all the relevant facts are given*. Still, this is quite different from being able to prove that the proposition is false, which is what Buridan appears to be claiming about the sophism in all cases in which it actually exists and refers to the time at which it is stated.

(b) Secondly, there is the case in which the sophism is stated at a certain time *t* but is intended and understood as making an assertion about some previous time *t'*. The possibility of a proposition's being used in such a way was mentioned at 7.4 and 7.5.1 (see these paragraphs and the commentary on 7.4). If the present sophism is taken in this way then it is possibly true, for it would be true at *t* if at *t'* there existed an equal number of true and false propositions, all non-self-referential. Buridan remarks that there are other present-tense propositions which are not possibly true if taken in the standard way but which must count as possibly true if understood in the way we have just been discussing. His example is 'Every proposition is negative'.

(c) Finally there is the case in which at *t'* the posited case obtains exactly as originally stated, and then at *t* someone states a proposition identical in wording with the sophism, but referring to *t'*, not to its own time of utterance *t*. Since the original sophism was, according to Buridan, false at *t'*, there were at t' two true and two false propositions, and so the proposition 'There are the same number of true and false propositions', spoken at t but with reference to t', is true at t; and the possibility of that situation shows that it is possibly true. The past-tense proposition 'There were (i.e. at t') the same number of true and false propositions', if spoken at t, would of course be true at t in a quite straightforward way.

SOPHISM 11

This is the *Liar* paradox in its classical and purest form – a proposition that directly asserts itself to be false and says nothing else. Note the care with which Buridan formulates the posited case. It is sometimes thought that the proposition 'What I am saying is false' by itself generates a paradox, irrespective of its context, but this is not so: if I were to *write* 'What I am saying is false' and at the same time *say* 'Peru is in Africa', then what I wrote would be simply and non-paradoxically true. So the statement of the case must make it clear that the proposition refers to itself and to nothing else, and the paradox is generated by the proposition and the case taken together.

The exposition in this sophism is not altogether in the orthodox form. The arguments in 11.1 and 11.2 are not directly for opposing answers to the question asked, but for the hypothetical conclusions that if the sophism is true it is false, and if it is false it is true, respectively; and in 11.3 and 11.3.1 these results are then developed into a self-contradiction. This is in fact one of the common ways in which the paradoxes of self-reference are presented in the literature of the subject. It is implicit in Buridan's treatment of the other sophisms in this group that this could be done for them too, but this is the only one where he does it quite overtly.

The arguments in 11.1 and 11.2 are only briefly stated, but follow lines that should be familiar to us by now. In 11.2 the 'terms' referred to are not, as my translation would suggest, 'what I am saying' and 'false', but rather 'I' and 'saying something false', since the Latin wording of the sophism (*ego dico falsum*) literally means 'I am saying something false'. The argument, however, is not affected by this.

In 11.3 the argument can be spelled out as follows:

(1) If the sophism is true it is false.   (11.1)
(2) If the sophism is false it is true.   (11.2)
(3) If the sophism is true it is both true and false.   (From (1).)
(4) If the sophism is false it is both true and false.   (From (2).)
(5) Either the sophism is true or it is false. (Principle of Bivalence.)

Therefore:

(6) The sophism is both true and false.   (From (3), (4), (5).)

11.3.1 then argues that (6) is self-contradictory. As in 7.4.3, it is noteworthy that Buridan thinks this needs to be proved. His proof is the same as the one he gave there.

11.4 notes, in a somewhat untidy position, that there are two further questions to ask about the sophism. These are the by now familiar questions of what its contradictory is and whether it is possible or impossible. The question of its contradictory is dealt with in some detail in 11.8–11.8.4, where earlier discussions of this topic are amplified. The half-promised discussion of possibility, however, never materializes at all.

The argument in 11.5 for the falsity of the sophism is somewhat condensed, but since it is essentially that given for the falsity of Plato's proposition in 9.3 it should not be difficult to follow.

11.6 replies to 11.2 on grounds based on the theory of 7.7.3. These should now be sufficiently familiar not to call for any further comment.

The standard formal pattern comes to an end at this point, but, as has happened in several other cases, there is more of interest in the material that lies outside the strict pattern than in what lies within it. This material is in two sections: 11.7 states a new argument for the conclusion of 11.2 and 11.7.1 replies to it; and 11.8–11.8.4 discuss various problems about contradictories.

11.7 tries to deduce the truth of the sophism from the hypothesis of its falsity in the following way:

(7) The sophism is false. (Hypothesis.)

Since a non-existent proposition is neither true nor false, (7) entails

(8) The sophism exists.

(9) The sophism and 'The sophism exists' together entail 'The sophism is true'. (Principle of truth-entailment.)

Therefore

(10) The sophism is true.

In his reply (11.7.1) Buridan says that he accepts the derivation of (8) from (7), and that he also accepts (9), but he points out that the argument totally fails in its attempt to deduce (10) from (7). In order to use (9) to derive (10) we need as premises both the sophism and the proposition that the sophism exists. Now (8) gives us the second of these premises, but nothing in the argument gives us the first one. The proponent of the argument has presumably confused the sophism itself with (7). Buridan's own position is that he accepts the validity of the inference stated in (9), but that since he rejects its first premiss (the sophism itself), he is free to reject its conclusion.

11.8–11.8.4 return to the topic of contradictories, which was discussed most fully in Sophism 8. We saw there that, according to Buridan, if p is a proposition and 'A' is a name of p, then a proposition equivalent to p can be formulated as 'p, and A is true' and a contradictory of p as 'Either not-p or A is not true', and moreover that if p is even potentially self-referential then these are the forms we should use in order to avoid certain paradoxical results (8.4.3.1–8.4.4). In the case of the present sophism, however, there is an additional complication; for if applied literally this recipe will yield (where 'A' names the sophism) 'What I am saying is false and A is true' and 'Either what I am saying is not false or A is not true' respectively, and it is clear that on the lips of another speaker these would not be equivalent to or contradictory of the sophism as originally spoken. In 11.8 Buridan imagines a somewhat simple-minded objection to the possibility of there being any proper contradictory of the sophism at all, made by someone who insists both that the terms shall be retained in their original verbal forms and also that they shall refer to the same things as they do in the original proposition. Clearly for a language that contains token-reflexive pronouns such as the English 'I' or the Latin 'ego', these are incompatible demands; and Buridan replies at 11.8.3 that the important thing about the contradictory of a proposition is that it should express the contradictory *thought*, i.e. that it should express the mental proposition which contradicts the mental proposition expressed by the original, and that the grammar of the language we are using may force us to change certain words in order to achieve this. Thus the proper contradictory of the present sophism on the lips of a second speaker would be 'Either what *you* are saying is not false or A is not true'.

This problem leads Buridan to offer some brief and not very systematic comments about the formation of contradictories, most of which are not specifically connected with the present sophism or even with self-reference in general. These remarks are certainly not intended as a systematic theory of how to construct contradictories, but they are too desultory to be likely to be mistaken for that in any case. The main points he makes are as follows.

Firstly, in a pair of mutually contradictory propositions one must be affirmative and the other negative. Here he may have had in mind primarily the traditional classification of propositions in syllogistic logic, whereby A and I propositions count as affirmative and E and O propositions count as negative; but he also speaks of forming the contradictory of a proposition by prefixing a negation-sign to it as a whole, and this too is to count as turning an affirmative proposition into a negative one or *vice versa*.

Secondly, in forming the contradictory of a proposition we have to introduce or remove some negative expression, but sometimes we may, and indeed sometimes we must, make other changes as well. He gives three examples.

1. The contradictory of 'Every man is running' is not 'Every man is not running' but 'Some man is not running'. Here there is a change in the syncategorematic word 'Every' to 'Some'.

2. The contradictory of 'It is possible that Socrates is running' is not 'It is possible that Socrates is not running' (for this is compatible with the original) but 'It is necessary that Socrates is not running'. Here we have a change in modalities from 'possible' to 'necessary'.

3. The third example is more complicated and presents problems to a translator. What is the contradictory of

(a) Every man who has a horse sees it?

This looks like an A proposition, and the standard rule that an A proposition is contradicted by an O proposition with the same terms would give us as its contradictory

(b) Some man who has a horse does not see it.

Nevertheless Buridan says that this is not correct, on the ground that (a) and (b) are compatible: they would, he says, both be true if every man had one horse that he saw and another horse that he did not see. It seems clear that he takes (a) to mean

(i) Every man who has a horse sees *at least one* horse that he has

and not

(ii) Every man who has a horse sees *every* horse that he has,

and that he takes (b) to mean

(iii) Some man has at least one horse that he does not see

and not

(iv) Some man who has a horse does not see *any* horse that he has.

Given these interpretations, he is quite correct in saying that (a) (= (i)) is consistent with (b) (= (iii)), and that its negation is equivalent to (iv), which must therefore count as its proper contradictory. What we have here, he remarks, is a change in the predicate in passing from a proposition to its contradictory, and this is often necessary when 'relative terms' are involved. But he sees that he is in danger of becoming entangled in a complicated topic that has little to do with the present sophism, and he breaks off with a promise of a fuller discussion elsewhere.

No such fuller discussion occurs in the *Sophismata* itself. The reference is probably to Tractatus IV of the *Summulae de Dialectica*, the fourth chapter of which is devoted to relative terms (see Reina [1957], pp. 336–42). In the present example the relative term in question is not, as one might at first suppose, 'man who has a horse', but 'it' (*illum*), which is called a relative term because it refers back to some previously occurring word in the sentence.

SOPHISM 12

This very brief sophism is the only one in the present group (7–12) that adds nothing of substance to the discussion of self-referential propositions. Its chief interest lies in the fact that the sophism itself is a complex (conjunctive) proposition, and that in 12.3 we are given examples of other complex propositions that can give rise to analogous paradoxes. Buridan leaves us to work out their solutions for ourselves on the basis of his earlier discussions. 'God exists' is of course merely a sample proposition assumed to be true. It is essential to the posited case that the stated sophism should be the only conjunctive proposition that exists at the time it is formulated.

This sophism also forms a transition to the next group, since at the end we are told that among the paradoxes not so far discussed are some in which epistemic terms such as 'know', 'believe' and 'doubt' play a central role. In the next three sophisms they do.

SOPHISM 13

Sophisms 13–15 form a group by themselves. In Sophisms 7–12 the paradoxical propositions asserted something to be true, or false. In the present group they assert something to be known, or doubted, or even known to be doubted. These sophisms may therefore be called *epistemic* paradoxes. The notions of truth and falsity, however, still play an important part in them.

Some comment is needed on how Buridan uses the words 'doubt' and 'doubtful' in these sophisms. Propositions are divided simply into the true and the false, not into the true, the false and the doubtful. There is no suggestion anywhere that doubtfulness might be a property of a proposition itself: when Buridan speaks of a proposition as doubtful, he always means that it is doubtful *to* someone, and that in turn means no more than that the person in question doubts, or is doubtful about, or is in a state of doubt about, that proposition. Someone is said to doubt a proposition when he considers it but has no belief about whether it is true or false. Doubting a proposition, therefore, is contrasted not only with knowing it to be true and knowing it to be false, but also with mistakenly believing it to be true and mistakenly believing it to be false, as well as with not considering it at all.

The structure of Sophism 13 is somewhat complicated. The exposition, down to the end of 13.2, proceeds normally; but there are two lengthy interpolations, one discussing a suggested solution that Buridan rejects (13.4–13.4.2), and the other discussing the nature of knowledge (13.5–13.6.2), before we reach the statement of his own view at 13.7 and the refutation of the contrary argument at 13.8. All this is followed by an appendix (13.9–13.9.1) on questions that arise if the posited case is varied. There is also another complication. The status of the paragraphs that, with some hesitation, I have numbered 13.3 and 13.3.1 is obscure. They can be taken as a continuation of the argument in 13.2; they can also be thought of as presenting arguments designed to lead into the discussion of knowledge that begins at 13.5. On the whole I am inclined to think that Buridan intends us to take them in both ways, but I am far from confident about this. My numbering is meant to indicate what I take to be their transitional status, but may obscure their connection with 13.2. This problem of interpretation is discussed more fully below.

As usual, the details of the posited case are important. The sophism must be the only proposition written on the wall, or else it may not be self-referential (the Latin is neutral between 'the proposition' and 'a proposition'). Socrates must not only doubt the proposition but know that he doubts it, otherwise the problem to be discussed will not arise.

It may be as well to make quite clear to ourselves at the outset just what the question being initially asked is. And this question is not whether Socrates knows the proposition written on the wall to be doubtful to him (for it is laid down in the posited case that he does), but whether the proposition on the wall, 'Socrates knows...', is true or not. It is laid down, that is, that its correspondence truth-conditions are satisfied; the crucial question will be whether or not, in conjunction with the case, it entails some impossibility.

13.1–13.1.3. Buridan is going – perhaps to our surprise – to reach the conclusion that in the stated case the sophism is true (13.7). The present arguments are therefore on his side, but it does not, of course, follow that he approves of them. While it is his regular and scrupulous practice to refute all the arguments advanced *against* his own position, he usually does not take the trouble to refute bad arguments *for* it.

In the present case, I think we can see easily enough that he ought to reject all three arguments. 13.1.1 argues from the satisfaction of the sophism's correspondence truth-conditions – from the facts being as by its formal meaning it says they are – to its truth, and Sophisms 7–12 have contained a sustained polemic against the validity of such an inference in the case of self-referential propositions. 13.1.2 maintains that equiform propositions must have the same truth-value, and we have seen in Sophisms 8 and 11 that that is not so. By the 'contradictory of the proposition' in 13.1.3 the simple negation, 'Socrates does not know...', is clearly meant, and again Sophism 8 has argued that we cannot safely infer from its falsity to the truth of the original.

13.2 states an argument for the falsity of the sophism, to which Buridan will reply at 13.8. When it is said that the sophism entails something impossible, it must be meant that the sophism and the proposition expressing the posited case together entail something impossible, and the appeal is once more to the principle numbered (A) on p. 120. This time, however, the 'something impossible' that is entailed is not that some proposition is both true and false but that some proposition (the sophism itself, in fact) is both known and doubted by Socrates. It is assumed that doubting a proposition is incompatible with knowing it. This leaves it to be proved that the sophism and the case do entail (i) that Socrates knows the sophism and (ii) that he doubts it. (ii) is established because it is asserted in the case itself. There is, however, something puzzling about the argument offered for (i). If I have construed it correctly, it involves the following steps:

(1) To know that things are as a proposition says they are is to know that proposition.

(2) Socrates knows that he doubts the sophism.

(3) Socrates knows that he knows that he doubts the sophism.

(4) What the sophism asserts is precisely that Socrates knows that he doubts the sophism.

(5) Socrates knows that things are as the sophism says they are. (From (3) and (4).)

(6) Socrates knows the sophism. (From (1) and (5).)

What is puzzling about the argument is this: Its aim is to derive (6) from the sophism and the posited case alone. Now (3) is certainly essential to the derivation of (5): (2) is not enough, for it only yields the result that things *are* as the sophism says they are, not that Socrates knows that they are. But whereas (2) is, correctly, claimed as given by the posited case, (3) is only claimed to be 'possible'. No doubt (3) *is* possible; but it did not form part of what was originally posited, and is *prima facie* stronger than anything that was.

Buridan will, of course, want to reject the argument we have just been looking at, so it is not surprising that there should be some faults in it. In his critique of it, however, at 13.8, he concentrates his whole attack on (1) and has no complaint to make about (3) at all; he says, indeed, that he accepts (5), which, as we have seen, depends on (3). In fact at 13.4.2, though admittedly in a different context, he quite explicitly says that he accepts (3) itself; and at 13.4.1.2 he even tells us that it has already been posited – though he then, perplexingly, immediately goes on to propose that we proceed to posit it forthwith.

There is, indeed, a recurring problem in this sophism about what Buridan's own attitude to (3) is and how he thinks it relates to the explicitly posited case, a problem to which I cannot think of any solution which seems to me wholly satisfactory. One suggestion that might be made, and which would relieve some of the perplexities, is that he accepted, and took it for granted that his readers also accepted, the principle that if anyone knows that *p*, and reflects on the matter, then he also knows that he knows that *p*; and that he therefore regarded (3) as deducible from, and hence implicitly posited in, the original case, even though it was not explicitly stated there. This would certainly explain his acceptance of (3) at 13.4.2, his failure to object to it at 13.8, and even his remark in 13.4.1.3 that it had been posited. Nevertheless, although a number of philosophers have accepted the principle in question, I am not inclined to think that Buridan was one of them. For one thing, if he did subscribe to it, why does he not tell us so? (The principle is not *obviously* correct, he is usually scrupulously careful to make his views explicit, and he was certainly sensitive to such distinctions as that between *knowing* and *knowing that one knows*.) More importantly, if he thinks that (3) is deducible from the posited case, why does he make the proponent of the argument in 13.2 merely claim that it is 'possible'? and why does he invite us in 13.4.1.3 to posit it 'since it is possible'?

I am inclined to think, therefore, that Buridan thought that (3) was *not* deducible from the posited case and that it represented a real, though quite consistent, addition to it. As far as 13.2 and his reply to it are concerned, what I suggest is that he was prepared to concede this addition without demur because in his view the important point was that even with this strengthening of the posited case the argument broke down because of its reliance on (1). I shall make some comments on 13.4.1.3 and 13.4.2 when we come to them.

I have already referred briefly to the problem of how 13.3 and 13.3.1 fit into the overall structure of this sophism. As we have seen, one important element in the argument of 13.2 as a whole is an argument for the sub-thesis that the sophism and the posited case together entail that Socrates knows the sophism. One way of looking at 13.3 and 13.3.1 is as two additional arguments for this sub-thesis; in that case we shall have three arguments for it, and the whole passage from 13.2 to 13.3.1 inclusive will form a single connected attempt to prove that the sophism is false. Against this interpretation, however, is the fact that when Buridan comes to answer the opposing argument in the standard place (13.8), what he replies to is precisely 13.2 and nothing else: 13.3 and 13.3.1 are refuted not there but at 13.6–13.6.2, at the end of the discourse of knowledge. On the other hand, this point is not quite conclusive, since by the time he has reached 13.8 he has already disposed of 13.3 and 13.3.1, and he may well have thought that even if 13.2 was not the whole of the argument for the falsity of the sophism, it was all he still had to deal with.

13.3 and 13.3.1 themselves parallel 13.1.2 and 13.1.3, except that whereas the earlier pair argued that the sophism is true, the present ones attempt to prove that Socrates knows it is true. More exactly, they contend that he will easily come to know this if he does a little simple reflection. The arguments look straightforward, but Buridan will give reasons later on for holding them to be fallacious.

So many easily confusable questions are raised in this sophism that it may be useful at this point to try to sort them out and indicate briefly what Buridan's answers to them are. At least the following six questions can be distinguished:

(a) Does Socrates doubt the sophism?
(b) Does Socrates know that he doubts the sophism?
(c) Does Socrates know that he knows that he doubts the sophism?
(d) Is the sophism true?
(e) Does Socrates know the sophism?
(f) Does Socrates know that the sophism is true?

Now affirmative answers to (a) and (b) are given in the posited case itself, so, on the assumption that the posited case is self-consistent (and Buridan does not suggest that it is not), these are not in dispute. In 13.4.2 he answers Yes to (c), though, as I have already pointed out, this answer appears to involve a strengthening of the posited case. (d) was the question posed at the outset, and in 13.7 he answers Yes to it. His answer to (f), however, is a firm negative, and that is why he has to refute 13.3 and 13.3.1, which argue for an affirmative reply to it. Finally, his comment on (e) is that it is ambiguous: taken in one sense it is equivalent to (f) and therefore must also have the answer No, but taken in another sense it is to be answered in the affirmative. We shall see his reasons for these contentions as we proceed.

13.4 expounds a view that Buridan thinks is incorrect, even though it leads to a conclusion that he agrees with. This view maintains that there are two propositions, not merely one, written on the wall, and therefore two propositions for us to consider. These are, firstly,

(7) Socrates knows that *the proposition written on the wall is doubtful to him*

and, secondly, the italicized part of (7), *viz.*

(8) The proposition written on the wall is doubtful to him (i.e. to Socrates).

About each of (7) and (8) we can ask whether Socrates knows it or is doubtful about it, and the theory being advanced is that he knows (8) but is doubtful about (7). The argument is presumably that firstly, the posited case says explicitly that Socrates is doubtful about the sophism, and (7) just is the sophism; and secondly, that the posited case also says explicitly that he *knows* that he is doubtful about the sophism, and what (8) says is precisely that he is doubtful about it. As far as the answer to the original question about the truth-value of the sophism is concerned, the conclusion is then drawn that it is true, since what it asserts is simply that Socrates knows (8) – which, according to the theory, he does.

Buridan has several objections to this solution. The first (13.4.1.1) is that it contravenes the view he put forward at 4.3.1, that a part of a proposition is not itself a proposition. The second objection (13.4.1.2) is more subtle. He accuses the theory of misquoting the sophism by replacing an infinitive phrase by a 'that'-clause. This may seem at first sight a trivial matter; but Buridan's point is that whereas embedded in (7) there is an expression that at least would have been a proposition if it had stood on its own, the sophism itself contains no such expression, and so, even if we were to waive the first objection, what is actually written on the wall consists of a single proposition only – the entire inscription. From this he draws the conclusion that if, as the theory under consideration maintains, Socrates knows *some* proposition written on the wall, then the proposition he knows must, contrary to what the theory says, be the entire sophism and not merely some part of it.

The third objection occupies 13.4.1.3, and its first two sentences pose a problem of interpretation to which I have already referred. On the face of it Buridan is claiming in the first sentence that he himself has already posited that Socrates knows that he knows that the sophism is doubtful to him. I find it quite incredible, however, that this is what he means, both because in fact he has up to this point posited no such thing, and also because in the very next breath, in the second sentence, he proposes that it be posited now, as if for the first time, 'since it is possible'. That being so, I can think of only two ways of making sense of these opening sentences, though I find neither of them entirely convincing. One is by supposing that 'it has been posited that...' means here no more than 'someone has suggested that...' Then we can take the second sentence to be saying, 'Well, it is certainly possible, i.e. consistent with the posited case, that Socrates knows that he knows...; so let us assume that he does and see where that leads us'. The other way is by supposing that *positum* is a scribal error for *possibile*. In that case the first sentence will mean 'It is possible that Socrates...', and the second will then follow on perfectly naturally. This reading has, I think, a considerable intuitive attractiveness, but it has no textual support at all: all the manuscripts unambiguously read *positum*.

No matter how we interpret the opening sentences, however, there is still a problem about what we are to make of the argument of 13.4.1.3 as a whole. It seems clear that Buridan is trying to refute the contention in 13.4 that Socrates does not know the entire proposition on the wall. But *prima facie* his argument misses the point. For he is arguing not from the posited case alone but from a possible extension of it, and so the most that his argument could give him would seem to be that it is *possible* that Socrates knows the whole proposition, not that he actually does know it.

I want to suggest, however, that Buridan may well have thought that this weaker conclusion was enough for his present purposes. For he may have taken 13.4 to be claiming that it *follows from* the posited case that Socrates does not know the entire sophism. Now to refute that claim, it is sufficient to show that the posited case leaves open the possibility that he does know it; and to show *that*, it is sufficient to show that some consistent extension of the posited case would entail that he does. If this way of understanding the argument is correct, then the principle being tacitly appealed to is the quite unexceptionable one that if p and q are mutually consistent and together entail r, then p cannot entail not-r. In the present instance, p is a proposition expressing the posited case, q is 'Socrates knows that he knows...', and r is 'Socrates knows the entire proposition on the wall'.

We should note, however, that Buridan does not categorically claim that it follows even from the strengthened posited case that Socrates knows the sophism; he only says that it 'seems to follow'. As I remarked earlier on, he thinks that the question 'Does Socrates know the sophism?' is ambiguous; but at this stage he is not yet in a position to spell out the ambiguity, and so his comments here have of necessity a certain rough and provisional character. What he would grant, and would claim to follow from the strengthened case, is that Socrates knows that the facts are as the proposition on the wall says they are; and this, I take it, is what he understands the proponents of 13.4 to mean by 'Socrates knows the proposition on the wall'. What he would deny, and would claim to be positively inconsistent with even the initially posited case, is that Socrates knows that the proposition on the wall is *true*, though this is of course also something that we might mean by 'Socrates knows the proposition on the wall'. It is, I think, his awareness of this ambiguity that lies behind his cautious use of 'it seems to follow'.

In 13.4.2, summarizing the position, Buridan reiterates that he dissents from the view expressed in 13.4, but acknowledges his agreement with some elements in it, *viz.* (a) that the proposition written on the wall is doubtful to Socrates, and (b) that Socrates knows that it is doubtful to him. He agrees, therefore, that Socrates does know (8), as 13.4.2 maintains, though he does not regard (8) as a part of the proposition on the wall. (Actually, (a) and (b) formed part of the originally posited case, so they were not really in dispute anyway.) He then adds that he holds that Socrates knows that he knows (8). This is a little puzzling; firstly because he gives no reasons for holding it, and as I have argued earlier on, it is difficult to believe that he thought it was entailed by the posited case; and secondly because it certainly did not form part of what was maintained in 13.4, and so cannot count as an item in his agreement with the view expressed there. I think his point may be that even if we say that Socrates knows that he knows (8), we do not thereby give an explicit answer to the question 'Does Socrates know the whole proposition on the wall or does he not?' That is the question to which he now proposes to turn; for an answer to it we have first to undertake an analysis of the concept of knowing, and that is his next topic.

13.5. Buridan thinks of knowing as a relation between a knower on the one hand and something known, an object of knowledge, on the other. He says, however, that whenever we know something there are two sorts of objects of knowledge involved, *primary* (or *immediate*) ones and *remote* ones, and that the relations in which we stand to these are different. A primary object of knowledge must be what in this paragraph he calls an *enuntiatio*, a word I have with some hesitation translated as 'assertion', though possibly 'judgement' would have captured the idea as well, if not better. He describes an *enuntiatio* as a certain kind of concept, a concept that must be complex and be of an assertive type. This seems to make an *enuntiatio* the sort of thing that in other passages he calls a 'mental proposition'. In 13.5.1 and 13.5.2, however, he also speaks of written or spoken propositions as capable of being primary objects of knowledge; so in what follows I shall refer to the primary objects of knowledge simply as 'propositions', using that word in the present context to cover indifferently both mental and linguistic propositions. (We must remember, of course, that written or spoken sentences must express mental propositions in order to count as propositions at all, so the *enuntiationes* at the conceptual level never drop out of the picture.) Propositions, Buridan maintains, are primary objects of knowledge in that without knowledge of propositions we have no knowledge of anything at all. But in knowing propositions we are also said to know other things as well, namely the things that are signified by the terms of those propositions; and these things are what he calls the *remote* objects of knowledge. I think we might express his idea by saying that the remote objects of knowledge are the things we know something *about*, and that we know about them by knowing (as primary objects) some propositions that refer to or make assertions about them.

What then is it to know a proposition (as a primary object of knowledge)? Buridan says it is firstly for the proposition itself to be true, and secondly for us to assent to it with conviction (*certitudo*) and good reason (*evidentia*). I think that by 'assenting to it with conviction' he means having a firm and sincere belief that it is true, and not merely, or even not at all, overtly assenting to it in a confident manner, which would be compatible with not believing it at all. If so, the theory of propositional knowledge that he is offering us is one version of the widely held view that knowledge is 'justified true belief'.

Propositions, then, are the only sorts of things that can be primary objects of knowledge, and all other things can be at most remote objects of knowledge. But it is important (and especially so in connection with the present sophism) to notice that propositions, unlike anything else, can be both primary and remote objects of knowledge. For one proposition may contain a term that refers to a second proposition; and then if the first proposition is a primary object of knowledge for someone, the second one will thereby become a remote object of knowledge for him. It may also in fact be a primary object of knowledge for him, but it need not be.

13.5.1 applies all this to the present sophism in an attempt to answer the question posed at the end of 13.4.2: Does Socrates know the proposition written on the wall or not? This question can now be seen to split into two: (a) Is the proposition on the wall a primary object of knowledge for Socrates? and (b) Is it a remote object of knowledge for him? To (a) the answer is obviously No: by hypothesis Socrates is doubtful about the proposition, and that is incompatible with his assenting to it with conviction. To (b), however, Buridan answers Yes, on the following grounds: The posited case lays it down that Socrates knows he is doubtful about the proposition on the wall. Now this presupposes that he has formed in his mind a mental proposition of the kind that he might express in words as 'That proposition on the wall is doubtful to me'. Moreover, his doubt about the written proposition on the wall is enough to make this mental one true, and his awareness of his doubt about the written one leads him to assent to the mental one with conviction and good reason. Thus the mental proposition is a primary object of knowledge for him; and so, since its subject refers to the proposition written on the wall, the latter is a remote object of knowledge for him. In short, he does not know the written proposition to be true, but he does know something about it via knowing some other proposition (the mental one) to be true.

13.5.2 develops this theme by envisaging the following situation: Socrates, who has inspected the proposition on the wall and (very understandably) found himself perplexed about its truth-value, hears Plato saying 'Socrates knows the proposition written on the wall to be doubtful to him', or comes across a piece of paper on which just those words are written; and his immediate and proper reaction is to think 'Well, that's certainly true anyway!' In other words he assents to what Plato says or what is on the paper with full conviction, and his perplexity about the proposition on the wall gives him good reason for doing so. Moreover, this proposition of Plato's (or the one on paper) is *true*; for it tallies with the facts, and since it is not self-referential – *it is not written on the wall* – this is enough to make it true. So Socrates knows it in the primary way.

The point illustrated here is that there can be two equiform propositions and yet someone can stand in different and opposed epistemic relations to them, knowing one to be true but being doubtful about the other. And in the case described this is not through inattention or misreading or mishearing or failure to notice their similarity. Nor is it because they refer to or speak about different things: each speaks of the same person, Socrates, and the unique proposition written on the wall, and asserts of the former that he knows he doubts the latter, and nothing else.

This is, I think, a peculiarly convincing example of a pair of equiform sentence-tokens that must count as two propositions, not as a single one written or spoken twice. Nevertheless Buridan acknowledges that people may feel there is a problem here: how, they wonder, *could* someone be so differently related to two propositions which he clearly recognizes to be equiform. His answer (13.6.1) is that the explanation lies in the fact that one of the propositions is self-referential and the other is not. He has argued in earlier sophisms that the truth-value of a proposition can be affected by whether it is self-referential or not: now he is showing that this fact can have epistemic consequences. In the present example Socrates, who is assumed to have been following the arguments of Chapter 8 so far, has come to realise that self-referential propositions raise grave truth-value problems. Noticing that the proposition on the wall is self-referential, and indeed more complicated than any of the earlier sophisms, he wonders what traps it conceals and is unable to see his way clearly through the problems it raises; but Plato's proposition poses no such problems, and once he has become aware of his own perplexity about the proposition on the wall he has no difficulty in seeing that what Plato says is true.

This explanation gives us Buridan's answer to 13.3. In 13.6.2 he gives a corresponding reply to 13.3.1. If, while Socrates is in his state of perplexity about the proposition on the wall, he hears Plato saying 'Socrates does not know the proposition written on the wall to be doubtful to him', then he certainly knows that what Plato is saying is false. What is wrong with the argument of 13.3.1, however, is that it assumed without question that Socrates knows that Plato's proposition is the genuine contradictory of the one on the wall – i.e. that the two propositions can be guaranteed on logical grounds to have opposite truth-values. But according to Buridan he may know no such thing. In Sophism 8 it was pointed out that the simple negation of a self-referential proposition may not be its genuine contradictory, but may have the same truth-value as it does, and that it is therefore unsafe to argue from the falsity of one to the truth of the other. In the present case the proposition on the wall is self-referential and Plato's is its simple negation, and Socrates knows all this; so it may be far from clear to him that they must have opposite truth-values.

13.7 resumes the main structure of the sophism with Buridan's own answer to the original question. By contrast with the previous paradoxical sophisms, this one, he says, is true. His reason is given in a very condensed form, but amounts to this. Clearly its correspondence truth-conditions are satisfied, for the posited case states that Socrates knows he doubts the sophism, and it itself asserts just that and nothing more. If it were not self-referential, therefore, we should conclude immediately that it was true. However, it is self-referential, and this creates in principle the possibility that although its correspondence truth-conditions are satisfied it may nevertheless, in conjunction with the context, entail a self-contradiction and be false for that reason. But although this possibility exists for self-referential propositions in general, it is not in fact realised in every case; and in the present instance, Buridan maintains, it is not realised. We cannot deduce from the sophism and the posited case that the sophism is both true and false, or that Socrates is both doubtful and not doubtful about it, or any other self-contradiction. The most we can deduce is that it is true and that Socrates doubts it, but this involves no inconsistency since people are often in a state of doubt about propositions that are in fact true. So in the absence of the deducibility of anything impossible from the sophism and the posited case, the fact that its correspondence truth-conditions are satisfied must be regarded as showing that it is true, though of course Socrates does not know that it is.

13.8 completes the formal pattern by replying to 13.2. The argument there was that the sophism, in conjunction with the posited case, entails the self-contradictory conclusion that Socrates both knows and doubts the sophism itself. The reply is that knowing and doubting the same proposition are incompatible only if by 'knowing' we understand knowing in the *primary* way; but, Buridan has argued, the sophism is only a *remote* object of knowledge for Socrates, and this is quite consistent with his doubting whether it is true. Socrates does indeed, as 13.2 contends, know that the correspondence truth-conditions for the sophism are satisfied; but in the light of earlier sophisms he may easily be unsure whether that is enough to make it true, and in that case he will not know it in the primary way.

The reply given in 13.8 assumes that Socrates is not as clear-headed as he might have been, that he is capable of becoming confused in his thinking and not seeing all the implications of the information at his disposal. As an addendum to the main discussion, 13.9 asks what the position would be if we were to disallow this possibility; if, that is to say, we were to write it into the posited case that Socrates is such an expert reasoner that he never fails to draw all the correct and relevant conclusions from the information he is given. Buridan's comment is that it is impossible to add this clause consistently to the case as originally posited. A perfect reasoner might of course be ignorant of a great many contingent facts, but in the case as envisaged there are no contingent facts, over and above those that are explicitly posited, that could be relevant to the truth or falsity of the sophism. So its truth-value could be worked out by logical reasoning alone from the facts as stated, and if Socrates is a perfect reasoner he will do this. That being so, he could not be in a state of doubt about the sophism, but it was part of the originally posited case that he was in such a state of doubt.

13.9.1 introduces another variant. In view of the inconsistency of the case envisaged in 13.9, we might try keeping the new clause that Socrates is a perfect reasoner but dropping the clause that says he finds the sophism doubtful. Given *this* posited case, if we ask afresh whether the sophism is true or false, the answer must be, Buridan says, that it is false, not true as it was in the case originally posited. The reason, which he does not state, is presumably that for the sophism to be true Socrates would have to be in a state of doubt about its truth-value, but it is inconsistent to suppose this and also that, as the new case posits, he is a perfect reasoner. So the sophism must be false; and, he adds, if it is false then Socrates, as a perfect reasoner, will know that it is.

Note. In the Latin text what Buridan says about Socrates in 13.9 is firstly that he is *sapientissimus* (literally, 'most wise') and then that he is *in arte doctissimus* ('most learned', or 'fully taught', 'in the art' – the art in question being presumably the art of logic). Another expression that he uses to essentially the same effect in Sophism 14 is *in omni arte et scientia doctissimus hominum* ('the most learned of men in every art and science'). The literal translations of these and similar phrases sound unidiomatic and stilted, so I have used a number of paraphrases which will, I hope, catch the essential point. Buridan does not, of course, suppose that there actually are in the world people who never make blunders in reasoning or fail to see the implications of what is said to them. When he describes one of the characters in his posited cases as *sapientissimus* etc., this is merely a way of ruling out as illegitimate, or irrelevant to the problem, remarks such as 'Perhaps he doesn't know because he is too stupid, or because such-and-such didn't occur to him, or because he didn't make good enough use of the information at his disposal'. In other words, he is making it clear that the problem he is concerned with is one about what follows from what, not one about the reasoning abilities of certain individuals.

The position is much the same in certain popular modern puzzles of a logical or mathematical sort. We may be given certain information and then asked whether X can tell whether something or other is the case or not. The question is never whether X is clever enough, but only whether the answer is deducible from the stated facts. In Buridan's terminology, X is always assumed to be *sapientissimus*.

SOPHISM 14

Again, the posited case needs to be read carefully. It is essential for the problem that the sophism be the only proposition, or at least the only disjunctive proposition, on the wall. (In the formulation of the sophism itself the Latin is neutral between 'the disjunction' and 'a disjunction', and does not imply uniqueness.) Plato is stipulated to be a perfect reasoner (see the Note at the end of the commentary on Sophism 13), and this is also essential. 'Socrates is sitting' is used by Buridan as a standard contingent proposition: a perfect reasoner is not assumed to be omniscient, and may be ignorant of many contingent facts. The question asked presents us with only three possibilities. In general the three mentioned are not exhaustive, for someone might mistakenly believe a proposition to be true or mistakenly believe it to be false. But Plato has been portrayed as the sort of person for whom these last two possibilities could not arise in a case like the present one. If it is possible to deduce the truth-value of the sophism from the facts at his disposal he will do so, and then he will know that it is true or false as the case may be; if this is not possible, he will know that too, and then he will simply suspend judgement, i.e. find the sophism doubtful.

The arguments in the exposition are presented as arguments *against* each of the three above-mentioned possibilities in turn.

14.1. Buridan tells us later, at 14.4, that he thinks this argument proves its point. It does, however, contain a logical error at the very beginning. It is correct to say that for a disjunction to be true at least one of its disjuncts has to be true, but it does not follow, nor is it always the case, that in order to *know* that a disjunction is true there has to be at least one disjunct that one knows to be true. The clearest exception occurs when one of the disjuncts is the negation of the other: in order to know, for example, that 'Either Socrates is sitting or Socrates is not sitting' is true one does not have to know either that 'Socrates is sitting' is true or that 'Socrates is not sitting' is true. Of course the disjuncts in the present sophism are not related in this way; and no doubt there are many disjunctions that one could not know to be true unless there was one specific disjunct that one knew to be true. There is, however, a nice problem here: just what are the conditions a disjunction has to satisfy for it to be possible to know it to be true without knowing of either disjunct that it is true? I do not know of any answer to this question, nor do I recall having seen it discussed. In the absence of any answer, the best we can do for Buridan's argument as it stands is to give him the benefit of the doubt and assume that the present sophism at least is a case where knowledge of the truth of one disjunct on its own is required for knowledge of the truth of the whole.

The argument of 14.1 is then this: since it is laid down in the case that Plato does not know the first disjunct to be true, what is needed is to show that he does not know the second one to be true either. This is accomplished by proving that the supposition that Plato does know it to be true would entail a contradiction. Let us call the second disjunct ('The disjunction written on the wall is doubtful to Plato'), 'B'. Then the proof being offered is this:

(1) Plato knows B to be true. (Hypothesis.)

Since whatever is known to be true is true, (1) entails

(2) B is true.

Since if B is true the whole disjunction is true, and since Plato is a good logician, we have:

(3) If Plato knows B to be true he knows the disjunction to be true.

We therefore have, from (1) and (3):

(4) Plato knows the disjunction to be true.

Since what one knows to be true one does not doubt, (4) entails

(5) Plato does not doubt the disjunction.

Since B asserts that Plato does doubt the disjunction, (5) in turn entails:

(6) B is false.

Thus (1), with the posited case, entails both (2) and (6), which together form a self-contradiction. Hence, given the case, we have to reject (1).

As I have pointed out, Buridan's overall argument in 14.1 is vitiated by a fallacy in its first step, so he has not really produced a disproof of the suggestion that Plato knows the disjunction on the wall to be true. It is possible, however, to devise an alternative disproof which does not commit this fallacy, in the following way. (I owe this argument to P. T. Geach.)

Let us suppose that

(7) Plato does know the disjunction to be true.

As in the step from (4) to (5) above, this entails

(8) Plato does not doubt the disjunction.

But as Buridan points out a little later on (at 14.3), even a moderately competent person, let alone an expert logician like Plato, knows whether or not he doubts any given proposition, provided he reflects on the matter – as by hypothesis Plato is in fact doing. So we can infer

(9) Plato knows that he does not doubt the disjunction,

and hence, since what B says is that he does doubt the disjunction,

(10) Plato knows that B is false.

Now Plato, as a good logician, knows that a disjunction with one false disjunct has the same truth-value as the other disjunct. Hence (7) and (10) yield

(11) Plato knows the first disjunct to be true.

This, however, plainly contradicts the posited case; so our starting-point, (7), must be false.

14.2.1 and 14.2.2 present two arguments to show that Plato does not know the disjunction to be false.

14.2.1 is brief and straightforward. To know a disjunction to be false one has to know each disjunct to be false (there seems no reason to doubt that *this* is a correct principle); but by hypothesis Plato does not know whether Socrates is sitting or not, so he does not know the first disjunct to be false.

14.2.2, however, is an argument that I think Buridan ought to reject as it stands. It argues that Plato does not know the disjunction to be false because it can easily be shown that he does not know its contradictory to be true. But the proposition cited as its contradictory is its simple negation (or more exactly, the equivalent of this negation by the de Morgan Law); and as Buridan argued in Sophism 8, and as he reiterates below at 14.6.1, in the case of a self-referential proposition its simple negation cannot be taken as its genuine contradictory. (At 14.4 Buridan claims that it has already been proved that Plato does not know the disjunction on the wall to be false. As I have just said, I do not think he ought to have regarded 14.2.2 as proving this, but perhaps he only means to endorse 14.2.1.)

14.3 completes the exposition with an argument designed to show that Plato does not find the disjunction doubtful. Since Buridan's own view is that Plato does find it doubtful, this is the argument he will have to refute, and he does so at 14.5. The argument runs:

(12) Plato doubts the disjunction. (Hypothesis.)

Since Plato is an expert – and indeed something much less than expertness would suffice – (12) entails

(13) Plato knows he doubts the disjunction.

Since the second disjunct says precisely that Plato doubts the disjunction, (13) entails

(14) Plato knows the second disjunct to be true.

Since the truth of one disjunct entails the truth of the whole disjunction, and since Plato is a good logician, (14) entails

(15) Plato knows the disjunction to be true.

Since one cannot doubt what one knows to be true, (15) entails

(16) Plato does not doubt the disjunction.

Thus (12), with the posited case, entails its own negation, i.e. (16), and so (12) must be rejected.

In 14.4 Buridan's view that Plato doubts the disjunction is argued for simply by elimination of the other possibilities: the arguments of 14.1 and 14.2.1 (and

14.2.2?) are accepted as cogent, and 14.3 will be refuted later at 14.5. But Buridan also maintains that not only does Plato doubt the proposition, he *knows* that he doubts it; and he seems to regard this as not sufficiently evident, or not sufficiently proved already, for he proceeds to give us an elaborate proof of it (14.4.1–14.4.1.1). I have to admit that it is not clear to me why he should think that such a proof is necessary at all. He believes he has sufficiently established that Plato does doubt the disjunction: why, one wants to ask, would it not be sufficient to appeal to Plato's expertness to show that if he doubts then he knows that he doubts? Moreover, it is worth noting that in the course of the very argument that he now offers, he makes use of the premiss ((21) below) that Plato *knows* he is doubtful about the first disjunct. Now this was not stated in the posited case, nor was it proved elsewhere. All that was said in the posited case was that Plato *is* doubtful about the first disjunct, so at this point Buridan himself seems to be trading on the principle that if Plato doubts then he knows that he doubts. Nevertheless let us analyse the argument.

Its overall form is one of which we have seen several examples already: a simple deductive inference with an initially assumed premiss which is proved later. In this case the assumed premiss is that the second disjunct of the proposition on the wall is false, and the proof of it is quite complicated. Let us call the first disjunct 'A', the second one 'B', and the whole disjunction 'D'. Then the initial argument is this:

(17) B is false. (Assumption, to be proved later.)

Since the proof of (17) will be a purely logical one, and Plato is an expert logician, (17) and the case entail

(18) Plato knows that B is false.

By the general theory of disjunctive propositions, (17) also entails

(19) A and D have the same truth-value.

Since, by (18), Plato knows (17), and (17) entails (19), we can then infer

(20) Plato knows that A and D have the same truth-value.

Next we have

(21) Plato knows that he is ignorant of the truth-value of A. (From the posited case?)

Finally, (20) and (21) yield the desired conclusion:

(22) Plato knows that he is ignorant of the truth-value of D, i.e. that he doubts D.

What remains, therefore, is to give a proof of (17); that is, a proof that, given the posited case, B is false. Buridan offers two proofs of this, in the latter part of 14.4.1 and in 14.4.1.1 respectively, and each consists of deducing a contradiction from B and the posited case taken together. This is of course a favourite technique of his for showing that a proposition is false.

The first proof claims to deduce the contradiction that the whole disjunction is both (i) doubtful to Plato and (ii) not doubtful to Plato. (i) is claimed to follow from B because it is just what B asserts, and that seems straightforward enough. But (ii) is simply said to follow 'for the reasons already given', and that is puzzling; for the only place at which any reasons have been given for Plato's not doubting the disjunction was at 14.3, and that is precisely the argument that Buridan rejects and which he will go on to refute at 14.5. In any case, 14.3 was not offered as a deduction of 'The disjunction is not doubtful to Plato' from the conjunction of B and the posited case, which is what would be needed here. I confess I do not know what to make of this first proof.

The second proof (14.4.1.1), however, is not open to this kind of objection, and in fact could stand on its own even in the absence of the first. It is this:

(23) B (Hypothesis.)

(24) B exists. (From the posited case.)

Therefore

(25) B is true. (From (23) and (24) by the principle of truth-entailment.)

Since Plato is an expert reasoner, it then follows that

(26) Plato knows that B is true.

But since B is one disjunct of D, and again since Plato is an expert, we can infer from this in turn that

(27) Plato knows that D is true.

Since one cannot doubt what one knows to be true, (27) entails

(28) D is not doubtful to Plato.

Now (28) denies what B asserts; hence (28) entails

(29) B is false.

B and the posited case therefore together entail both (25) and (29), which contradict each other, so B must be false. Thus (17) is proved and the gap in the initial argument is thereby filled in.

It is worth noting that this second argument does at line (28) deduce from B and the posited case precisely what was needed for (ii) in the first one; so if I am right in my complaint of a defect in the first argument, the second could be used to patch it up.

All that is now necessary to complete the formal pattern is to reply to the argument of 14.3. The step Buridan rejects is that from (13) to (14). From (13) – 'Plato knows he doubts the disjunction' – it indeed follows that Plato knows that the correspondence truth-conditions of the second disjunct are satisfied. But as we are well aware by now, the satisfaction of these truth-conditions is not enough in Buridan's view to establish the truth of that second disjunct; and in fact, as we have just seen (14.4.1.1), that disjunct (with the posited case) entails a self-contradiction and must therefore count as false, not true. And if it is false, then Plato cannot know it to be true, as (14) alleges he does. Indeed, since Plato is the expert he is, he will not merely not know it to be true, but will also positively know it to be false.

14.6 and 14.6.1 form an appendix in which Buridan considers a further objection that might be brought against his view that the sophism is doubtful to Plato. This objection is based on the principle that anyone who is doubtful about the truth-value of a proposition will also, if he is clear-headed, be doubtful about the truth-value of its contradictory; for, since contradictories must have opposite truth-values, any clear-headed person who has no doubt about the truth-value of one of them will have no doubt about the truth-value of the other. But now, the argument proceeds, the contradictory of the sophism is 'Socrates is not sitting and no disjunction written on the wall is doubtful to Plato' (this is what we obtain by negating the whole sophism and applying the de Morgan Law). Yet if Buridan's own view is correct, Plato knows that the second conjunct of this conjunction is false, since he knows that there *is* a disjunction on the wall that he is doubtful about; so since the falsity of one conjunct entails the falsity of the whole conjunction, he must know that the whole conjunction is false. This means that he is not doubtful about it, and therefore he cannot be doubtful about its contradictory, the original sophism, either.

Buridan's reply, in 14.6.1, refers back to his account in Sophism 8 of how to form an adequate contradictory of a self-referential proposition. The proposition on the wall is self-referential, and so its proper contradictory will have to be not the conjunction just cited but rather 'Either (Socrates is not sitting and no disjunction written on the wall is doubtful to Plato) or A is not true' (where 'A' names the proposition on the wall). Now this is a disjunction, and Buridan admits that it was correctly shown in 14.6 that Plato knows that its first disjunct is false. But consider the second disjunct ('A is not true'). We have shown that Plato is doubtful about the proposition on the wall, i.e. that he does not know whether A is true or not; and this means that he is doubtful about 'A is not true'. So what we have in the proper contradictory of the sophism is a proposition of the form 'Either p or q', where Plato knows that p is false and does not know whether q is true or false. By the general theory of disjunction, if p is false, p-or-q must have the same truth-value as q; so since Plato does not know whether q is true or false, he does not know whether p-or-q is true or false either. In this way we preserve the principle that if a proposition is doubtful to someone, so is its contradictory.

SOPHISM 15

This is probably the most difficult of all the sophisms in Chapter 8. It also contains, at 15.5.1–15.5.2, the hardest and most complicated single argument in the whole of the *Sophismata*. Once we recognize this long argument as an explanatory comment on Buridan's statement of his own view at 15.5, the overall structure of the sophism is, however, easy to discern. The orthodox pattern continues down to the end of 15.6 and finishes there. Then we have statements of two further objections to the view Buridan has come to, with his replies and comments (15.7–15.8.2.1). Finally, at 15.9.1–15.9.2, we have a discussion of some variants of the originally posited case.

15.0. Literally, the sophism means 'To someone there is being propounded a proposition that is doubtful to him'. I despair of finding a natural-sounding English sentence that conveys the exact sense of the Latin and is also neat enough to bear, stylistically, the frequent repetition with which it has to occur in the course of the discussion. The translation I have given is far from literal, but I do not think it should cause confusion provided that the precise sense of the original is borne in mind throughout. It is also worth recalling the point made near the beginning of the commentary on Sophism 13, that when Buridan speaks of a proposition as doubtful, he always means that it is doubtful *to* someone, i.e. that the person in question is in a state of doubt about whether it is true or false.

One of the main interests in Sophism 15, and also one of the chief sources of the difficulties in it, is that we are deliberately not given enough information to be able to tell whether the sophism itself is or is not self-referential, i.e. whether or not it asserts its own doubtfulness to someone. If at the time when it is spoken no other proposition happens to be being put to anyone, then it has to be taken as self-referential since the only proposition whose doubtfulness it can be asserting is it itself. On the other hand, if even one other proposition is being put to someone else, the doubtfulness of that other proposition would make the sophism true in a straightforward way, and in that case it would not be claiming that it itself is doubtful. It is, however, explicitly laid down in the posited case that you, to whom the sophism is addressed, have no information about whether any other proposition is being put to anyone or not; so you do not know whether or not it even asserts its own doubtfulness to you. Buridan's contention – to anticipate – will in outline be that if someone else is doubting a proposition, the sophism is true, that if no one else is doubting any proposition, it is false, and that since by hypothesis you do not know which of these situations obtains, it must be doubtful to you.

It is laid down in the posited case that, like Plato in Sophism 14, you are an expert reasoner, and this is essential to many of the arguments that follow. As was explained at the beginning of the commentary on that sophism, this also means that we have only three possibilities to consider: that you know

COMMENTARY

the sophism to be true, that you know it to be false, and that you find it
doubtful. Buridan presents arguments against each of these possibilities in turn.

15.1.1. At first sight this argument looks as if it ought to be invalid on
Buridan's own principles. To say that no one is doubting any proposition is
merely to say that the correspondence truth-conditions of the sophism are not
satisfied. In Buridan's view, of course, a proposition whose correspondence
truth-conditions are satisfied would nevertheless be false if it entailed a
self-contradiction, and you could know it to be false by knowing that it
entailed one. However, although Buridan does not mention the point, this
way of knowing that a proposition is false cannot be available here. For in
his view it is only self-referential propositions that can be false in this way,
so in order to know that the sophism was false in this way you would have
to know that it was self-referential; but it follows from the posited case that
you do not know this.

An analogous qualm might be felt about 15.1.2, and an analogous defence
is available. The argument is that you cannot know that the contradictory
of the sophism is true, and therefore cannot know that the sophism itself is
false. But the proposition that is cited as the contradictory of the sophism is

(1) No one is doubting any proposition,

whereas according to Sophism 8 its 'safe' contradictory is rather

(2) No one is doubting any proposition or A is not true

(where 'A' names the sophism). However, in Buridan's view there are only
two ways in which (2) could be true: one is by (1)'s being true, and the other
involves the sophism's being self-referential. And it seems clear from the
posited case that you cannot know that either of these conditions is satisfied;
so Buridan might argue that you cannot know that (2) is true any more than
you can know that (1) is.

At 15.5 Buridan claims that it has been proved that you do not know that
the sophism is false. Presumably this is meant as an endorsement of both 15.1.1
and 15.1.2.

15.2 presents the argument to show that you do not know the sophism
to be true. Let us again call the sophism 'A'. Then the argument can be
analysed as follows:

(3) If you know that A is true then either you know that someone else
is doubting some proposition or you know that you are doubting A.

(4) You do not know that someone else is doubting some proposition.

Therefore

(5) If you know that A is true then you know that you are doubting A.

But

(6) If you know that A is true then you are not doubting A,

146

and

(7) If you know that you are doubting A then you are doubting A.

By standard propositional logic we then have from (5), (6) and (7):

(8) If you know that A is true then you are both doubting A and not doubting A.

But clearly the consequent of (8) is self-contradictory; hence

(9) You do not know that A is true.

This argument is also given approval at 15.5.

15.3 is the argument that Buridan will refute, at 15.6. It attempts to disprove the hypothesis that you are doubting the sophism by deducing its negation from it. It runs thus:

(10) You are doubting the sophism. (Hypothesis.)

Therefore

(11) You know you are doubting the sophism.

Therefore

(12) You know that someone is doubting some proposition.

But what the sophism asserts is precisely that someone is doubting some proposition. Therefore (12) entails

(13) You know that the sophism is true.

Finally, since you do not doubt what you know to be true, (13) entails

(14) You are not doubting the sophism.

– which is the negation of (10).

15.4 simply remarks that, given the posited case, the conclusions of 15.1, 15.2 and 15.3 cannot all be correct.

15.5 states Buridan's own view that you are in fact doubtful about the sophism, and moreover that you know you are, and gives as a reason a simple elimination argument that accepts 15.1 and 15.2 and by implication refers us forward to the refutation of 15.3 at 15.6. And then at 15.5.1 begins the long and involved argument that I mentioned earlier on.

It is, I think, a mistake to regard this argument as an attempt to give a proof of Buridan's own view (that you are doubtful about the sophism) by some more positive method than the mere elimination of alternatives. For one thing, if that is what it was it would flagrantly beg the question at issue, for in the course of the argument, at 15.5.1.3, he uses 'you know you are doubting the proposition (i.e. the sophism)' as a premiss, and this would be to assume the very thing to be proved. And secondly, he does not call the argument a *probatio* (proof) but a *causa*, which is I think best taken to mean 'explanation'. I am inclined, that is, to think that the passage is best understood as Buridan's response to someone who accepts the conclusion of 15.5 that you know you are doubting the sophism, but is puzzled about how this can possibly be so, or about what precisely the source of your doubt is.

As a first step to understanding the argument we have to notice that the whole of 15.5.1.1–15.5.1.4 is intended as a proof of one of the statements made in 15.5.1, and that 15.5.2 then resumes the overall argument where 15.5.1 left off. So I shall first of all piece together 15.5.1 and 15.5.2, and then analyse the proof that is sandwiched in between them. The overall argument can be spelled out as follows, (15)–(17) being in 15.5.1 and (18)–(19) in 15.5.2.

(15) Either (a) someone other than yourself is doubting some proposition or (b) no one other than yourself is doubting any proposition. (Law of Excluded Middle.)

Now if (a) holds, then the sophism will be non-self-referential and its correspondence truth-conditions will be satisfied. Hence we have:

(16) If (a) holds then the sophism is true.

Next we have:

(17) If (b) holds then the sophism is false. (To be proved in 15.5.1.1–15.5.1.4.)

From the posited case we have:

(18) You do not know which of (a) and (b) holds.

All this explains why

(19) You do not know whether the sophism is true or false.

Now (19) does not deductively follow from (15)–(18), but I do not think that Buridan is claiming that it does. (19) does not follow deductively because there is nothing in (15)–(18) to rule out the possibility that you might have some other way of finding out the truth-value of the sophism. But all that I think is being claimed is that in the light of the given case we have in (15)–(18) an explanation or rationale which makes it intelligible how you come to be in doubt about the sophism.

Now let us turn to Buridan's proof of (17), i.e. to paragraphs 15.5.1.1–15.5.1.4. This *is* intended to be a deductively valid argument. What we want to prove is that given (i) that the posited case (or more accurately a proposition expressing it) is true, and (ii) that no one other than yourself is doubting any proposition (i.e. (b) above), then the sophism is false. By the principle he has so often appealed to already – that if a proposition, together with something true, entails something false, then it itself is false – it will be sufficient if we can deduce something false from the sophism in conjunction with (i) and (ii). The 'something false' he proposes to deduce is the self-contradiction that the sophism is both true and false.

The deduction of the *truth* of the sophism from these premisses is given at 15.5.1.2, and consists simply of an appeal to the principle of truth-entailment; for the posited case itself gives us the information that the sophism exists, and therefore it and the sophism together (even without (ii)) entail that the sophism is true.

The deduction of the *falsity* of the sophism occupies 15.5.1.3, and is much harder. To make its analysis a little easier I shall use some of the terminology I employed in the Introduction and say that a proposition is *inconsistent in a certain context* if from it, together with a proposition expressing that context, a self-contradiction can be deduced. It is of course one of Buridan's characteristic doctrines (first stated in Sophism 7 but reiterated many times later) that it is possible for a context, such as a posited case, to be such that a certain proposition can have its correspondence truth-conditions satisfied and yet be inconsistent, and therefore false, in that context. He also holds that this can happen only with propositions that are self-referential. (In the present sophism the assumption that you are a perfect reasoner or expert logician is taken to include the assumption that you agree with these Buridanian doctrines.) The argument can now be set out as follows:

(20) You know you are doubting the sophism. (Presumably this is assumed to have been already proved.)

Since the sophism asserts no more than that someone is doubting some proposition, and you are a good logician, (20) entails

(21) You know that the correspondence truth-conditions of the sophism are satisfied.

Next, again since you are an expert logician (and hold the Buridanian views mentioned above), we have:

(22) You know that if the correspondence truth-conditions of any proposition are satisfied, then that proposition is either true or contextually inconsistent.

(21) and (22) then yield

(23) You know that the sophism is either true or contextually inconsistent.

Now one of the complications in the present example is of course that you are ignorant of some relevant features of the context in which the sophism is uttered. (23) does, however, mean that we can at least assert this:

(24) You know that the context in which the sophism is uttered is either one that makes it true or one that makes it contextually inconsistent.

The question now arises: could there be any context that would make the sophism inconsistent? Buridan thinks we can answer Yes to this for the following reason: The question whether there could be any such context (as distinct from the question of whether the actual context is of this kind or not) is a purely logical question, and therefore is one to which you can be presumed to know the answer; so we have

(25) Either you know that some context would make the sophism inconsistent or you know that no context would do so.

Now (24) entails

(26) If you know that no context would make the sophism inconsistent, then you know that the sophism is true.

However, it has already been shown (at 15.1) that

(27) You do not know that the sophism is true.

From (26) and (27) we therefore have

(28) You do not know that no context would make the sophism inconsistent,

and (25) and (28) then give us

(29) You know that some context would make the sophism inconsistent.

What kind of context, however, might that be? All contexts can be divided into (a) those in which someone else is doubting some proposition and (b) those in which no one else is doubting any proposition. Now clearly

(30) You know that in any context of kind (a), the sophism is true, and therefore not inconsistent.

Hence by elimination,

(31) You know that any context that would make the sophism inconsistent would be of kind (b).

Now (29) says that you know that some context *would* make the sophism inconsistent, so from it and (31) we can certainly infer

(32) You know that some context of kind (b) would make the sophism inconsistent.

Buridan, however, wants to draw the apparently stronger conclusion

(33) You know that *every* context of kind (b) would make the sophism inconsistent,

and at first sight this seems to be a *non sequitur*. I think, however, that he would claim, and with reason, that contexts of kind (b) could differ from one another only in ways that are irrelevant to the truth-value of the sophism, and that therefore as far as the present question is concerned what holds for one of them must hold for all; and in that case he is entitled to infer (33) as he wants to.

The rest of the argument is simple. Since whatever is known to be the case is the case, (33) gives us

(34) Every context of kind (b) – i.e. every context in which no one other than yourself is doubting any proposition – would make the sophism inconsistent (and therefore of course false).

But by hypothesis (ii) at the beginning of the argument

(35) No one other than yourself is doubting any proposition.

Therefore we have finally the desired conclusion:

(36) The sophism is false.

Thus from the sophism and hypotheses (i) and (ii) we have deduced that the sophism is false, and this is what 15.5.1.4 claims we have done. With this the whole proof of (17) that was begun in 15.5.1.1 is completed.

15.6 rounds off the main formal pattern of the sophism by replying to 15.3. The step that Buridan challenges is the one from (12) to (13). All that (12) assures us of is that you know that the correspondence truth-conditions of the sophism are satisfied, but you need to know more than that in order to know that the sophism is true, as (13) claims you do. You need also to know that it is not contextually inconsistent, and that is precisely what you do not know: for, as we have just shown, it would be inconsistent in some contexts but not in others, and by the posited case you do not know which of these contexts actually obtains.

15.7.1 and 15.7.2 raise additional objections against the view for which Buridan has been arguing in the main body of the sophism, viz. that you find the sophism doubtful. Both of these objections argue that on the contrary you know it to be true.

15.7.1 pursues a line that should be familiar to us by now, arguing that you know the contradictory of the sophism to be false and therefore must know the sophism itself to be true. Buridan's answer at 15.8.1 also takes a familiar form which by now needs no explanatory comment.

15.7.2, however, merits more attention. An *expository* syllogism is one in which the middle term is a singular one, and the form of expository syllogism to which Buridan is referring here is 'X is (a) B, X is (an) A, *therefore* Some A is (a) B', where 'X' is a term that designates some individual. Suppose, the argument runs, that I present you with the following inference of that form:

(37) You are doubting a proposition;
(38) You are someone;

Therefore

(39) Someone is doubting a proposition.

You cannot fail to recognize the validity of this inference. If Buridan's main contention – that you know you are doubting the sophism – is correct, then you must know that (37) is true. You can hardly have any doubts about the truth of (38). So as an expert logician – or even a modestly competent one – you must also know that (39) is true. (39), however, is just the original sophism itself.

The reply given in 15.8.2 consists in admitting that you do indeed know that (39) is true, but denying the identity of (39) with the original sophism. This is not a quibble or a verbal trick. The point is not simply that (39) is an utterance or inscription that is physically distinct from the sophism initially stated. In the situation being envisaged you stand towards (39) in a crucially different way from that in which you stood towards the sophism in the originally posited case. There it was explicitly laid down that the sophism *and no other proposition* was being put to *you*, and that you did not know whether any other proposition was being put to anyone else at all; thus you did not know whether anyone – yourself or anyone else – was doubting any proposition other than the sophism itself. As we saw, if you had known that anyone was doubting any other proposition, you would have known that the sophism was non-problematically true. The new case that is being envisaged, however, is that, while you are doubting the sophism, I present the expository syllogism, and in particular (39), to you; so in this situation, far from its being the case that you do not know whether any proposition other than (39) is being doubted you positively know that there is one that is, *viz.* the sophism itself. You therefore know that (39) is made straightforwardly true by the fact that you are already doubting, and know that you are doubting, that other proposition. The fact that it and (39) are equiform is immaterial. (This is the point made in 15.8.2.1.) The situation, in fact, is analogous to the one described in 13.4.2, where Socrates doubted the proposition written on the wall but had no doubt about an equiform proposition spoken by Plato or written on paper.

Buridan drives home his reply by a reference to the theory expounded in Sophism 8 of how to construct a proposition equivalent to one that is or could be self-referential. This theory would give as an equivalent to the sophism,

(40) Someone is doubting a proposition and A is true

(where 'A' names the sophism). If it could be shown that you know (40) to be true, it would indeed follow that you know the sophism to be true. But the acknowledged fact that you know (37) and (38) to be true does not demonstrate that you know (40) to be true; for (40) does not follow from (37) and (38) – its first conjunct does, but its second does not.

The remaining paragraphs consider some variants of the initially posited case.

15.9.1 presents a situation that combines elements of the original case and of the one envisaged in 15.8.2.1. In 15.8.2.1 it is supposed that X says 'Someone is doubting a proposition' to you, and that while you are reflecting on what he has said, Y then also says to you 'Someone is doubting a proposition'. And Buridan's contention is that you find X's proposition doubtful, but that when you hear Y's proposition you understand it as referring to X's and made true by your doubt about the latter. 15.9.1 varies this by supposing that X and Y (now called, in Buridan's more customary way, 'Socrates' and 'Plato') speak simultaneously and that you for your part give equal attention to what each of them is saying. This brings the situation closer to the originally posited case, in that there is no already established state of doubt in your mind by the time either of them speaks. It seems clear, too, that Buridan wants us to suppose, as in the original case, that you do not know whether any proposition is being put to anyone else, and also that Socrates' and Plato's propositions are the only ones that are being put to you. There seem therefore to be two possible lines we could take about this case: (a) we could try to assimilate it to that of 15.8.2.1 and suppose that you doubt, say, Socrates' proposition and that your doubt about it verifies Plato's and thus gives you knowledge of its truth; or (b) we could assimilate it to the case posited at the beginning and say that you are in a state of doubt about each of the two propositions equally.

In 15.9.1.1 Buridan comes down firmly in favour of (b). Let us call Socrates' proposition 'S' and Plato's proposition 'P'. Then his argument against (a) is as follows. By hypothesis S and P are spoken simultaneously and you are attending to them simultaneously and equally. So if we were to suppose, as (a) suggests, that you knew, say, S to be true because it refers to P, it would be irrational not to suppose that you also knew P to be true because it refers to S. We must therefore suppose that

(41) Either you do not know either S or P to be true, or you know that both S and P are true.

Now let us suppose

(42) You know that both S and P are true.

Since each of S and P asserts that someone is doubting some proposition, (42) entails

(43) You know that someone is doubting some proposition.

Since, however, (42) also entails that you are not doubting either S or P, and since these are the only propositions that you yourself are considering, (42) and (43) entail

(44) You know that someone other than yourself is doubting some proposition.

But by the posited case you do not know whether anyone else is even considering any proposition. So (44) is false, and therefore (42), which entails it, is also false. And this means that the first disjunct of (41) must be true, i.e. that

(45) You do not know either S or P to be true.

We have thus refuted (a); and (b) is the only reasonable alternative.

15.9.1.2, as an addendum, underlines the dependence of the above argument on the simultaneity of S and P. If you are already in a state of doubt about anything at all, then any *subsequent* statement to the effect that someone is doubting something, provided it is made while your state of doubt persists, will be verified by your already established doubt and you will therefore know it to be true.

Buridan's contention in 15.9.1.1 that whatever you know about S you must know about P, and *vice versa*, may remind us of his discussion of Sophism 8, where he maintains that Socrates' and Plato's propositions must have the same truth-value. It is a persistently recurring theme in his thought that if two propositions are to have different truth-values there must be some *basis* for this difference: if two propositions are related analogously in every way to their contexts, it is, he thinks, irrational to hold that one of them is true but the other false.

15.9.2 raises a question of a quite different kind. It takes us back to the original posited case but asks us to delete the clause that says you are a perfect reasoner. The effect of this is twofold. It transforms the question from being one about what logically follows from what into one about what your state of mind might be. And it opens up other possibilities than the three originally envisaged (that you know the sophism to be true, that you know it to be false, and that you are doubtful about it): for now it is being admitted not only that you might be ignorant of some contingent matters but that you might commit logical blunders as well. You might therefore be mistakenly convinced that the sophism was true or be mistakenly convinced that it was false, and each of these states of mind is different from either knowledge or doubt. These are now, Buridan remarks, quite open possibilities, and that is all one can say about the matter. Who can tell what any ordinary muddle-headed, or even reasonably clear-headed, person is likely to think when confronted by a nasty problem like Sophism 15?

The Aristotelian reference in 15.9.2 is to the *Nicomachean Ethics*, 1146^b, 25–30.

SOPHISM 16

After the intellectual rigours of Sophism 15 one can almost hear Buridan breathing a sigh of relief as he begins the final batch of sophisms (16–20). His style becomes more relaxed and, especially in Sophisms 17 and 18, more anecdotal and entertaining. These five sophisms may conveniently be called 'pragmatic paradoxes', since they are concerned with problems of self-reference that arise in connection with action-directed activities such as promising, intending or wishing. They fall naturally into two groups: the problems raised by 16 and 17 are closely connected with each other, and so are those raised by 18–20.

Sophism 16 is set in the context of a mediaeval academic exercise known as *Obligation* (*obligatio*). The 'game of obligation', as Hamblin ([1970], pp. 125ff.) calls it, required two participants, an 'opponent'. (the teacher) and a 'respondent' (the pupil). In what appears to have been the commonest form of the exercise, the first step was for the opponent to propose to the respondent that for a specified period of time he should 'accept the obligation' of maintaining the truth of a certain proposition, which would normally be one that was in fact known to be false. The respondent might, for good reason, decline the proposed obligation; but if he accepted it, the next step would be for the opponent to question him by putting to him a sequence of other propositions and asking him whether they were true or false. The task of the respondent was at all costs to avoid inconsistency, i.e. to avoid saying anything from which, together with the initial proposition and his previous replies, a self-contradiction could be deduced; but otherwise he was expected to give true responses whenever possible. The aim of the opponent, on the other hand, was to trap him into inconsistency. In the version referred to in the present sophism the respondent is given not a proposition to maintain but a rule to observe in his replies. One of Buridan's purposes is to show how an apparently innocent obligation becomes unfulfillable if the opponent uses certain self-referential propositions in his interrogation.

Brief and straightforward accounts of the obligation exercise will be found in the passage in Hamblin referred to above, in de Rijk [1974], and in Spade [1977]. Note that Buridan uses the technical term 'opponent' at 16.7.

16.0. The situation envisaged in the posited case is that Buridan, in his role as opponent, has proposed to you, as respondent, the obligation to reply with a simple 'Yes' or 'No' to each proposition that he will put to you – 'Yes' if the proposition is true and 'No' if it is not. This has seemed to you to be an obligation that you could comply with consistently, since every proposition must be either true or not true, and so you have accepted it. Of course the proposal does not tell you how to reply if you are ignorant of whether the proposition put to you is true or not, but in order to simplify his exposition of the problem Buridan ignores this possibility for the moment (he brings it in later on, at 16.5). The essential point is that it seems as if there must at least *be* a correct way of responding to each proposition in terms of the obligation. The proposition he puts to you, however, is 'You are going to answer in the negative', and immediately you are in trouble.

16.1 and 16.2 expound the problem by showing that both 'Yes' and 'No' are incorrect answers, since by answering 'Yes' you make the proposition false and by answering 'No' you make it true.

16.3 states Buridan's own view. By contrast with his treatment of most of the other sophisms, in which he sides with one of the proposed answers to the question posed and takes issue with the other, this time he agrees with both of the arguments in the exposition and gives it as his view that in spite of its innocent appearance the proposed obligation was one that you ought not to have accepted, since it has turned out to be unfulfillable. It is not that there is any difficulty, apart from the obligation, in making a correct comment on the truth-value of 'You are going to answer in the negative'. Several correct replies are in fact open; if, for example, you were to say 'That is false', you would be giving an affirmative answer and therefore making the sophism false; so your answer would be correct, since it just says that the sophism is false. But the terms of the obligation forbid such a response, and leave you with only incorrect replies to make. The trouble arises because of self-reference. In a concealed way, each of the permitted answers is indirectly self-referential, much as were Socrates' and Plato's propositions in Sophisms 8 and 9. For by the conventions agreed to, replying 'Yes' acts as a claim that the original proposition is true, and that proposition itself makes an assertion about your reply; and analogous considerations apply to the answer 'No'. Mere self-reference, however, does not automatically generate a problem. The response 'That is false' would be equally self-referential, but it could be used to make a correct reply. So Buridan speaks cautiously about a 'self-reference that would inevitably make your answer false'. He maintains that if you want to accept an obligation of the proposed kind then you should make it a condition that no proposition is to be presented to you that would give each permitted answer that kind of self-reference. But, he seems to be implying, you need not insist that all kinds of self-reference be ruled out.

16.4 is the formal reply to the contrary argument, which in this case is of course the argument given in 16.0 for the acceptability of the obligation. That argument began by saying that every proposition that might be put to you is either true or false. Buridan does not dispute that, even as far as the sophism itself is concerned. What he does dispute is that it follows that you can always make a correct reply in terms of the obligation, and his reason is this: Even if we count saying nothing at all as a permissible response, there are only three responses you can make, and the truth-values of the sophism and the reply in each case will be as in the following table:

Response	Truth-value of the sophism	Truth-value of the response
None	False	None
'Yes'	False	False
'No'	True	False

It can easily be seen that although the sophism itself is false in some cases but true in others, no response can be true; and that is why you ought not to accept the obligation, except with the qualification mentioned in 16.3.

16.5 begins with the trivial point that if the obligation had specified 'That is true' and 'That is not true' as the only permitted replies, the same problem would have arisen; but then it adds the not-so-trivial point that you would still be in trouble if you were in addition allowed to say 'I find that doubtful'. We are not told why this is so; but presumably the reason is that if you respond to the sophism by saying 'I find that doubtful', then your response is an affirmative one, and so the sophism is false; and since you can hardly fail to know that it is false, it follows that you do not find it doubtful after all.

16.6 raises an ingenious objection and 16.6.1 gives an equally ingenious reply to it. Buridan has claimed that each of the two replies to the sophism, 'That is true' and 'That is not true', would be false. But, the objection runs, 'That is true' and 'That is not true' form a pair of contradictories, and contradictories must have opposite truth-values. So how could both replies be false?

Buridan's reply is first of all to remind us that what is impossible is that a pair of contradictories should both be false *at the same time*; and of course for two propositions to be false at a given time they must both exist at that time. He then runs through the possible cases. (a) Suppose you reply to the sophism by saying 'That is true' and nothing else. Then your reply, as we have seen, is false; but at the time when it is false its contradictory does not even exist, and so we do not have a pair of contradictories both being false at the same time. (b) The same holds if you reply 'That is not true' and nothing else. (c) Suppose the point is pressed that you might make both replies simultaneously (perhaps by speaking one and writing the other?), so that both *would* exist at the same time. Then, he says, the position is this: The sophism only said you were going to answer in the negative, not that you were not going to answer in the affirmative as well. Now one of your replies (*viz.* 'That is not true') was in fact negative, and that means that the sophism has turned out to be true. Therefore your reply, 'That is true', was itself true, and your other reply, 'That is not true', was false. So this time we do have a pair of contradictories existing at the same time, but they have opposite truth-values as contradictories should.

16.7 does no more than introduce an alternative notation for the problem and raises no new issues.

SOPHISM 17

Sophism 16 was concerned with the acceptance of an undertaking or obligation. The present sophism is concerned with the making of what Buridan more or less indifferently calls a promise or a vow or an oath. It seems clear that these two topics have close logical affinities and can give rise to similar problems. In Sophism 16 Buridan did not call the sentence expressing the acceptance of the obligation a proposition, though he might well have done so. Here, however, he does speak of the words used to make a promise (vow, oath) as a proposition, and hence as true or false: true if the promise is fulfilled, false if it is not. Many people will no doubt have qualms about this terminology on the ground that promising to do something and asserting that something is the case are two very different sorts of speech-acts. I do not think that Buridan need, or would, deny that. But what he here calls a *promise* (*promissum*) is not an act of promising but a verbal formula in which an act of promising is expressed (just as what he calls a *proposition* is not an act of asserting something but a verbal formula in which an act of asserting is expressed – see Sophism 6). And such a verbal formula can plausibly be said to have at least a propositional aspect. If, for example, I say to you 'I shall come to the meeting this evening' in a context that makes my use of these words count as the making of a promise, then even if what I am doing by means of this utterance is inadequately described as making an assertion about my future movements, there is certainly the question of whether I shall in fact go to the meeting; and if I do go, then what I said tallies with the facts in a way at least very analogous to that in which a proposition can tally with the facts. By going to the meeting I 'make my words come true'.

17.0. The promises that Sophism 17 deals with are conditional in form. What Plato says in the posited case in fact consists of two conditionals, though Buridan refers to them both together as a single promise. We are clearly meant to understand Plato's throwing Socrates into the water and his letting him cross as mutually exclusive alternatives. Note that the question posed at the end of 17.0 is only one of three that are listed in 17.2 as raised by the sophism.

From a structural point of view 17.1 can be thought of as running together the *pro* and *contra* arguments that are found at this point in most of the other sophisms. First we are told why Plato should not throw Socrates into the water, then we are told why he should not let him cross. Of course these are not the only courses of action open to Plato; but he has said he will do one or other of them if Socrates utters some proposition, and Socrates has done that.

17.2 lists three questions raised by the posited case, 17.3–17.5 answer each of these in turn, and the sophism then comes to an end. It thus does not conform very strictly to the usual orthodox pattern; in fact the sophisms in this final group are more loosely constructed than most of their predecessors.

17.3. *Is Socrates' proposition true or is it false?* The position is that his proposition is a contingent one and that we are not given enough information in the posited case to be able to determine its truth-value. So given only the case as stated, we cannot *know* that it is true or *know* that it is false. The question can be raised, however, whether it *is* true or false at all, i.e. at the time at which it is spoken. The problem of the truth-value of contingent propositions about the future has been intensively debated since the time of Aristotle (in 17.4 Buridan refers us to the *De Interpretatione*, presumably to the much-discussed passage about the sea-battle tomorrow in chapter 9). Some philosophers have held that propositions about future contingencies have no truth-value at all, or have some third truth-value distinct from truth and falsity. Some others have held that they have no truth-value at the time they are formulated, but acquire a truth-value when the predicted event occurs or fails to occur. It seems clear that Buridan does not hold either of these views. According to him, Socrates' proposition *is* either true or false, and the time of its truth or falsity is the time of its formulation. As we have seen, he holds that a proposition is true or false only if it exists, and only *while* it exists. What is distinctive about a proposition about the future is that it is true or false in virtue of what is not yet, and if we cannot know how the relevant things will turn out then we cannot now *know* whether it is true or false; but this does not mean that it *is* not true or false. Buridan says in 17.4 that such propositions are not *determinately* true or false until the occurrence or non-occurrence of the predicted event, but again this does not mean that they are not true or false at all. In the present case Socrates' proposition *is* true if Plato *will* throw him into the water, and *is* false otherwise. Buridan comments that it is therefore within Plato's power to determine whether it is true or false. This of course is what contributes to the problem; for it means that it is for Plato himself to determine which of the two conditionals in his promise has a true antecedent and is thus the operative one, and the trouble is that whichever choice he makes his promise commits him to making the opposite one.

17.4. *Is Plato's proposition (his promise) true or is it false?* We have seen what it is in general for a promise to be true. But what in particular is it for a *conditional* promise to be true? A conditional promise is expressed by a sentence of the form 'If *p* then *q*', where *p* asserts that something is or will be the case and *q* says that the speaker will perform some action. (This formulation is too rough to be really accurate, but the needed refinements would only unnecessarily complicate the issue here.) For Buridan, therefore, a conditional promise is just one sort of conditional proposition. He now says that there are two ways in which we can understand conditional propositions, and two corresponding accounts of their truth-conditions.

(a) We can interpret 'If *p* then *q*' as meaning that *q* logically follows from *p* (i.e. that the inference '*p*, therefore *q*' is a valid one), and therefore count it as true if *q* is deducible from *p* and false if it is not. Buridan calls this the *strict* sense of a conditional, and it is in this sense that he uses 'if...then...' almost exclusively throughout the *Sophismata*. Now it is clear that if we understand Plato's conditionals in this way then both of them must count as false: 'Plato will allow Socrates to cross' just is not logically deducible from 'Socrates' next proposition will be a true one', nor is 'Plato will throw Socrates into the water' deducible from 'Socrates' next proposition will be a false one'; and, as Buridan was at pains to stress in Sophism 3, nothing in the rest of the posited case can have any bearing on this. It is, however, as he admits, most unlikely that we intend to use conditionals in this sense when we make promises, vows or the like; and the truth-conditions for conditionals in this 'strict' sense do not in any case fit in well with the idea that a promise counts as true when it is fulfilled.

(b) The second sense in which conditionals can be understood Buridan describes as 'less strict', but he says it is the usual one in which conditional promises are understood. In this 'less strict' sense we count a conditional promise 'If *p*, then *q*' as true when *p* is true and the speaker performs the action specified in *q*, and false when *p* is true but the speaker does not perform that action. His account of the truth-conditions of such conditionals is incomplete, in that we are given no rules for the truth or falsity of the conditional when *p* is not true. Nevertheless, the rules he gives are sufficient to enable him to answer the question he is asking here, *viz.* 'Is Plato's conditional promise true or false when interpreted in this second way?' His answer is that it is false. The promise took the form of a double conditional, and all that is necessary for the stated truth-conditions to be applicable to one or other conditional is that Socrates should say something that is either true or false; and Socrates did precisely that. We cannot of course tell whether Socrates' proposition is in fact true or false, but whichever it is, the antecedent of one of Plato's conditionals will be satisfied. Then the question is whether Plato does what is specified in the consequent of that conditional; and the answer is that he does not, so the conditional is false. Admittedly the reason why he does not perform the specified action is a peculiar one: it is logically impossible both that he should perform it and that the antecedent should be true. Still the fact remains that he does not perform it, and by the truth-conditions that have been stated that is enough to make the conditional false.

At the end of 17.4 Buridan says that Socrates' proposition makes Plato's promise self-referential, but it is difficult to see in what precise sense this is so. In Sophisms 8 and 9 we had clear cases of indirect self-reference, since Socrates' and Plato's propositions each contained a term that stood for the other. In the present case it is easy to see that Plato's conditionals contain a term ('the next proposition you utter' or 'what you say') that stands for Socrates' proposition, but it is hard to see how Socrates' proposition contains any term that stands for either or both of Plato's conditionals. The position is, however, similar to the straightforward cases of indirect self-reference in that there is no shadow of paradox about Plato's conditionals on their own, but with the addition of Socrates' proposition to the situation we can plausibly derive a 'classical' paradox of the form '*p* if and only if not-*p*'. The derivation might run thus: Given that Socrates says what he does, Plato's first conditional entails

(1) If Plato is going to throw Socrates into the water, Plato is going to allow Socrates to cross.

On the assumption that letting Socrates cross and throwing him into the water are mutually exclusive, this in turn entails

(2) If Plato is going to throw Socrates into the water, Plato is not going to throw Socrates into the water.

Given again that Socrates says what he does, we have

(3) If Plato is not going to throw Socrates into the water, then Socrates' proposition is false,

and this, with Plato's second conditional, entails

(4) If Plato is not going to throw Socrates into the water, Plato is going to throw Socrates into the water.

(2) and (4) then clearly combine into

(5) Plato is going to throw Socrates into the water if and only if Plato is not going to throw Socrates into the water.

Perhaps in saying that Socrates' proposition made Plato's promise self-referential and thereby made it inevitably false, Buridan meant no more than what I have just tried to spell out. It may be worth noting that at the end of 17.5, instead of speaking of self-reference, he uses a more cautious mode of expression.

17.5. *What ought Plato to do to keep his promise?* That 'ought' implies 'can' is a principle usually associated with Kant, but not of course confined to his thought. By contraposition it yields the principle that what one cannot do one has no obligation to do. This is what Buridan appeals to for an answer to his third question: there is nothing that Plato can do to fulfil his promise, so he has no obligation to keep it at all. He adds that Plato ought not to have made his promise in the first place (except with some suitable qualification that would have ensured the possibility of his keeping it), and here he seems to be making an implicit appeal to a further principle, *viz.* that if doing A commits one to doing B, then if B is impossible one ought not to do A.

Buridan's example in Sophism 17 has the same structure as a number of paradoxical anecdotes that date from ancient times. Two of the best-known are the following.

1. Protagoras trained a pupil, Euathlus, as an advocate, on the understanding that the latter would pay his fee when he won his first case. Euathlus, however, decided not to practise law, whereupon Protagoras sued him for payment of his fee. The problem usually developed from this example is this. Protagoras argued: 'If I win my case I shall get my fee because that is what I am suing for; and if I lose, I shall still get my fee because then Euathlus will have won his first case'. But Euathlus argued: 'If Protagoras wins I shall not have to pay because I shall still not have won my first case; and if he loses I shall also not have to pay because the judge will have ruled against him'. Now which of the two argued correctly?

2. A crocodile stole a woman's baby and promised to return it to her if she told him truly whether he would eat it or not. The woman then replied, 'You are going to eat it'. She argued thus: 'If what I have said is true, I shall get my baby back because the crocodile has promised to give it back if I speak truly; and if what I have said is false, I shall still get it back because in that case the crocodile is not going to eat it'. But the crocodile argued: 'If what you have said is true, you will not get your baby back, because you have said that I am going to eat it; and if what you have said is false, you will not get your baby back because you have not spoken truly'. Now which of the two argued correctly?

It is easy to develop Buridan's example along the same lines. For Plato could say to Socrates: 'If what you have said is true, I shall throw you into the water, since that is what you said I would do; and if it is false, I shall still throw you into the water, because that is what I said I would do if you spoke falsely'. And Socrates could reply: 'If what I have said is true, you will not throw me into the water, because you promised to let me cross if I spoke truly; and if it is false, you will still not throw me into the water, because what I said was that you would do so and I spoke falsely'. Again, the question can be raised: which of them argued correctly? The interesting thing is that Buridan does not formulate this problem at all.

SOPHISM 18

We now move from conditional promises to conditional wishes. In this sophism, as in many of the others, the posited case can be made to generate, or to seem to generate, a paradox of the form 'p if and only if not-p' (18.1). Buridan's solution will turn on making clear an ambiguity in sentences of the form 'X wants to φ if p'. Such a sentence can be understood to mean that X has a certain wish of a conditional kind, i.e. a wish whose content is that if it is the case that p then he (X) will φ. In that case the whole sentence will be a categorical proposition, and it is only the content of the wish that X is (categorically) said to have that is conditional in nature. Alternatively, 'X wants to φ if p' can be understood to mean that if it is the case that p, then X wants to φ. In that case the whole proposition is a conditional one, with p as the antecedent and 'X wants to φ' as the consequent; and the wish that is (conditionally) attributed to X in this consequent is not itself a conditional one but a plain wish to φ. We could bring out notationally the difference between the two interpretations by writing 'X wants (to φ if p)' for the first and '(X wants to φ) if p' for the second. In the example used in the sophism, the situation is complicated by the fact that p itself asserts that someone has a certain wish. It is, indeed, because of this that the paradox arises.

18.0. 'Eat' has to be understood to mean 'eat at some determinate time and place'. This is why at some points in the discussion Buridan uses the phrase 'to eat here and now' (*hic comedere*). The two conditionals in the posited case are deliberately ambiguous: they can be interpreted in either of the ways just mentioned.

18.1, like 17.1, corresponds structurally to the *pro* and *contra* arguments of most of the other sophisms. The paradox is generated by taking the propositions in the posited case in the second of the two ways described above, i.e. as conditionally attributing to Plato and Socrates a wish to eat and a wish not to eat respectively, and by regarding a conditional proposition as making a claim that the consequent follows logically from the antecedent. Buridan says at 18.2 that this is the 'strict' way to interpret the propositions in question, perhaps because grammatically they have the overall form of conditional sentences.

18.2 gives Buridan's solution to the problem posed in 18.1, by making explicit the ambiguity I have mentioned. The self-contradictory result in 18.1 is indeeed derivable if we take the conditionals in the posited case in the second way. But this is not to be wondered at, since then the conditionals themselves are not merely false but impossible: 'Plato wants to eat' simply does not entail 'Socrates wants to eat', etc.; and, in the terminology of Sophism 3 (see 3.2), every false inference is an impossible one. If, however, we understand the conditionals in the posited case in the first way, there is nothing impossible in the case itself and no self-contradictory conclusions can be drawn from it. Take the first element in the posited case: 'Socrates wants to eat if Plato wants to eat, but not otherwise.' This will now be held to mean that Socrates has a wish whose content could be expressed by the proposition 'If Plato eats then Socrates eats too, and if Plato does not eat then Socrates does not eat either'; and moreover the occurrences of 'if...then...' in this proposition will be interpreted in the way that was explained for promises in Sophism 17 and is extended here to apply to the expressions of wishes. What this amounts to is that what Socrates wishes is that 'Plato eats' and 'Socrates eats' should have the same truth-value. Analogously, what Plato wishes is that they should have opposite truth-values. Now there is not the slightest inconsistency in supposing that Socrates and Plato do have these wishes, and so the posited case, thus understood, is a perfectly possible one; and with this interpretation of the case, the deduction of the self-contradiction in 18.1 cannot be carried through. It is, of course, impossible that both of the wishes mentioned should be *fulfilled*, but the case does not say that they are.

It will almost certainly occur to the modern reader that there is a third way in which the propositions in the posited case could be interpreted: they could be taken as conditional propositions but not as expressing entailments. They could, for example, be taken as material conditionals. In that case, 'Socrates wants to eat if Plato wants to eat' would mean 'Either Plato does not want to eat or Socrates does want to eat', and the others would be understood analogously. In that case the position will be that no one of the conditionals in the posited case will itself be impossible, but the whole set of them taken together will be impossible; so the case as a whole will be impossible, though not for the reasons that Buridan gives. Moreover we can still carry through the deduction of the paradoxical conclusion of 18.1. So the upshot is that Buridan's overall position, *viz.* that the case is impossible and a paradox can be deduced from it, holds if we interpret the propositions as conditionals at all, even in the weakest sense, rather than as categorical assertions of conditional wishes.

18.3. The reasoning in 18.2 may solve the problem posed in 18.1 but it does not answer the original question, *viz.* whether in the posited case (assuming it is interpreted in a consistent way) Socrates does or does not want to eat. Buridan's comment is that there is not enough information given in the posited case to enable us to tell whether he wants to eat or not. We are told that he wants to-eat-if-Plato-wants-to-eat, but that is not the same thing as wanting to eat *simpliciter*. Buridan gives an analogous example. I may want to-go-to-Rome-if-Socrates-is-going-there. But my reason may have nothing to do with Rome; it may simply be that I want to be with Socrates wherever he may be, and I may even regret that it is Rome he has decided to go to. In that case it will be misleading, or even downright false, to say that what I want to do is to go to Rome. The point is that to say what wish a person has one has to specify what it is a wish *for*. There is no other way of discriminating between wishes; wishes for different things count as different wishes, and a 'wish' that is not a wish for anything is not a wish at all. So a wish to-eat-if-Plato-wants-to-eat does not by itself qualify as a wish to eat. Therefore if we are asked whether, on the assumption that the posited case states all the wishes that Socrates and Plato have, Socrates wants to eat or not, we shall have to reply that he does not; and the same goes for Plato.

The objector in 18.3.1 then tries to argue that the same cannot go for Plato; for one clause in the posited case says that Plato wants to eat if Socrates does not want to, and so, if we hold, as 18.3 concludes, that Socrates does not want to eat, we shall have to infer that Plato does. Buridan's comment is that this is to lapse back into the confusion he has been at pains to clear up. The objector's argument turns on taking the cited clause in the posited case as a conditional proposition about wishes rather than as the attribution of a conditional wish; but as we have seen, we must not take it in that way if the consistency of the case is to be ensured.

SOPHISM 19

This sophism follows closely the lines of the previous one. The paradox is developed in very much the same way, and the solution is reached by making an analogous distinction. Curses, however, are different from wishes in that a curse is an overt verbal utterance whereas a wish is a state or attitude of mind. One difference in Buridan's treatment of the two cases is that he is willing to countenance calling an utterance of the form 'May X be cursed if *p*' a cursing of X, albeit only a conditional (or conditioned) one, whereas in Sophism 18 he refused to call a wish to φ if *p* a wish to φ at all. This is of little consequence, however, since he says that whether a conditional curse should be called a curse at all is just a matter of arbitrary verbal convention.

The derivation of the paradox in 19.1 is presented in a very condensed form, and I shall try to spell it out in detail. When Socrates says 'May Plato be cursed if he is cursing me, but not otherwise', it is at least tempting to say that what Socrates is doing is cursing Plato if and only if Plato is cursing him. And then it looks as if the first clause of the posited case can be reformulated as

(1) Socrates is cursing Plato if and only if Plato is cursing Socrates.

Similarly, the second clause would give us

(2) Plato is cursing Socrates if and only if Socrates is not cursing Plato.

Then one way of reaching the conclusions of 19.1 is as follows:

(3) Socrates is cursing Plato. (Hypothesis.)

Therefore by (1):

(4) Plato is cursing Socrates.

Therefore by (2):

(5) Socrates is not cursing Plato.

Therefore by (1) again:

(6) Plato is not cursing Socrates.

But the conjunction of (4) and (6) is self-contradictory; and therefore (3) is false. Secondly, we have:

(7) Socrates is not cursing Plato. (Hypothesis.)

Therefore by (2):

(8) Plato is cursing Socrates.

Therefore by (1):

(9) Socrates is cursing Plato.

So (7), with the posited case, entails (9), which is its own negation. Therefore (7) is false. (3) and (7), however, are contradictories, and so cannot both be false; and that constitutes the problem.

In 19.2 Buridan produces a solution very like that of 18.2. If we take (1) and (2) above as formulations of the posited case and interpret them as entailments (two-way entailments, in fact), then each will be false, and indeed impossible. To curse someone is to *say* something, such as 'May he be cursed', or 'May he come to harm' (see 19.2.1). So (1) would have to be construed as claiming that 'Plato is saying "May Socrates be cursed"' entails 'Socrates is saying "May Plato be cursed"' and conversely. But it is clear that from the fact that Plato is saying something, nothing whatever follows about what Socrates is saying, or even about whether he is saying anything at all; and the same goes for the converse. On this interpretation, then, the posited case is impossible, and the conclusions of 19.1 are correctly drawn but unsurprising.

The alternative is to take the first clause in the posited case as asserting categorically that Socrates is saying the whole of the following, 'May Plato be cursed if he is cursing me and may he not be cursed if he is not cursing me', and to understand the second clause in an analogous way. Moreover, although he does not explicitly say so, I think Buridan must take the occurrences of 'if' in these utterances of Socrates and Plato not as expressing entailments but in the way explained for conditional promises and wishes in Sophisms 17 and 18. This is indeed, one would think, the most natural way to interpret the statements in the posited case anyway; but be that as it may, if we understand them in this way, then certainly there can be no inconsistency in supposing that Socrates and Plato are in fact saying the things they are thus portrayed as saying. And of course the argument of 19.1 cannot then be carried through. The only question then remaining – it is indeed how we now have to understand the question originally posed in 19.0 – is whether these utterances of Socrates and Plato count as curses or not.

According to Buridan (19.2.1 and 19.2.2) this is a purely verbal matter about which there are no clearly established conventions. If we do call these utterances curses we shall at least have to make it clear that they are curses with conditions attached, not absolute or unconditional ones. Some people, however, might want to reserve the word 'curse' for the absolute variety and so decline to call curses with conditions curses at all. Using the word in one way, therefore, we shall have to say that Socrates and Plato are each cursing the other, and using it in the other way we shall have to say that neither of them is doing so. And if anyone protests (19.2.1.1) that according to the second clause in the posited case Socrates and Plato cannot both be cursing each other or both be failing to curse each other, then the reply is that to argue in this way is to lapse back into construing that clause in the sense of (2), which is an interpretation that we have already rejected.

SOPHISM 20

This brief final sophism adds very little to the previous one, and indeed Buridan calls it merely an amplification of the discussion there. His point seems to be to make it clear that his treatment of Sophism 19 did not essentially depend on the fact that curses are overt verbal utterances, and would apply equally to the corresponding wishes even if they were not expressed in words. In this way the topic of Sophism 19 is linked with that of Sophism 18, which dealt explicitly with wishes.

The problem and solution are only sketchily outlined, and we are expected to do our own filling-in by referring back to the previous sophism. The task is not a hard one.

One interesting, though minor, point is that at the end of the sophism Buridan says that Socrates' wish *is* a wish that Plato should come to harm, though of course only a conditioned one; and this seems out of line with his insistence in 18.3 that Socrates' wish to-eat-if-Plato-wants-to-eat does not count as a wish to eat.

REFERENCES

Only works referred to in the text are listed here

BURIDAN, JOHN (JOHANNÉS BURIDANUS)

(1) *Summulae de Dialectica (Summulae Logicales)*. This is a lengthy work, divided into eight Tracts, and written in the form of a detailed commentary on a much shorter text. The text appears to be by Peter of Spain (d. 1277), but modified by Buridan himself whenever it suits his purpose. Many Mss. and printed versions exist, but some contain only the basic text, and in some others Buridan's commentary is replaced by one by Johannes Dorp. No critical edition has yet been issued, except of Tract IV (see Reina [1957] below).

(2) *Sophismata (Tractatus de Sophismatibus)*. For the relation of this work to (1), see Introduction, pp. 31–2. See also Scott [1966] and [1977].

(3) *Consequentiae (Tractatus de Consequentiis)*. See Hubien [1976].

(4) *Commentary on Aristotle's 'Metaphysics'*.

(5) *Commentary on Aristotle's 'Physics'*. Facsimiles of editions of (4) and (5), dated 1518 and 1509 respectively, were published by Minerva (Munich) in 1965. (On the title-page of the facsimile of (4) the date is incorrectly given as 1588.)

Ashworth, E. J. [1974]. *Language and Logic in the Post-mediaeval Period*. Dordrecht, Reidel.

Black, M. [1948]. The Semantic Definition of Truth. *Analysis*, Vol. VIII, No. 4.

Bocheński, J. [1961]. *A History of Formal Logic*. University of Notre Dame Press. Translated and edited by Ivo Thomas. (Original German edition, *Formale Logik*, Verlag Karl Alber, Freiberg/München, 1956.)

Faral, E. [1949]. Jean Buridan: Maître ès Arts de L'Université de Paris. *Histoire littéraire de la France*, Vol. XXXVIII, pp. 462–605.

Hamblin, C. L. [1970]. *Fallacies*. London, Methuen.

Hubien, H. [1976]. *Iohannis Buridani Tractatus de Consequentiis*. Louvain, Publications Universitaires (Critical edition of Buridan (3), with an Introduction.)

Kneale, W. and M. [1962]. *The Development of Logic*. Oxford University Press.

Moody, E. A. [1953]. *Truth and Consequence in Mediaeval Logic*. Amsterdam, North Holland.

Pinborg, J. (ed.) [1976]. *The Logic of John Buridan*. Copenhagen, Museum Tusculanum.

REFERENCES

Reina, M. E. [1957]. Giovanni Buridano: 'Tractatus de Suppositionibus'. *Rivista critica di storia della filosofia*, Vol. XII, pp. 175–208, 323–52. (Critical edition of Tract IV of Buridan (1), with an Introductory Note.)

Rijk, L. M. de [1974]. Some Thirteenth Century Tracts on the Game of Obligation. *Vivarium*, Vol. XII, No. 2, pp. 94–123.

Scott, T. K. [1966]. *John Buridan: Sophisms on Meaning and Truth*. New York, Appleton-Century-Crofts. (Translation of Buridan (2), with an Introduction.)

Scott, T. K. [1977]. *Johannes Buridanus: Sophismata*. Stuttgart, Fromann-Holzboog. (Critical edition of Buridan (2), with an Introduction.)

Spade, P. V. [1977]. Roger Swyneshed's 'Obligationes'. *Archives d'histoire doctrinale et littéraire du moyen age*, Vol. XLIV, pp. 243–85.

Tarski, A. [1944]. The Semantic Conception of Truth and the Foundations of Semantics. *Philosophy and Phenomenological Research*, Vol. IV, pp. 341–76.

INDEX

For some very frequently occurring topics (e.g. self-reference, truth) only a few basic references are given.

Printed in the United Kingdom by
Lightning Source UK Ltd., Milton Keynes
138379UK00001B/29/P